In this lively and timely book Charles Areni and Stephen Holden offer a constructive response to one of the trickiest modern dilemmas: how to get fathers doing more of the housework and childcare. Refreshingly, they are not afraid to name the problem – many fathers simply do not do their fair share – nor to offer concrete solutions: in the home, men must step up, and women must let go. Advocating a domestic equivalent of women 'leaning in' at work, they outline numerous practical steps that could be taken, and convincing reasons why parents should follow them. The book is well structured and easily readable, full of interesting and apposite anecdotes. It is refreshing to read a book from the point of view of a father ready to claim competence in the private sphere and to stake a claim as a knowledgeable equal parent. Without downplaying the inequity of most mothers' work-care load, the authors make a convincing plea for recognition that dads too are capable parents. Having noticed that there is nothing like being in sole charge to engender proficiency, they argue that mothers ceding the field (to a resident or non-resident co-parent) is probably the quickest route to gender equality, skilling dad up in the domestic arts and freeing mum to pursue other activities, including paid work. The solution requires give and take on both sides, but as the authors convincingly argue, the potential gains to fathers' family relationships and to mothers' economic independence are surely worth a try!

Professor Lyn Craig, Social Policy Research Centre,
University of NSW

Charles and Stephen have created a challenging yet inspiring guide for all current or aspiring mothers and fathers. This work is rich with both meaningful research and stories that we can all relate to and is truly a must read. Fathers are challenged to truly lift their game in the domestic realm and mothers are encouraged to both motivate and let this happen. *The other glass ceiling* requires us to reflect on our own behaviours and values and presents us with a view of what we can do to be both better parents and ultimately happier people. A must read. Simple as that.

Daniel Petre, AO, author of *Father time:*
making time for your children

The other glass ceiling explores a topic that is pervasive in society: the lack of work–family balance. Drawing on years of research, the book highlights how fathers avoid childcare and home responsibilities with strategies like feigning incompetence or being absent 'breadwinning', and how mothers sabotage themselves by not leaving space for men to contribute to the home in their own way and own time. In the same way women experience a glass ceiling in the workplace stemming from deeply ingrained social, cultural and institutional factors, men experience the 'other glass ceiling' in the home based on many of the same factors. The authors implore the unrelenting CEO of the home, who expects things to be done in a certain way and at a certain time, to let go and create space. Men are invited to step up, be creative, build a lifelong relationship with their children and contribute to the home so that women can have more time to work, rest and play ... Actually, removing the 'other glass ceiling' supports the wellbeing of mothers, fathers and kids, so the whole family benefits.

Dr Rosina McAlpine, author of *Inspired children:*
how the leading minds of today raise their kids

The other glass ceiling

Fathers stepping up, mothers letting go

Charles S. Areni and Stephen S. Holden

Illustrations by Gaye Dell

DARLINGTON PRESS

First published by Darlington Press
Darlington Press is an imprint of SYDNEY UNIVERSITY PRESS

Fisher Library F03
University of Sydney NSW 2006
AUSTRALIA
Email: sup.info@sydney.edu.au
sydney.edu.au

National Library of Australia Cataloguing-in-Publication Data

Author:	Areni, Charles S.
Other Authors/Contributors:	Holden, Stephen S., author.
Title:	The other glass ceiling: fathers stepping up, mothers letting go
ISBN:	9781921364235 (paperback)
	9781921364242 (ebook: epub)
	9781921364563 (ebook: mobipocket)
Notes:	Includes bibliographical references and index.
Subjects:	Sex role
	Sexism
	Glass ceiling (Employment discrimination)
Dewey Number:	305.3

Cover image by Gaye Dell
Cover design by Miguel Yamin

Contents

Acknowledgments

Charles

The cover of this book lists two authors, implying that two men were responsible for it. But writing a book is a team effort, and I had a lot of important players on my team. I can't thank them all, but there are some people I must acknowledge, first of all my ex-wife and her partner. I think it's very cool that my kids have the love and security of two mums and two dads. Four loving parents – that's got to be a good thing. Second, I must mention Peter McDonald, my friend and collaborator who gave me encouragement and connected me with the right people to start this journey on the right path. Nigel Marsh, a brilliant and successful writer in his own right, took time away from his busy schedule to meet with me, and comment on earlier chapter drafts. Richard Denham, who I met at my very first single fathers support group meeting, was a constant source of support along the way. I also want to thank my editor, Agata Mrva-Montoya for having the vision and faith in this project from the outset. Finally, and most importantly, I want to thank my family – Glory, Tiffany, Shane and Jacqueline. Without them, none of this or anything else I do, matters.

Stephen

Two women in particular deserve special acknowledgement for their contribution to this book although neither probably realises how much they contributed, and in the case of the first, never will know. My paternal grandmother, Doreen Stephens, died in March 2001, months before the birth of my son. She actively campaigned for the rights of women in the 1940s and 50s, and herself broke through the glass ceiling in 1960s (long before it was so named) becoming one of the first women to hold an executive position in the BBC. She taught me that humans are not even-handed in how they deal with other human beings, and more importantly, that the power to challenge inequity (be it based on sex, colour, ethnicity, religion, etc.) rests with the individual her- or himself. The other woman I wish to thank is the one who delivered to me the greatest gift of my life – a son. Both mother and son have given me the experiences and the lessons that motivated me to write this book. Finally, I thank the many who have provided encouragement, listened to my ideas, viewed chapters, made comments, and challenged my thinking as this book has come to fruition: Charles Areni, Bettina Arndt, Lynley Casey, Matthew Casey, Liberty Cramer, Gaye Dell, Paul Flaherty, Sue Frohlick, Sharon Kyme, Bénédicte Larrieu, Mark Spence and Max Sutherland.

Two dads, one voice

We are two dads. We have many personal stories and a common experience both as fathers and single fathers.

Between us, we have three children from two mothers – or so we think as we have not taken DNA tests of those we think are ours and we may have fathered other children that we do not know! Our children spend half their time with their mothers, the other half with their respective fathers. Between us, we have many ex-partners, one ex-wife, one current wife, and one step-child. Since separating from the mothers of our children, they have had two marriages, one divorce and added another child to the pool. Confused? You might have to get used to that: complexity is a feature of modern mended and blended families.

The point is that here, we wish to tell our various personal stories at the same time as sharing our common experience as dads, and single dads in particular. Communicating the personal along with the shared experience does not work if we use 'we' and 'our', or worse 'first author' and 'second author'! Just as we object to the parents that say 'We are pregnant' (she is, he is not!), we two single dads wish to speak about personal experiences without presuming that one speaks for two. So this book is written in one single, personal voice: here 'I' tell 'my' story, speak about 'me' and what is 'mine'. This means that you will never know whether it is Stephen or Charles who is telling his story. Nor will anyone else – which may be a good thing. Two dads, one voice.

Prologue

Becoming a first-time parent was the most stand-out day of my life, which is kind of ironic given that men are so often defined by the work they do. I did very little of the work to become a parent. Mum did all the work! It is striking how on the entry of a baby into the world, dad's contribution is so limited. Maybe the world of professional success is the compensation for a man's limited input in the reproduction domain: a big fish in the world of work, a tiny fish in the world of the womb!

Still, from the very beginning I was determined to be an involved dad even if Nature would have me standing by as a pretty helpless observer at the beginning of the event. I was all in – 100 percent committed to being the best father in the whole universe!

But what really forced me to assess my priorities was not the day that I became a father, but the day that I became a *single* father. Phew, now that was a challenge! Not only did I have a child to take care of, but it seemed that much of the world aligned with Nature in trying to make my role smaller than I thought it should be.

Single parenthood is tough on both mums and dads – but in different ways. Single mums are now seen as a normal part of the demographic landscape. By way of sheer numbers throughout the years, single mums are viewed with far less suspicion and derision than they were decades ago.

Not so single dads. Single dads who are actively involved in parenting still represent a small proportion of separated homes. As a result they are less visible, and when they do appear on the public radar screen, it is often as 'deadbeat dads' who walk away from parental responsibilities, or 'deranged dads' who spray-paint over portraits of the Queen, break into Buckingham Palace dressed as Batman[1] or climb Sydney Harbour Bridge.[2] But this is changing,[3] and this book is about the new world order.

Becoming a parent, and then a single parent, has taught me some interesting things. Perhaps one of the big insights was to see up close and personal the operation of sexism, the differentiation between gender that was unnecessary, artificial, contrived, exaggerated, and most importantly, damaging. It was quite an epiphany. I realised perhaps for the first time what it might feel like for women who suffer at the whims of unrealistic public expectations about what they can and cannot do, what they should and should not do.

---

1   Holden 2013.
2   Court bans protesting father from going near bridge or his children. *Sydney Morning Herald*, 13 May 2011. Retrieved 28 August 2013 from http://www.smh.com.au/nsw/court-bans-protesting-father-from-going-near-bridge-or-his-children-20110513-1elx4.html.
3   Berlatsky 2013.

Women are still confronted by the impossible expectations of being perfect mothers, while at the same time pursuing successful careers. The phrase 'at the same time' is critical here. There are, after all, only 24 hours in a day. If mums are busy being perfect parents, where do they find the time to pursue careers?

But this kind of thinking can hurt men too. Here, the problem is the expectation that fathers fulfil the 'breadwinner' role in the family. They are defined solely in terms of professional success. As parents dads are second best at best, and incompetent boobs at worst. Mums have too many roles in which they are expected to excel, and dads do not have enough roles in which they are expected to excel. While one challenge is to expand the role of women in professional life, the other challenge is to expand the role of men in domestic life.

This is my account of what it's like to be a homemaker and a breadwinner at the same time. Mothers have been juggling these conflicting responsibilities for decades, whether they are single or not, but this is still very much new territory for dads like me. This book is about my desperate attempt at this balancing act.

Introduction: reflections on the glass ceiling

In her concession speech at the 2008 National Convention of the Democratic Party, Hillary Clinton made the following statement:

> As we gather here today in this historic magnificent building, the 50th woman to leave this Earth is orbiting overhead. If we can blast 50 women into space, we will someday launch a woman into the White House.
>
> Although we weren't able to shatter that highest, hardest glass ceiling this time, thanks to you, it's got about 18 million cracks in it … and the light is shining through like never before, filling us all with the hope and the sure knowledge that the path will be a little easier next time.[1]

The 'highest, hardest glass ceiling' to which she was referring is, of course, the presidency of the United States, a position no woman has ever held. More generally, the glass ceiling metaphor captures the reality that women are vastly underrepresented in top government, management, legal, educational and religious institutions around the world. For instance, it is reported that women constitute almost half of the US

---

1   Hillary Clinton's exit speech. Retrieved 13 December 2013 from http://www.nydailynews.com/news/politics/ full-text-hillary-clinton-exit-speech-article-1.296790.

workforce and hold more than 50 percent of all middle-management positions, but they make up only two percent of Fortune 500 and Fortune 1000 CEOs.

Europe offers a similar story with women representing 44 percent of the workforce, 30 percent of managerial positions and only three percent of company CEOs. Within the EU, women comprise just over ten percent of the top executives in the top 50 publicly quoted companies, and in the US, less than 16 percent of corporate officers and less than 15 percent of members of boards of directors within Fortune 500 companies.[2]

Of course, here in Australia a woman broke through that 'highest, hardest glass ceiling' when Julia Gillard became prime minister. But don't let that individual achievement fool you. In the aggregate, the glass ceiling seems as impenetrable as ever in Australia, and the pattern is unmistakable. The more power, prestige, and financial compensation associated with a profession or position, the fewer women you will see.

Australian women make up 45.3 percent of the overall labour force, and roughly 44.6 percent of managerial and professional positions. So far, so good. But when we look at board members of ASX Top 200 companies, only 8.4 percent are women. CEOs of these same companies? Only 3.0 percent. Board Chairs? Down to 2.5 percent.

The numbers in the public sector tell a similar story although slightly better perhaps. Despite comprising almost half the total labour force, women account for 33.4 percent of all government board positions, 30.1 percent of Federal Parliament positions, and 17.9 of all university vice chancellorships. These percentages haven't changed much over the last decade; and this is just a brief snapshot.[3] As we move from one industry to the next, we find women underrepresented at the highest echelons of management.

There are innumerable causes of the glass ceiling and I can't possibly go into all of them here. I will, however, make an observation about one insidious cause. Men simply don't do their fair share of domestic labour or 'housework', and when children enter into the equa-

---

2 Barreto et al. 2009, 4. See also http://www.economist.com/displaystory.cfm?story_id=4197626 [Accessed on 12 December 2013].
3 Equal Opportunity for Women in the Workplace Agency 2010.

tion, the gap in domestic workload between mothers and fathers increases . . . a lot!

Indeed, my research shows a fairly consistent pattern across what might be called the family life cycle of men and women. I examined a 'week in the life' of 702 Australian men and women, who were classified as either single, married with no children, married with children, or divorced with children. Research participants were then asked what they were 'currently doing' several times throughout the week, and the activities reported were classified into domestic labour, paid labour, child care, leisure, or 'other' categories.

The pattern that emerged was unmistakable.[4] When I compared single men to single women, there were no differences in frequencies for any of the five categories of activities. Single men and women spent their weeks doing more or less the same things. When I compared married men and women with no children, however, wives reported doing domestic labour more frequently than husbands. None of the other categories differed.

The big differences in roles and responsibilities became apparent when I compared married fathers and mothers. Mothers reported doing domestic labour and being involved with child care far more frequently than fathers, who reported paid work and leisure activities more frequently than their wives did. Other research reflects this same basic reality for married mothers. They are twice as likely as fathers to pay household bills, almost five times as likely to prepare family meals, ten times as likely to do the household cleaning, and oh yes, seven times as likely to do the family shopping.[5]

Things actually *improved* for mothers who divorced their husbands. Single mothers still reported doing domestic labour more frequently and leisure less frequently, but the differences in childcare and paid-labour activities disappeared, probably because single mothers spend more time on the job and rely on professional childcare services more extensively than married mothers do. Other researchers, using different methods and sources of data, have drawn largely the same conclusions.[6]

---

4   Areni 2014.
5   Taffel 2003, 27.
6   Craig 2005, 2006a, 2006b; Chesters, Baxter & Western 2009.

So the traditional stereotypes of the homemaker wife and the breadwinner husband systematically emerge as women and men progress through their family life cycle. To some extent divorce represents a move away from the traditional female stereotype, which may in part explain why women initiate 70–80 percent of all no-fault divorces.[7] Staying home all day changing nappies, doing the laundry, and cleaning the house, etc., may not seem quite as nice as flying to Melbourne for the big, industry conference this weekend. More on that later.

This book will not solve the problem of the glass ceiling, but it may make some serious headway into the uneven allocation of domestic labour and child care in the traditional family household. As a single father, let me be clear about one thing. Much of the problem is that fathers simply do not 'step up' to their responsibilities as parents. The 'deadbeat dad' phenomenon is real.

Fathers stepping up

Barack Obama, the man that defeated Hillary Clinton and went on to win the Presidency of the United States, was raised by a single mother, and he had this to say about it:

> I came to understand that the hole a man leaves when he abandons his responsibility to his children is one that no government can fill. We can do everything possible to provide good jobs and good schools and safe streets for our kids, but it will never be enough to fully make up the difference.
>
> That's why we need fathers to step up, to realize that their job does not end at conception; that what makes you a man is not the ability to have a child but the courage to raise one.
>
> As fathers, we need to be involved in our children's lives not just when it's convenient or easy, and not just when they're doing well – but when it's difficult and thankless, and they're struggling. That is when they need us most.[8]

---

7 Brinig & Allen 2000.

President Obama is right; much of the problem lies with men simply being unfair to women and children. But if that were all this book was about, it would be an angry, depressing read. I am not apologising for the lack or paternal contribution to child care, nor am I attempting to justify it. What is presented in this book is nothing more and nothing less than the personal views of two single fathers, doing their best in the simultaneous roles of homemaker *and* breadwinner.

But it must be said that one of the key themes of this book is how society implicitly sanctions my role as breadwinner and denigrates my role as homemaker. I'm seen as a successful man in terms of my profession, but a hopeless idiot in terms of being a parent. Gender stereotyping can work against men or women, depending on the situation. A simple study I conducted shows how insidious gender stereotypes are in colouring perceptions.

Consider the following scenario.

Chris is a single parent of two, a seven-year-old boy and a three-year old girl, and also the director of marketing for a medium-sized electronics firm. Today, Chris is scheduled to present key results from the quarterly sales report to the Board of Trustees but arrives for the meeting 15 minutes late due to having to drop the older boy at school, and the younger girl at day care. In addition to dishevelled hair, there is a noticeable stain down the left side of Chris' suit, the result of the young girl vomiting at the end of her car trip after a hurried breakfast.

Why do you think Chris is late for this meeting? Is Chris a good parent? A good employee? More importantly, which sex have you assumed Chris to be as you answer these questions? Did you think that Chris was a man or a woman? In research I conducted, I simply asked these initial questions to encourage people to reveal their assumptions about the sex of Chris.

---

8   Barack Obama, 'We need fathers to step up'. Retrieved 13 December 2013 from http://www.parade.com/104895/presidentbarackobama/ barack-obama-we-need-fathers-to-step-up/.

Chris' sex was not identified in the above scenario. Go ahead and check. No personal pronouns, no identification of gender. I used the gender-neutral name Chris for the fictitious parent for exactly that reason. However, you probably filled in this blank automatically based on assumptions you made about how the world works. In the scenario presented, most people (95 percent) infer that Chris is a woman.[9] Both men and women make this assumption, a result consistent with previous research using similar approaches.[10] Why is Chris presumed to be a woman?

Given that Chris is identified as a director of marketing, it is more likely, based on this information alone, that Chris is a man. We know from our discussion of the glass ceiling that men are significantly more likely to be in management than women.

So why is it assumed Chris is a woman? Perhaps it is the mention of Chris being a single parent. Somehow this seems to apply more to mothers than fathers. But why? If a couple with children divorce, don't both of them become single parents? So strictly, this adds no information to whether Chris is man or woman.

However, the scenario mentions the dropping of children at school and day care. Women generally take on the majority of the burden of child-bearing in the home, and mothers become primary custodians for children in 80–85 percent of divorces.[11]

So if we make the broad assumption that men are as likely to over-represent women at the executive level (say 85:15) as single mothers are to over-represent single fathers in the duty of dropping children at a day-care facility (say 85:15), then our best guess is exactly that, a guess.

In other words, Chris being an executive should skew our expectations toward him being a man, but this would be more or less offset by Chris being a custodial single parent, which would lead us to believe that she is a woman. The rest of the information in the vignette (vomit stain, dishevelled hair, tardiness, electronics, etc.) contains little additional information beyond associating Chris with parental and executive roles. So Chris' gender should be a coin toss.

---

9   Holden & Areni 2013.
10   Deutsch & Saxon 1998.
11   Farrell 2000, 153.

But people are not flipping coins. Overwhelmingly, people assume Chris is female. Why is this? Intuitively perhaps, the story seems to describe a woman more than a man. It falls in line with stories that it is the lot of women, and especially single mothers, to be engaged in a struggle to be a good parent to the children while pursuing a career at the same time.

The strength of fit is perhaps helped by the storyline that both of the struggles experienced by Chris as a woman reflect a glass ceiling created by men. For one thing, men do not pull their weight in home duties, and for another, they discriminate against women at work.

Additional responses of research participants suggest that Chris the mother is 'not really serious about her career'; that she needs to 'get her priorities in order'. And exactly what order is this?

These responses suggest that society persists with the stereotype that women are primarily mothers and only secondarily executives, so any role conflict should be resolved by reducing the amount of time and effort devoted to the 'secondary' role.[12] Why did the research participants implicitly assume this? Why shouldn't Chris the mother reduce the amount of time devoted to being a mother? More importantly, why can't she?

Now imagine Chris is a man. Is he perceived to be struggling? Hurting his career? If he is helping in childrearing as well as working his way up the corporate ladder, research suggests that if Chris was a man he would be viewed as a hero of sorts. Chris the father is viewed solely as an executive.[13] Any role conflict created by also acting as a father is viewed as going above and beyond the call of duty.

This is clearly an unfair standard that operates against women, and one that is clearly reflected in the data capturing the weekly activities of Australians. Why are women viewed as mothers first and executives second, whereas fathers are viewed almost solely in terms of their roles as providers? The net effect of these stereotypes is that mothers wind up doing more child care, more domestic labour, and less paid labour than fathers.

---

12 Petre 1998, 25; Deutsch 1999, 91–93; King 2008; Valimaki, Lamsa & Hiillos 2009.
13 Cooper 2000; Marsh & Musson 2008.

These stereotypes are biased and unjust for women. Why should they be viewed as the main nurturers of children in the typical Australian family? But is there another side of the story? Does this same stereotype sometimes work against men? To examine this, I asked research participants about another scenario.

> Terry is a single parent of a four-year-old boy called James. James spends some of his time with Terry and some with his other parent. Today, three police-officers and two child-safety officers have just arrived unannounced at Terry's home. The child-safety officers indicate that specific allegations have been made that Terry has been abusing James. They insist on entering the house to interview first Terry, and then James. While the accusations have been made anonymously, it is perhaps significant to note that the separation of James' parents was acrimonious.

Why is Terry being confronted by these allegations? Is Terry a good parent? What do you think this time?

Well, it probably depends on which sex you imagine Terry to be. Most people (82 percent) tended to see Terry as a man. Again, this is interesting by itself. Why assume Terry is a man? Single mothers have roughly 80–85 percent of the total custody time with their children compared to single fathers who get the remaining 10–15 percent. So a single mother would have more opportunity to care for, but also to mistreat, her child.

Additional responses suggest that people believe Terry the father is guilty of abusing his son. You might argue that this conclusion just makes sense since men are naturally more aggressive than women. Accordingly, husbands harass, abuse and beat their wives, and fathers are more likely to be child abusers. Women as mothers on the other hand are natural caretakers. A woman would never harm a child. Women simply know and understand the needs of children.

As it happens, these gender stereotypes are not terribly relevant. Across all categories of child abuse, women make up a greater proportion of child abusers than men: 54 percent female versus 46 percent male. And when we consider only parents as offenders, mothers are much more likely to be abusers of children than fathers: of all child abusers 45 percent are mothers and 24 percent are fathers.

On the other hand, it is true that men are more likely to be sexual abusers than women, but sexual abuse is relatively rare as a form of abuse. Sexual abusers represent only 7.2 percent of all child-abuse perpetrators and only 2.4 percent of parental abusers. In short, the probability of a mother abusing a child is 20–50 times as high as the father sexually abusing a child.[14]

Presumed perverted

It was a Monday and I was shopping in a department store. Given the time and day of the week, the store was relatively lacking in shoppers, and almost all of the ones there, except me, were women. I hadn't really planned to shop. Indeed, single and other involved parents rarely have the luxury of planning anything. Rather, what happens is that some unexpected circumstance affords a sudden opportunity to go shopping. In this case it was the cancellation of a 1.30 meeting that gave me a two-hour window after lunch.

Another thing about being a single parent is that one rarely shops for a specific thing or even category of things. One chains together multiple shopping trips to take advantage of a precious opportunity. In this case, I knew both my kids needed clothes, but it was also time to do some grocery shopping, which meant I would have to swing by the house on the way back to work to put spoilable foods in the fridge or freezer. For this same reason, I would have to buy the clothes first. I decided to start with my then three-year-old girl.

Now one of the limitations of this approach to shopping is that one doesn't always have a list of needed items when the

---

14 See *Child maltreatment 2007* published by the US Department of Health and Human Services. The gender of perpetrators is reported at http://www.acf.hhs.gov/programs/cb/resource/child-maltreatment-2007 [Accessed 13 December 2013]. The relationship of the perpetrator to the child in child fatalities is given in Table 4.5, page 62.

opportunity to shop arises. You have to rely on memory quite a bit. One thing I remembered from the previous week was having to do a load of laundry because my daughter was running low on undies, and I wasn't sure I would make it through the school week. So girl's undies seemed like a good place to start shopping.

But no sooner had I started then I became aware of a presence. I was being watched. I looked over my shoulder at an approaching security guard who said. 'Excuse me, but what are you doing?' 'I'm buying clothes for my daughter,' I answered, somewhat surprised. 'Don't you have somewhere to be?' he asked. 'Yes, I do!' I responded, this time with some anger in my voice, as I became aware of what was happening and why.

It became clear that the security guard did not see a father shopping for his child's clothes. He saw a pervert. Just my imagination? Right. So if I had been in the, oh I don't know, let's say automotive section of the store examining spark plugs the security guard would have done the same thing? Really? If you honestly believe that then read no further. This book is not for you.

If a working mum had been doing the same thing for the same reason, I seriously doubt there would have been any intervention at all. When I told some male colleagues with young children about the episode, one responded that he never shops for his daughter's clothes without a female around for exactly that reason. I was stunned to hear this, and the entire experience triggered a series of questions in my mind.

First, why was I compelled to go shopping for my daughter's clothes on a Monday afternoon in the first place? Would the same thing have happened on a Saturday afternoon, a more plausible part of the week for dads to shop for their little girls' clothes? Why do I have to juggle my responsibilities as a parent and an employee, and what does this say about the assumptions society makes about the 'proper' roles and responsibilities of mothers and fathers?

Why can't I buy clothes for my three-year-old girl, or any three-year-old girl for that matter? Why do fathers find it necessary to have women along to make these purchases? Are we incapable of selecting girls' undies, or are we all assumed to be Humbert Humbert in Nabokov's *Lolita* until we can establish otherwise? Sounds like gender discrimination to me.

So, many good men are categorised as villains based on the gender profile of a thankfully rare offender and despite considerable evidence to suggest that women abuse children overall at a higher rate than men. If mothers are the designated nurturers of the world, then fathers are implicitly assumed to be second-rate parents, or even worse, depraved, abusive criminals.

Intriguingly, I found that some of the few who identified Terry as a woman still saw the father as the villain. She was described as the victim of an angry ex-husband making false claims against her, even though the accuser was described as anonymous, a surprising result given research showing that mothers make over 90 percent of all false accusations in divorce trials involving child custody disputes and that over 95 percent of all false accusations are against fathers.[15]

In other words, he's a scoundrel either way. Here is another double standard resulting from the very same gender stereotype. Men are not good parents or not parents at all. This double standard, which has been demonstrated in several studies examining gender stereotypes,[16] operates against men.

This 'other' glass ceiling can be interpreted in at least two ways. First, it's an additional barrier that mothers face. After being discriminated against on the job, where male values, orientations and interests are implicitly recognised and promoted over her own, she gets to come home to a second job where she must do more than her fair share of the menial labour.

But a second view of the 'other' glass ceiling is as a constraint on fathers who genuinely want to be more involved in raising their children and, more generally, in participating in household activities. Most fathers have felt this kind of discrimination to some degree, but it is rarely acknowledged.

---

15   Farrell 2001, 79, 218.
16   Rosenwasser et al. 1985; Wentworth & Chell 2001.

How do I know? Well, for one thing I am a father. And I have experienced it. I have often been judged to be a lesser parent than a mother. As a single father, I have had others express surprise or even indignation that I am raising my family without any maternal guidance. Older women, and even childless teenage girls, have admonished me for not doing things 'the right way'.

I am also Chris and Terry. Both scenarios are based on my actual experiences. I have been accused of abusing my son by an anonymous person. Facing false accusations is a tough challenge under any circumstances. Doing so over an issue about how you treat your own children which threatens and undermines your relationship with your children is one that still makes me shudder.

But I have also turned up late for a major meeting at work with my child's vomit down the front of my suit; a far more trivial experience, but one that allowed me to see gender discrimination at work in the other direction. I don't know if I was a 'hero' but I certainly intimidated the (mostly) men in the room. It could have been the smell of the vomit, but I suspect it had more to do with me juggling my professional and personal responsibilities in ways that they never even contemplated. I also suspect that a woman in the same situation would have been treated very differently.

So, I have bumped into both glass ceilings from opposite directions. I have been the traditional male breadwinner in the predominantly male professional world far from parenting issues and responsibilities. Like so many women who have been done this juggling act for some many decades, I have also been a single parent who has to manage the task of raising my family.

Mothers letting go

Society's assumption that mothers know better than fathers about caring for children, and more generally about running a household, is the other glass ceiling in a nutshell, and as we've seen already, it can work against men and women. How does society reinforce this stereotype?

The stereotype that mothers are the essential parents and fathers are optional, expendable, irrelevant, incompetent, menacing and dangerous can be found everywhere, from abortion rights, paternity fraud, DNA testing, artificial insemination, sperm banks, child support payments, and adoption laws, to Homer Simpson, parent–teacher committees, and birthday parties.

You've come a long way, Daddy!

The other day I was walking around Darling Harbour with my kids during the Latin Festival. As we walked past the toilets, I noticed a sign for a Parent's Room. Below the sign, there were various graphics of the amenities provided in the facility. In very small letters at the bottom of the sign it read 'Fathers Welcome'. Nice to know that we fathers qualify. You've come a long way, Daddy!

To be sure, there are differences in the parenting approaches of fathers and mothers. This is as it should be. Not only is the parenting of mothers and fathers 'equal but different', but the difference itself is of value.

Admittedly, mothers, and women in general, may find some of the ideas expressed in this book to be confronting. But this is simply a reflection of their difference. For instance, mothers wield 'influence power', even if only by fiat. And much of this book is about voluntarily relinquishing that power.

How does influence power work exactly? Well, Ron Taffel interviewed hundreds of mothers and fathers about parenting activities and decisions, and some of the responses are quite illuminating in this regard.[17] Mums say things like 'It was almost easier when men had *nothing* to do with the kids. At least then things were done *right*'; or 'Mine doesn't contribute at all. It's like living with *another child*'.[18]

And how does it feel to be on the other side of these old fashioned gender stereotypes? Dads feel like 'Nothing I do is right. It's got to be done her way' and 'She wants me to do fifty percent of the work but she wants *one hundred percent* of the *decision-making power*'.[19]

---

17 Taffel 2003, 18.
18 Taffel 2003, 25.

We dads get the idea. She is management; he is labour, or even worse, just another child who needs looking after. The last quote in particular is quite illuminating; she is the boss and he is the personal assistant.

First-time mothers will tell first-time fathers what to do, even though she has no more training than he does. The presumption is that having breasts and a vagina, and having delivered the baby means that she understands the child's needs implicitly. I question this assumption. And this authority by fiat continues as the child matures. Mothers determine what children wear, eat, do and watch, far more than fathers do.[20] Fathers are merely ciphers, a stand-in parent for when mum is busy, tired or otherwise disengaged. And even here, their temporary authority is easily destroyed by a mother who interferes with his attempts to discipline his own children.

Letting go involves letting dads do things their own way, and this will be painful because dads do things differently, but different does not necessarily mean 'inferior'. This will be the toughest lesson for the mothers reading this book. Dads have preferences just like mums, and when these preferences collide neither parent should assume that their way is the 'right' way. This may sound simple enough, but it's really difficult to do in day-to-day domestic life.

This was a constant battle I had with the mother. She insisted that the kids have a bath every night; I thought it was alright if they skipped a night every now and then. I thought the kids needed to be in bed at 8:30 pm on school nights; she let them stay up later if they were having fun. She made my son do homework every night, but I let him do a whole week's worth the night before it was due. I dropped the kids off and picked them up from school on time, without fail; she was continually late for drop off and pick up. Did I mention that we divorced?

Some of you may reject the idea that mothers are somehow preventing fathers from being involved around the house. Mothers needn't let go of anything; fathers simply need to step up. Is it all about husbands being unfair and lazy? Well, in some parts of the world, attitudes and social policy toward fatherhood have changed

---

19   Taffel 2003, 25.
20   Lamb 2004, 13; Levine 2000, 9.

rapidly, and the amount of time and effort devoted to being a dad has changed at the same pace. In Norway, the implementation of father-friendly policies in the workplace led to an increase in paternal leave from three percent of all working dads to 90 percent in a single decade.[21] Does this sound more like deadbeat dads, or fathers who were waiting for permission to raise their children? Why would unfair, lazy men become just and diligent so quickly?

I'd put forward an additional argument for why the denigration of dads is not in the best interests of mothers, and women in general. There is a surface or peripheral level where legal victories of mothers over fathers in child custody battles can be interpreted as advances for women. After all, mothers are women and fathers are men. But these same 'victories' may also inadvertently reinforce the stereotype that women are uniquely suited to domestic life; that a woman's place is indeed in the home. Somebody has to do all that parenting, and if he's incompetent then she's got to do it.

Women have quite vigorously and justifiably attacked traditional stereotypes linking women to domestic roles and excluding them from the professional world, but this is only half the battle. We must also question the traditional stereotypes linking men to professional roles and excluding them from the domestic world. Continuing to denigrate fatherhood and assuming female superiority in everything related to parenting is probably not the best way to proceed if we are to have more female prime ministers, CEOs, Nobel Prize winners, Supreme Court justices, and, well, hopefully you get the picture. If these potential female leaders are at home compensating for an obviously ill-equipped father, how are they going to scale these professional heights? How will the playing field ever be level?

Men are not the common enemy of women seeking to break through the glass ceiling. Nor are women the common enemy of men who wish to shatter the other glass ceiling by seeking equal status in matters of family life and children. Neither glass ceiling is strictly a battle between the genders, but contemporary debate is almost always framed in these terms.

---

21   Kvande 2009.

Even as you read this now, many women are happy to stay at home looking after the kids and wonder what all the fuss is about women running major corporations. Which side of the debate do you suppose they are on? And as hard as this may be to believe, some men get it. Some men are genuinely indignant that women have been prevented from attaining top positions in public institutions and private organisations. Both glass ceilings are 'maintained' by those who want to restrict opportunities and choices of others, men *and* women, because of gender stereotypes. It's time to start seeing beyond gender.

As a single, career-oriented father, I understand the challenges facing many women: work–life balance, role conflict, family friendly policies, parental leave, just to name a few. My lifestyle is far more similar to a single, career-oriented mother than it is to most of the men I know, who I often struggle to identify with. These are not 'women's' issues; they are family issues, and despite what the media and courts have been saying, or more pertinently not addressing, fathers are very much a part of the family.

In many areas some men and women are on the same side, and some men and women are on the other side! So differences notwithstanding, the common goal is breaking down traditional gender stereotypes, particularly those that restrict the life choices of either women or men. To do that, it is time to look at the *other* glass ceiling in a little more detail.

The book begins with a chapter, 'Reflections on the glass ceiling', that identifies the uneven distribution of domestic labour and child-care responsibilities in the typical Australian home as a major cause of the glass ceiling. Fathers simply do not contribute their fair share. This book unveils the biases, myths, stereotypes and taboos underlying this gender inequity, and offers a potential solution that requires more trust, respect, delegation and cooperation between mums and dads.

The first half of the book, 'Fathers stepping up', addresses internal, psychological barriers fathers create for themselves. In many respects, fathers have nobody to blame but themselves for their often secondary status within the family. Research indicates that while mothers choose to allocate additional discretionary time to family activities, fathers choose . . . golfing! Fathers aren't as involved in the lives of their children, often by choice. The chapter 'Deadbeat dads' explores why this is the case and what the costs are for mothers and children.

Nobody ever went to their deathbed wishing they had spent more time in the office. That's how the old saying goes. 'The deathbed paradox' explores the unexpected pitfalls of the traditional male stereotype as the breadwinner of the family. From Willy Loman in *Death of a salesman* to George Bailey in *It's a wonderful life*, popular culture offers glimpses of what men often lose while focusing on their careers.

Being a father is easy. You don't need a degree, a diploma, a licence, or even a permit. But being a good father is a lot of hard work. Why go through with it? 'The toughest job you'll ever love' explores all the emotional rewards of being a father, and parenthood in general.

The second half of the book, 'Mothers letting go', addresses the external, sociological barriers fathers face. As it turns out, the world is not always very encouraging to dads who want to play a central role in the lives of their children. And mums are often the ones creating these external barriers. 'We're pregnant! (No I'm not!)' explores the decisions made by mothers – and fathers – throughout various stages of reproduction from conception through to lactation. It shows how, even before baby is born, paternity is being marginalised relative to maternity. 'The second parent' examines how mothers come to dominate fathers in the parenting of the children. The chapter combines personal anecdotes with television programs, news stories, public policy and academic research to examine how society tends to marginalise and even denigrate fatherhood. It explores the consequences for mothers, fathers, and especially children.

Until recently, single parent meant single mother. The fact is that children of divorces have two parents; it's just that they usually spend a lot more time with mum than dad. In 'Weekend warriors' you'll find out how single dads compensate for this lack of time in order to maintain strong bonds with their children. Surprisingly, married fathers may actually spend less time with their children than their divorced counterparts!

Fathers bring a unique set of skills to the parenting table, and research is beginning to uncover the unique benefits for children who spend a lot of time with their dads. No matter how hard mothers work at being great parents, they simply cannot provide the complementary sets of skills that fathers can. 'The compleat child' reviews academic research on the unique contributions of fathers to the physical, emotional and intellectual wellbeing of children, and argues for a more balanced approach to parenting in Australian families.

But this book is not just about single dads. It is relevant to any man who chooses to prioritise fatherhood over career aspirations. It is for mothers who want to smash through the glass ceiling in pursuit of the highest echelons of professional success without compromising their commitment to their children. It is for *any person* – male or female – who chooses to act contrary to gender norms, or who defies the requirement to choose between career and children.

This book challenges the sexism that expects a mother to care for her family and doubts her commitment to a career, and equally, the sexism that requires a father to provide for his family financially and doubts his ability to look after his own children. This is the other glass ceiling – the one reflected in gender inequity in the family home. As we'll see, these two forms of sexism are inextricably linked in subtle yet complicated ways. To see how, let's first examine the original glass ceiling – the one that operates in the boardroom.

Part 1
Fathers stepping up

Make no mistake about it. When it comes to gender inequity in the typical family home – the imbalance of workload and responsibility for the needs of family members – dads must shoulder more than their fair share of the blame for this sad state of affairs. How can husbands casually fob off all this toil and hardship onto the women they say they love?

Men are deluded. They tell themselves a series of half-truths and outright lies to justify not making an equal contribution to the care of their own children.

The first part of this book exposes this self-deceit and identifies the specific psychological barriers that fathers impose on themselves to become separated from their children. It challenges fathers to reconsider the assumptions they make about themselves and about how the world is supposed to work in general.

For the dads that heed this call, the rewards will far outweigh the inconveniences; they will wonder what they were doing with their lives before they became 'real' dads. Those that don't, will go to their deathbeds wondering 'what if', as so many fathers have done before them.

Deadbeat dads

There isn't, and has never been, a known society where men do the majority of domestic and childcare labour.

Deutsch 1999, 4

When the terrible moment of birth arrives, its supreme importance and its superhuman effort and peril, in which the father has no part, dwarf him into the meanest insignificance; he slinks out of the way of the humblest petticoat, happy if he be poor enough to be pushed out of the house to outface his ignominy by drunken rejoicings. But when the crisis is over he takes his revenge, swaggering as the breadwinner, and speaking of Woman's 'sphere' with condescension, even with chivalry, as if the kitchen and the nursery were less important than the office in the city.

Shaw 1903, 18

No woman ever killed a man while he was washing the dishes.

Sign hanging in a quaint little café in the Hunter
Valley wine region of Australia

A fairy tale gone wrong

Once upon a time, there lived a beautiful princess with long, flowing golden locks and big, round sapphire blue eyes. From the time she was a little girl, she dreamed of one day marrying a handsome prince, living in a magnificent palace, and becoming the queen of a vast, splendid kingdom, er, queendom, er, you know what I mean! One day she learned of a fabulously wealthy prince who lived in the kingdom on the other side of the Misty Mountains, and decided to pay the young royal a visit – incognito of course. This is a fairy tale after all.

Disguised as a simple washerwoman, she joined a caravan headed for the kingdom on the other side of the mountains. After arriving and spending time among the townspeople, she heard a loud horn blast. Looking up, she saw the prince riding his royal white stallion with a palace guard on either side of him. So preoccupied was she with the approaching prince, that she lost her footing and, twisting an ankle as she fell, let out a loud yelp. Instantly, the prince dismounted his horse, ran over to her, and helped her to her feet. Finding the prince to be kind and gentle, even though he thought she was nothing more than a lowly washerwoman, she was more determined than ever to become his bride.

She had learned from the townspeople of the annual ballroom dance held in the palace on the night of the first full moon after the winter snow had completely melted from the ground, and through her father's connections, secured an invite to the gala event. As her horse-drawn carriage cleared the last turn of the mountain pass, she could see the royal palace in the distance, its magnificence ever increasing as she approached.

It was the most elegant and beautiful place she had ever seen! Gold walls and marble floors, or was it gold floors and marble walls? Anyway, some really seriously awesome floors and walls defined every room, with carpets displaying a rainbow of every imaginable colour, and furniture made from the finest woods and fabrics!

The royal garden was a veritable cornucopia of flowers and fruit trees, and the imperial pool featured six porcelain fountains, arranged in two rows of three, which sprayed water ten metres into the air in four different directions, creating the impression of a light, misty rain. In short, the prince had a way cool bachelor pad.

The two met on the dance floor during the community dance, where each man and each woman were paired off and on throughout. When she was due to partner with the prince, she looked down in deference, until he touched her hand; then she looked up and their eyes met. Time both stopped and flew as she gazed into his eyes.

Immediately afterward, the prince asked her for the next dance, and by the end of the evening they had fallen in love. They married two months later in an elaborate ceremony, and all the townspeople were invited to share in the festivities. Afterward, the princess moved into the magnificent palace, where she lived happily ever after.

Well, not exactly 'ever after'. Actually, it was more like a year or so; then the prince began to change.

He began joining his friends at the Royal Golf Course more and more often, and this was usually followed by a lengthy visit to the Ye Old Village Tavern. Then there were the weekend hunting expeditions. It was rather surprising how little game the prince and his mates actually brought back with them.

And he became somewhat, eh, less romantic than he had been initially. Once, when she had returned early from a trip to the village market, she saw a young woman exiting through the side gate of the palace. She didn't know what to think. Actually, she *did* know what to think, she just wasn't sure what, exactly, to do about it.

Supposing that having a child together might provide just the spark their marriage needed, the princess bore the prince a son, and then another, and then a daughter, then another son, but this actually made things worse. The prince was hardly ever around. Trips to Ye Old Village Tavern became more frequent, and when he returned, he was usually in no condition to do anything but pass out in bed. And, of course, the children greatly increased the amount of work that needed to be done around the palace. The princess was constantly exhausted, lacking in sleep, and increasingly irritable.

By now the spacious beauty of the palace had lost its allure and become instead a source of angst and frustration. Keeping everything clean and tidy had become an onerous ritual. Sure she had many servants to help, but they had to be told what to do, and knowing what needed to be done was usually more than half the problem. Looking after the palace had become a struggle and a juggling act that directly contributed to the sense of mental exhaustion and stress.

The garden, once admired for its beauty and bounty, had by now become just another source of drudgery. Plants had to be watered, trees pruned and harvested, weeds cleared, and then there was the fertiliser – animal poop really. Now when she looked out the palace window into the garden she saw not flowers, fruits, and a rainbow of colours, but rather weeds and undergrowth, dirt and filth, and the hours and hours of labour they implied.

The pool, previously a source of inspiration and awe, now offered no solace. Leaves, sticks, bird droppings, and other debris had to be removed constantly. Two of the six fountains had become clogged and no one in the village had the faintest idea of how to repair them.

Depressed, demoralised and defeated, the princess had finally had enough. After several meetings with the finest and noblest counsellor in the village, she filed for divorce, and was granted the palace, custody of all the children, and 50 percent of the prince's future earnings in perpetuity. And she lived happily . . . ever after!

Fathering – the bare minimum

One day, my son and I were having one of those silly conversations where I speculated on where various of his characteristics originated. I thought it might be fun to include him in the speculation. So I asked him . . .

'Where did you get your good looks?'
'Mummy.'
'Where did you get your intelligence?'
'Mummy.'
'Where did you get your charm?'
'Mummy.'
'Well, what did you get from me then?'
'All you gave for me was your sperm.'

Sadly, this is often how the modern fairy tale of romantic love, marriage and parenthood actually turns out. A man's home may be his castle, but he is often not fit to be king! Husbands, and particularly fathers, simply do not contribute their fair share to running the family household and raising their own children. The wife/mother eventually exhausts herself making up the difference, giving up sleep, leisure, personal pursuits and, of course, her career in the process.

A woman's place?

By and large, 'women are still expected to take care of the children in our society'.[1] The very nature of the post-industrial workplace had this expectation built into it. Men 'went' to work. They left the home to sell their labour to organisations that, more often than not, were in the position to dictate how and when that labour would be delivered. Men worked outside of the family home, where, when and how their employer demanded, and with this arrangement came the implicit assumption that male labourers would have little or no childcare responsibilities back home.[2]

Eventually things began to change; women ventured into the world of professional work and this certainly changed the dynamic of the typical family household – but not as much as you might think. Men helped out a little more at home – but not much. Perhaps more importantly, not much changed at the office to accommodate this influx of career-oriented women.

To say that women have historically faced many invisible barriers in the workplace that have inhibited their equal participation in various professions is to make the understatement of the last half-century.[3] These barriers are often put in place by a good ol' boys club that makes sure the rules of professional success favour the interests, styles, motives and preferences of men over women. 'No girls allowed' still very much captures the world of professional success, at least at the very uppermost levels of public and private organisations.

How do the organisations that hire labour reflect the interests of men rather than women? Just imagine, for example, women designing an organisation where the clerk reports to an assistant manager, who reports to a store manager, who reports to a district manager, who reports to a regional manager, who reports to the vice-president of mar-

---

1 Kymlicka 1991.
2 MacKinnon 1987.
3 Kolb et al. 2011.

keting, who reports to the president of marketing – whoops, sorry – chief marketing officer, who reports to the chief executive officer (i.e., the alpha male).

If this kind of hierarchical organisational structure doesn't reflect a male obsession with status and dominance, I don't know what does. One could just as easily imagine an organisation with no official titles, no ranks, and no levels of hierarchy, where there are no official lines of reporting and everybody just kind of discusses everything with everybody else, sort of like a great, big Tupperware party.

What about the many professions involving career paths wherein the employee must survive a 'trial by fire' early on before they reap any real professional rewards? Law firms demand excessive hours from junior associates in order for them to later make 'partner'. The same basic approach holds in consulting firms and various agencies. Young doctors must endure a brutal 'internship' before they can officially practise medicine. Junior academics at universities must disproportionately produce research publications during a five-to-seven-year period following the award of their PhD or other terminal degree in order to 'make tenure'. Similar examples abound in other sectors of the professional world.

The commonality here is obvious. In order to succeed in the professional world, an individual must disproportionately sacrifice time and labour during their 20s and 30s, typical childbearing years for women. This seems like another rather obvious example of a male-dominated institution rigging the rules of the game to favour men over women.

One could easily imagine an institutional environment where the need to bear and raise young children was given greater primacy. Employees in their 20s and 30s wouldn't be pushed into 'make or break' positions, but rather, would be seen as investments in the future of the organisation. The real weeding out process wouldn't start until the late 30s and 40s, stages in the typical family life cycle when mothers and fathers would be in better positions to make more even contributions of their time to professional and domestic labour.[4]

In retrospect, it makes equally intuitive sense, the idea that the 'make or break' years in any career path should occur when children are

---

4   Craig & Sawriker 2009.

typically in high school, not when they are in nappies. But this did not become the norm in these professions. Why not? What organisational processes led to this and other policies that resulted in a systematic under-representation of women in senior roles – the glass ceiling? Well, men making biased decisions, of course. But how, exactly, do men come to these capricious, discriminating decisions?

The (not so) secret life of men

As a personal observation, I'd like to point out that husbands are not particularly sophisticated when it comes to withholding information from their wives. Research is pretty clear that women transmit and detect subtle non-verbal forms of communication better than men. Men like things stated, explicit, and straightforward; women go for a more subtle, nuanced form of communication.[5]

I've always found the movie *True lies* to be rather fantastical in this regard. In it, Arnold Schwarzenegger plays a secret agent who has managed to keep his alternative existence a secret from his wife, played by Jamie Lee Curtis, over many years of marriage. Right. Does anybody really believe that a man could pull this off? In reality, a wife would detect the subtle cues of deception immediately. She'd start asking questions like 'Where *were* you last night?', 'I *called* the office but you weren't there,' 'Is there somebody else?', after the first missed dinner or late night at the office. No, not a chance on earth he pulls this off.

On the other hand, Jennifer Garner in the television show *Alias* is much more credible as a secret agent who is able to conceal her identity from one boyfriend after another. That's more like the universe I live in, the one where men are more easily duped by women when it comes to secrets and subterfuge. As long as dinner is on the table when he gets home from work, it would never even occur to him that she is off saving the world from international criminals.

I think it very unlikely that the men who have run major private and public institutions have deliberately created policies that dis-

---

5   Hall 1978.

criminate against women. Maybe in the past, but not now. Yet, women are still discriminated against in the professional realm and all the evidence points to men as the instigators. What, then, is the process by which men have universally prevented women from achieving equality in labour markets? Here's a stab at an explanation. Whether it's a dictatorship, a democracy, or something in between, decisions in major public and private institutions have been made from a male perspective, with the motives and priorities of men paramount; not necessarily with the intent of disadvantaging women, but nevertheless, with that effect.

In a room full of men, adopting a policy of testing the new talent early on, before making them partners, or awarding them tenure, or allowing them to practise medicine, etc. made a lot of sense. They either decided this as individuals 'in charge' of policy, implicitly discussed this at meetings and built a consensus for the idea, or explicitly voted for this at a designated committee meeting. The problem was that no women were around to ask the simple question of how all that new talent would go about starting families if they were being pushed so hard at work? Whoops! None of the blokes thought to bring that up!

Men talking the talk (but not walking the walk)

However men came to dominate the public and private organisations comprising the seat of power in modern society – whether deliberate or incidental – they are not ready to relinquish their authority just yet. Women have been demanding these top spots for over half a century now, but as we learned in 'Reflections on the glass ceiling', *very* little has actually changed.

What's even sadder is that male leaders have learned to navigate the treacherous waters between the Scylla of giving up power and the Charybdis of admitting to chauvinistic, discriminating attitudes, policies and behaviours. They've learned how to proclaim the latest politically correct attitudes with a straight face and a stern expression.

For example, give men a survey about their attitudes toward doing housework and looking after children, and you will get a virtual testimony to gender equality in the family household. But if you examine time diaries of what mothers and fathers actually do throughout the week, you'll find that she changes nappies and mops floors far more often than he does.[6]

And this disparity holds even when taking into account that fathers often exaggerate the amount of time they spend with their children.[7] In one rather notorious example of exaggeration, the husband of former US Congresswoman, Pat Schroeder, gave an interview to talk about how important a role he played in his wife's political career by being the go-to guy at home with the children. It was a phone-in show; the first caller was his wife. Ms Schroeder asked him a series of questions like the name of the family doctor, shoes sizes, names of teachers, best friends, etc. Needless to say, dad did not pass the little quiz. This was perhaps a cruel lesson, and I seriously doubt that this little episode motivated him to become a more involved dad – more on that later. But it drove the point home nicely. Don't talk the talk if you can't walk the walk.[8]

Ask male CEOs about 'family-friendly' work policies, paternity leave, flexible hours, equal opportunity, affirmative action and the gender pay gap, and you'll get a carefully rehearsed litany of political correctness. Women should be equal in this; women should be equal in that; companies should give priority to hiring women in senior executive positions; parental leave policies should be gender neutral. You name it, and they've learned the 21st-century, feminist-sanctioned, politically correct response.

But ask these same men to describe the perfect daughter-in-law for their aspiring sons, and you'll get a lock, stock and barrel description of Suzie Homemaker. She cooks, she cleans and, most importantly, she supports his career. In reality, nothing much has changed over the last half century. Men still have the expectation that their wives will cook the meals, clean the house, do the laundry, change the dirty nappies, wake up at two in the morning to tend a sick child. This expectation is perhaps less explicit than it was 50 years ago, but it's still there.[9]

---

6   Baxter & Smart 2010, 142–43.
7   Pleck & Pleck 1997, 33–48.
8   Schroeder 2000.
9   Tracy & Rivera 2010.

Even when the traditional gender roles have reversed; when she is the breadwinner and he is the part-timer earning 'supplementary' income, the views around the office are not likely to fully recognise this. She will be viewed as underqualified relative to her male peers, but he will be viewed as overqualified relative to his female peers. In short, the world will still be of the view that he *should* be earning more and she *should* be earning less.[10] To a large extent, what the last 50 or so years have taught male leaders is how to look like they are making changes to promote gender equality without actually changing their fundamental attitudes at all.

We can talk all we want about how the public and private institutions that hire labour have to change to eliminate the glass ceiling facing women in pursuit of career success, but we better also consider the changes necessary in that little institution we call the family household. There are only 24 hours in a day. If she's doing more housework and child care than he is, she has less time to devote to her career. She can compensate somewhat by giving up sleep and leisure, and research indicates that career mothers do exactly this.[11] But at the end of the day, she won't have as much time for her career as he does.

Indeed, if one were to examine the last 50 years of research on how men and women allocate time to paid labour and domestic labour, certain trends would become apparent. Some of these trends are, perhaps, not surprising. Women do more paid labour now than in the past, whereas the amount of paid labour that men do has not changed considerably over the last 50 years. Yet men still do more paid labour than women overall even when occupations and positions are comparable. In general, the traditional male stereotype as the breadwinner is still reflected in contemporary labour statistics.

The changes in domestic labour show a different pattern. Men do slightly more domestic labour now than in the past, and women do less domestic labour now than in the past. But overall women still do far more domestic labour than men. One US study suggests that married mothers who work full time do 48 more minutes of domestic labour

---

10   Triana 2011.
11   Craig 2005, 521–40; 2006a, 125–43; 2006b, 259–81.

per day than their full-time employed spouses.[12] The traditional female stereotype as the homemaker is still very much apparent.

Not only are there differences in the *amount* of domestic labour mothers and fathers do, but there are rather important differences in the *type* of work performed around the house. She tends to be saddled with the more frequent, inflexible necessities of family life that must be performed in a daily basis, whereas he performs tasks that are less frequent and that have quite a bit of discretion around when they get done.

She must have dinner on the table at 7 pm every night, whereas nobody notices whether he cuts the lawn on Saturday morning or shows up at the golf course for an early tee off time. She must change the nappy when the little one poops; he can fix the gate in the back yard whenever it suits him. Beds must be made every day. Snow must be shovelled from the drive way only once or twice a year. Who do we think will have the more difficult time juggling professional and domestic responsibilities?[13]

Parenthood introduces an additional category of activity into the household, caring for children. Once more the literature suggests a clear pattern in the gender differences over time. Mothers do less child care now than in the past. Fathers spend more time looking after their own children now than they did in the past, but studies vary considerably in terms of how much child care fathers do relative to mothers, with research in some countries indicating almost equal contributions, and research in others suggesting wide disparities.[14] However, the general consensus is that fathers still do not do their fair share when it comes to looking after children.

---

12   Miley & Mack 2009, A1–A22, A27.
13   Blair & Lichter 1991. Research also suggests a link between how much domestic labour is segregated along the lines of gender and gender inequity in terms of total time devoted to domestic labour – the more segregated the domestic labour, the less he does overall. Wives looking for a fair shake in running the family household would do well to get their husbands to do more cooking, cleaning, laundry, and bed-making.
14   Lunn 2008; Miley & Mack 2009; Baxter & Smart 2010, 25, 28; Fathers spend only a minute a day alone with their children, Melbourne *Herald Sun*, 20 October 2008. Retrieved 16 December 2013 from http://www.news.com.au/news/dads-are-gone-in-60-seconds/story-fna7dq6e-1111117797917.

Moreover, as with domestic labour in general, fathers seem to get the easier, more enjoyable, less routine, childcare activities. He gets to play games, teach sports, and do other kinds of recreational activities, whereas she has to deal with day-to-day care, sick children, and personal problems.[15] Given this division of labour it is perhaps not surprising that the contributions fathers make to child care tend to come on the weekends, when it's far more acceptable and convenient to be away from the office, than during the work week, where things like school drop off and pick up, soccer training, piano lessons, parent–teacher conferences, etc., tend to happen.[16] Fathers seem to have the luxury of compartmentalising their lives into distinct work and non-work segments, whereas mothers are left to continually juggle the roles of parent and employee on a moment-by-moment basis.[17]

When domestic labour, paid labour, and childcare labour are considered together, women have increased their total amount of labour considerably over the last half century, whereas men have increased their total workload far less. The net effect is that women do more total labour than men, and experience leisure less often than men as a consequence. In other words, the increase in domestic labour by men has been minimal by comparison to the increase in paid labour by women. In sum, women do more domestic labour, more child care, less paid labour, and experience less leisure than men; they may also get less sleep and have less time for personal care, depending on their circumstance.[18]

In addition to a loss of leisure, another cost of this uneven allocation of labour is stress. Research indicates that mothers report higher levels of stress than fathers in general, with the highest levels experienced by married mothers who work full time. This may, in part, be due to the fewer hours of sleep reported by married mothers compared to

---

15   Howard, McBride & Hardy 2003, 6.
16   Maume 2011.
17   Thompson 1995; Deem 1996; Areni 2008.
18   Craig 2006a; 2006b; Monna & Gauthier 2008; Burnett et al. 2010; Durbin & Fleetwood 2010; Watson 2010; Gimenes-Nadal & Sevilla-Sanz 2011; Vijayasiri 2011.

married fathers.[19] All work, no play, and no sleep makes Jill a very, very stressed-out girl.

How husbands avoid housework (and what to do about it)

It turns out that fathers use a number of tactics to get out of doing their fair share of parenting.[20] The most basic approach is to simply ignore their responsibility. Dads sort of play a game of 'chicken' when something needs to be done around the house. If he holds out longer than she does, she does the work and he wins. Ignoring children's pleas, walking past the spill on the floor, tossing used undies on a pile of dirty clothes with a bin buried underneath are all (not so) excellent ways that dads play this hand.

My advice to women married to such men? Bolt. Not permanently. I'm not talking divorce here. I mean just leave for the weekend. No advance warning. Call up your girlfriends and plan a trip. Then when he comes home from work on Friday just tell him point blank that you're off to the airport. Better yet, make sure the fridge is empty and the house is a complete mess. Throw him into the deep end of the parenting pool and see if he can learn to swim. He will. Mummy strikes are terribly effective for getting daddies to do more around the house.[21]

A variation of the ignorance tactic is the whinge and moan approach. Here, dads will do the odd household task from time to time, but the idea is to put up such a stink about it that she won't bother asking him again. I have some sound advice for mums married to these kinds of dads. First, buy a full-body leather suit with metal spikes and a proper, circus-quality, lion taming whip. Don't worry. All the leading department stores carry them – in the sado-masochistic, sexual role-play department – right next to intimate apparel and sleepwear. Anyway, before he wakes up in the morning, ring his boss and tell him your husband is too sick to go to work today. Then dress up in the leather suit and wake him by cracking the whip in his ear, and tell him *you're* the boss today!!! In short, fight fire with fire!

---

19   Craig 2007; Miley & Mack 2009.
20   Deutsch 1999, 74–80.
21   Taffel 2003, 62.

Of course, some dads are cleverer than this. They use the old feigned incompetence act. Here the idea is that he ostensibly tries to contribute to household and parenting duties, but he either intentionally or carelessly messes everything up. Ruined laundry, inedible meals, well-organised but filthy bathrooms, are all ways to play this game.

My advice to mums married to dads using this tactic should be rather obvious – feign a little incompetence yourself! The mother[22] of my children taught me this one. I'll have to admit that doing the laundry wasn't always – how do I say this – a major priority for me. So I just didn't do very much of it. One day, fairly soon after we were married, she put a $1500 Hugo Boss suit in the wash. Then – to add insult to injury – she put it in the dryer.

Do you know what happens to wool/polyester blends when you do this? When it came out of the dryer it was the size, shape and hardness of a cricket ball. When I asked, no *confronted*, her about it, she pulled one of the best incompetence acts ever seen. Oscar-worthy I'd say. She simply did not know that you could not put business suits in a washing machine or a dryer. I bought it – and more or less took over laundry duties for the remainder of the marriage.

And let's face it men. How hard is it to load a dishwasher, run a vacuum, or do the laundry? Give me enough time and bananas, and I'll teach a Rhesus monkey how to do the laundry properly! Men are *way* smarter than Rhesus monkeys! Hard as that is for women to believe sometimes, we really are, so the feigned incompetence bit should fail on the face of it.

Then we have a subtle variation of feigned incompetence called the lower standards ploy. This is when fathers do things around the house. They do them technically correctly, but at a far lower standard than she would. One mother, for example, explained that every time it was her husband's turn to prepare dinner he made pasta. This consisted of boiling and draining the pasta, opening a jar, and stirring through the sauce – every single meal!

---

22 I could say 'ex'. For some time post-separation, I even referred to her as 'X', a reference of her being an unknown quantity. But this puts her not all that far from Voldemort in the Harry Potter books, (s)he who must not be named. In fairness, it takes two to tango, and 'mother' seems a lot more respectful than other appellations.

The lower standard ploy is often used when it comes to cleaning bathrooms. Men aren't exactly known for leaving the loo spotless, and for fairly obvious reasons. The male philosophy of peeing in the toilet is very much like playing a game of horseshoes – getting close is usually good enough. It's hardly surprising then that when it comes to cleaning the toilet, his 'filth tolerance threshold' for lack of a better term, is much higher than hers. The net result is that he does a lousy job of cleaning up.

Women married to men like this have at least two strategies for evening the score. The first is to fight fire with fire. He puts the seat up and then pees everywhere, right? Fine. You put both seats down and really pee all over everything! Just let it flow! Tell him that *your* preference is for both seats to be left down, and that it's his turn to clean the bathroom. Now this strategy can admittedly cause a little friction in a relationship, so here's another approach.

Improve peeing accuracy by changing the game. Not horseshoes, but archery. Just put one of those mesh targets with the rubber suction cups in the bottom of the toilet. They have them. You can order them online. One mother even commented 'Your product is amazing! I am the only woman in a family of five and this is my favourite product to tell people about. Also, I gift it whenever appropriate! Thanks so much!'[23]

Post the house rules on the wall nearby. Bull's eye = 50 points; 25 bonus points for a five-second stream in the scoring area; lose 100 points for peeing outside the scoring area!!! Then just hang a score board over the commode so the men in your life can compete with one another. Keep track of high scores, personal bests, house records. Solve the problem just like that!

Then there is the most awful, insidious, form of subterfuge for avoiding domestic responsibilities – compliments! That's right. When he tells you that you've just cooked the most incredible meal he's ever tasted, he may mean it, but he also wants to make sure that you'll prepare the next meal as well. It's difficult to detect whether meal compliments are legitimate or not, but if he starts complimenting you on

---

23   Just go to: http://www.pottytarget.com.

how clean the floor is, or how bright his dress shirt looks, tell your man you're on to him and that *he* can do the cleaning next time!

To sum up, husbands have developed rather sophisticated psychological ploys to avoid doing their fair share of work around the house. Learn to recognise them and confront your husband when he uses them. Better yet, use these same tactics yourself. Deliberately ruin his favourite shirt in the laundry (one you secretly can't stand anyway)!

Dads in absentia

While they may rule the boardroom and the upper and lower houses of government, men are hardly the poster-children for parenting. Their record of achievement in the professional domain may be laudable, but in the domestic domain men come in for a lot of criticism, and they've earned it.

I use the term 'deadbeat dads' more broadly to describe the men that have abandoned their domestic posts, both before and after divorce. This definition is, of course, expanded beyond its normal use, where it describes dads who, post-divorce, simply leave behind all their responsibilities. But the truth of the matter is that they had already walked away from the responsibilities long before the divorce came through. He did not become a deadbeat dad because of divorce; he became divorced because he was a deadbeat dad!

Married fathers are often absent fathers. They are simply not around to look after their children, clean up around the house, prepare meals, change nappies, do laundry and other things that pretty much need to get done for a family household to function properly. They are elsewhere – in the office, at the golf course, at the pub, etc. – doing other things like working, playing, or just getting drunk with their mates. At home, they simply don't do enough.

How much is 'enough'? Um, that'd be 50 percent. Your wife, remember her, that woman you said you'd love and honour till death do you part or some such nonsense? She does the other half. There is perhaps nothing more infuriating than hearing a so-called father tell his mates, 'Hey, can't join you guys for the footy, I'm babysitting Saturday night.' Babysitting? Who's kids we talking about, mate? Yours? That's not babysitting. That's called being a parent!

One study even suggests that older daughters actually spend more time caring for their younger siblings than their fathers do.[24] Research also shows that married fathers, if given the possibility of having a free

24   Baxter & Smart 2010, 40–41.

day, think of personal leisure over family activities with the children. Fishing with his mates wins out over spending a day at the beach with his kids.[25] Men, this is not good enough! As the title of the book suggests, it's time to step up.

Wisdom from the great prophet

Gandhi always held that women needed to be freed from household slavery – and he did this when establishing his first ashram in South Africa by having men and women share domestic tasks. Gandhi's notion was that women, free of the household chores, would be free to participate as equals with men in social and political activities.[26]

I'm constantly struck, or rather dumbstruck, by how fathers define their roles and responsibilities in the family household, or perhaps more precisely, how they deny their roles and responsibilities. The breadwinner mentality essentially becomes an excuse for not doing much else. This was brought home one evening when the main fuse on the electrical switchboard blew out. Standing there in a pitch black house, I had to figure out something pretty quickly.

Now I'm, admittedly, not the handiest of men when it comes to electrical problems, but I'm not a complete idiot either. I reset the main fuse switch, but within seconds it tripped again. I even, get this, replaced the main fuse, reset the switch, and – nothing – the main fuse tripped again. At this point all my hypotheses had been falsified. That's fancy academic talk for not having any idea what the problem was. But by now it was 9:30 pm. Where was I going to find an electrician this late on a Friday night?

I called somebody. I called somebody else. I called a third, then a fourth, then a . . . Finally, I found somebody who was already out on a job in the next suburb and was willing to stop by afterward. Now this is dedication folks. He arrived at 10 pm and quickly fixed the problem. (For you electricians out there, the problem was that one of the heaters had a tear in the electrical cord, which was creating a short).

---

25 Petre 1998.
26 Collins & Lapierre [1975] 1997, 478–79.

Anyway, afterward at roughly 10:15 pm, we started chatting. I may have offered him a beer, I can't remember. My co-author was due to arrive any minute, so I know I had some beer in the now functional fridge. It turned out that the electrician's son was the same age as mine, and midway through the beer, I discovered that the two boys played in the same soccer competition, and had a match against one another the following morning. On his way out the door, I told him that I'd see him at the soccer match, to which he replied, rather sheepishly, that he wouldn't be there because he was playing golf with his mates. I got the impression that this was the norm for Saturdays.

Here was a man willing to work at 10 pm on a Friday night, something I wouldn't do unless I was being paid triple-time – no quadruple-time – yet he had no intention of watching his son play soccer the next morning, something I wouldn't miss for the world. Well, maybe for the whole world, but I don't miss his matches very often. A simple matter of priorities? More on that later. By the way, I know you readers can't stand the suspense, so I'll tell you. My son's team won a 3–2 thriller, but no, my son did not score the winning goal. He's a defenceman.

To be fair, perhaps the electrician felt that he had earned his 18 holes of golf by working late on a Friday, but we must really question the choices fathers make about what to do with their time, which often involve not being around their own children! These choices are often couched in terms of the need to provide for the family, but as we've touched on already, this may be more subterfuge than substance, and the net effect of these kinds of decisions is that fathers don't spend all that much time around their own children.

One researcher created quite a sensation by estimating that the typical Australian father spends roughly one minute per day looking after his own children. Don't get me wrong – I'm sure it's a 'quality' minute – but I think it's really time for men to ask themselves honestly whether they're getting the job done as fathers. Interestingly, this research led to much angst and outrage among many 'men's rights' groups, until, that is, it was revealed that earlier research put the estimate at 37 seconds per day. Seems like the modern notion of an 'involved' father amounted to adding 23 seconds of child care per day.[27]

So the breadwinning role may be nothing more than a convenient excuse or giant cop-out when it comes to fathers not doing their fair share of child care. And as we'll see in the next chapter, many men live to regret playing this card. And so the question naturally arises – how do dads get away with it – with not doing their fair share around the house and with their kids?

The research reported in the prologue links this uneven distribution of domestic and professional labour in the household to progression through various stages of the family life cycle. As young singles, the lifestyles of women and men are similar with respect to the amount of time devoted to paid labour and domestic labour. Distinct breadwinner and homemaker roles are not yet apparent in the day-to-day activities of single men and women. Hence, younger, childless women earn, on average, the same as their male counterparts.[28]

Gender differences in professional and domestic labour begin to emerge when couples get married and move into the same domicile. Married men tend to do less domestic labour compared to when they were single, whereas the reverse is true for married women, resulting in a small but apparent gender gap. Additional research suggests that the gender difference in domestic labour has more to do with marriage than sharing a domicile. Married men do less housework than cohabiting men in romantic relationships, whereas married women do more housework than cohabiting women.[29]

The major change that causes lifestyle differences between men and women is having children. Married mothers do more domestic and childcare labour and less professional labour compared to childless wives. Married fathers also increase the amount of time they devote to domestic labour and childcare labour, giving up leisure time in the process, but these changes in time allocation are not as pronounced as for mothers, which results in a widening of the gender gap for domestic labour, and the creation of a gender gap in paid labour, childcare labour and leisure.[30] Compared to married fathers, married mothers do more domestic and childcare labour, less paid labour, and have less leisure time. These gender differences in time allocation abate as children, par-

27 Millar 2008; Lamb 2000, 23–42.
28 Porter 2011.
29 Davis, Greenstein & Marks 2007; Devetter 2009.
30 Baxter & Smart 2010, 141; Burnett et al. 2010.

ticularly the youngest child, moves from pre-school, to school-age, to post-school ages.[31]

Another way of looking at this is that career-oriented mothers do 'double-duty' or a 'second shift', bearing the brunt of the domestic and childcare labour after a hard day at the office. This is the 'price' of parenthood for women – a price that men do not pay. Mothers do the domestic work, and without being freed from that, do not have the time and resources to commit to their careers as fathers do. Or conversely, fathers do *not* do their share of domestic duty – giving them more time and resources to pursue worldly status and wealth. Amazingly, studies show that even unemployed husbands do less housework than wives who work a forty-hour week.[32]

Executive orders

'They've just had a new baby ... and I made sure that Jay-Z was helping Beyoncé out, and not leaving it all to mom and the mother-in-law.'[33]

Barack Obama, advising Jay-Z to not become a deadbeat dad

At this point I must sheepishly admit that this basic family life cycle pattern almost exactly characterises the changes in my life after my son was born. Prior to the birth of my older child, my son's mother and I pursued career success without compromise. But when she became pregnant it was as if some auto-pilot program took over. I got a promotion. She quit her job. I worked 50+ hours in the office, and she took over almost complete responsibility for all things domestic. It was not a happy time in our marriage.

What seems utterly amazing is that married couples often do not explicitly discuss adjustments in paid and domestic labour allocations prior to having children. Rather, research suggests that married couples

---

31   Craig & Sawriker 2009; Baxter & Smart 2010, 142; Vijayasiri 2011.
32   Hochschild & Machung 1989; Kymlicka 1991.
33   Heard on the trail, *The Economist*, 27 October 2012. Retrieved 13 December 2013 from http://www.economist.com/news/united-states/21565262-heard-trail.

drift into parenthood without formulating who will do what labour when around the house and at the office. First-time married parents seem to drift into the traditional gender roles of homemaker and bread-winner without really planning to do so.[34]

Indeed, it is only external pressure on the family household, in the form of exhausting work schedules, long periods away from children, inflexible bosses, etc., that forces married parents to reconsider this cul-turally prescribed arrangement. As one 'breadwinning' father described it:

> Twelve hours a day – gone from home. A lot of people do, but after doing it for a little while my wife and I sat down and said 'this is not an everyday life', and we made a decision based on the fact that the children were young, they weren't in school. We were trying to pay a mortgage which we weren't successfully getting ahead on. It's like, 'Why live this lifestyle at the moment when the kids are young and gorgeous and doing all these wonderful things? Why not do that in ten year's time when they are both in high school and looking after themselves and we can work like idiots and pay something off and it won't affect their lifestyle as much?' And so we made the decision and I got out of the business.

However, in the absence of extreme external pressures on family life, the male breadwinner and female homemaker roles seem to be the de-fault values for parents.

Ex-fathers

But what if mum wants to continue pursuing her career? What if she doesn't want to be the homemaker, or more likely, what if she wants him to be every bit the homemaker that she is? A 50/50 split? Although there are many complicated reasons for divorce,[35] many a marital dis-solution has stemmed from dissatisfaction over the division of labour within the family home.

---

34 Deutsch 1999.
35 Kitson 1992; Stevensen & Wolfers 2007.

Divorce is a tough place for both men and women. It tests them. And if there are children, it is even more testing. But in general, women are more proactive and men are more reactive. Women initiate 70–80 percent of all separations and divorces. This is of course a staggering statistic showing a very large disproportion between men and women. To say it another way, it is the exception rather than the rule when the man steps up and says: 'Honey, I think we need to call this quits.' In most cases she plays the divorce card and he reacts with surprise, shock and genuine befuddlement.[36]

Make no mistake about it – she tends to divorce him, and it is difficult not to interpret this general pattern in terms of the benefits of divorce outweighing the costs from her perspective. What are the costs? Well, we've heard a lot about this already. Much mass media content and academic research has focused on the problem of women's post-divorce welfare – or more specifically, lack of. While women predominantly initiate divorce, women also tend to be the biggest losers in terms of income post-divorce.[37]

Moreover, many mothers make a decision to divorce knowing that they are likely to have to carry the can as regards the children.[38] That is, they part knowing that they may have to sacrifice much in their life to raise their children as a single parent. Sure, many of these women will re-partner, but at the time that she is leaving, the future is unknown and uncertain.

Indeed, there is considerable evidence that, for mothers, divorce is very much the lesser of two evils. It's not very nice. It's just better than the alternative – staying married to him. After divorce, the women's standard of living drops, whereas the men's standard holds steady or sometimes even rises.[39] In addition, she is more likely than him to default on mortgage and other debt payments following divorce, and will find it more difficult to get access to credit.[40]

Divorced mothers will find it exceedingly difficult to find a job with flexible enough working hours to accommodate her now impossibly

---

36 Hetherington & Stanley-Hagan 1997.
37 Smock et al. 1999.
38 Horwitz & Lewin 2008.
39 O'Neill 1992; de Vaus 2004; de Vaus et al. 2009; Gadalla TM 2009.
40 Lyons & Fisher 2006.

complicated schedule. Childcare facilities will either be inadequate, too expensive, or too far away. Her now increased childcare responsibilities, assuming she gets primary custody, which is overwhelmingly likely, will result in the loss of mobility and maybe the loss of supportive extended families.

Alimony or spousal maintenance payments are increasingly rare, and child support payments have declined in real terms. Then there is the difficulty of ensuring the collection of court-mandated payments. And finally, even if she does find a job, the loss of employment currency and human capital (i.e., connections, expertise, up-to-date knowledge, etc.) during the '(not so) happy homemaker' years means any chance of a career is limited![41]

Don't get me wrong. I'm not saying that divorce is a picnic for fathers either. I've been there, done that, and it ain't pretty at all! More on that later. But let's put to bed, once and for all, this silly, sexist, 'gold digger' stereotype of a woman who divorces her spouse for financial gain. The hard facts say otherwise. Financial gain is not likely to be a primary motivation for a mother.

So why does mum quit if she's looking at potential poverty,[42] an unattractive job, limited career prospects, and an unmanageable portfolio of responsibilities? This is a pretty harsh indictment of dads. Moving several rungs down the socioeconomic ladder is evidently preferable to staying married to him, or in other words, no matter how much bacon he's bringing home, he's such a pig that overall it's not worth it. Indeed, research suggests that married men may even create more domestic labour than they actually perform.[43]

Mothers are perfectly capable of performing a basic economic analysis of costs and benefits of having him around, and will call the shots as to whether he stays or goes. This notion of a cost–benefit analysis may seem far removed from romantic notions of love, till death do us part, for better or for worse, and all that, but at the end of the day it seems like a pretty low bar to clear. Just contribute slightly more than you take; yet many a married father has failed to clear the bar.[44] It

---

41 Kymlicka 1991.
42 US Census Bureau 2009.
43 Mauldin & Meeks 1990.
44 Lancaster 1989; Mauldin & Meeks 1990.

should hardly come as a surprise then that, after initiating a divorce, mothers look for an alternative, economically viable partner to help raise her (their) children. And yet, fewer women than men re-partner after divorce, suggesting that the pickings are slim indeed.[45]

So what are the actual benefits to mothers who divorce their spouses? Well, if parents divorce or become single for other reasons, the gender differences in time allocation actually diminish compared to married parents, mainly because single mothers do less domestic labour than married mothers. Although primary custody of children after divorce is usually awarded to the mother, single mothers are more likely than married mothers to purchase childcare labour from the marketplace, allowing them to work full time. In effect, single mothers trade childcare labour for paid labour, which reduces the gender difference in time allocated to paid labour.

Married mothers can make similar trade-offs between child care and paid labour, but they may be more reluctant to do so if their husbands work full time. The breadwinner stereotype may insinuate that a married father's income is essential, whereas a married mother's income is not, leading married mothers to reduce the amount of paid labour they contribute to the marketplace. By contrast, single mothers experience less ambiguity about their need to work, even if they receive child support payments from their ex-spouses, so they work full time. Hence, the gender gap in paid labour observed for married parents is largely eliminated for single parents.

So divorce may actually allow single mothers more time for their careers, further education, financial planning, travel, hobbies and just getting more sleep. Having a more 'balanced' lifestyle may be worth a loss of financial status for many divorced women.[46] Ex-wives may essentially be saying: 'I didn't start it, he did! He didn't do his fair share when we were married!' To her, divorce is the end not the beginning of the problem.

Men tend to dismiss domestic work as not real work. The reality is that if she did not do it, it would not get done. As the quote from George Bernard Shaw makes clear at the beginning of this chapter, the male disdain for domestic labour is the ugly side of marriage; it is the

---

45   Kitson 1992; Stevensen & Wolfers 2007.
46   Craig 2005; Davis et al. 2007; Devetter 2009; Areni 2014.

blueprint or prototype of a deadbeat dad. This is men getting an over-inflated view of the 'bigger picture' tasks that occupy their time at the office. Well, boys, proceed at your own risk.

In effect, men have gone off to work to earn salaries and then paid their wives to do the housework, much like they could pay a maid to do the same thing. The irony is that fathers often stop paying for this labour at the very point in time when a court order makes their now ex-wives wage rates rather explicit. The term 'deadbeat dad' comes from ex-husbands who fail to pay child support and/or spousal maintenance payments to their ex-wives – who are still doing the bulk of the domestic labour! Becoming an ex-husband is not the same as becoming an ex-father, yet divorced men do not have a great record when it comes to meeting their financial obligations to their children.

There are a number of ways to measure the extent of the problem; we could look at the percentage of unpaid dollars relative to the total dollar value of all court orders, or the percentage of fathers that fail to fully comply with court orders relative to the total number of ex-husbands with court ordered obligations. Either way, there is considerable variability as we move from one country or even one state to the next. Much bad press has been given to 'deadbeat dads', the fathers who have abandoned their children and give little time, money, affection or even respect to their children after divorce. This is shameful, whether they are the secondary custodians (i.e., every other weekend and holidays) or not.

Can there be worse? Unfortunately yes. To add bile to their vileness, some fathers well capable of caring financially for their children step away even from this responsibility by (a) disguising their income through the cover of a business from which they draw a meagre salary while paying all their living expenses through their own company, (b) not declaring cash income to the ATO, (c) quitting or cutting back on employment, (d) going overseas, (e) salary-sacrificing, and (f) putting assets in the names of other relatives.[47]

Perhaps the saddest reality of all is that mothers are not really asking for all that much. Of course, the only fair arrangement is for men to do 50 percent of the work around the house. But research suggests that

---

47   Braaf & Meyering 2011.

the wife of a father who contributes 34 percent of the total childcare labour hours in the household is likely to be satisfied with this arrangement. But fathers who do only 27 percent of the work are likely to have discontented partners.[48] Guys, for an additional seven percent you can be in a happy marriage. Isn't it worth it?

---

48   Baxter & Smart 2010, 61.

The deathbed paradox

Each day has 24 hours and every day dads make decisions about how that time will be spent.

If they are playing golf with their mates on a Saturday, they are not in the stands cheering their son in his grand final soccer match. If they are at the pub watching the footy, they have missed their daughter's picnic in the backyard. Short of the introduction of a new cloning device for busy parents, fathers must choose where, when and with whom they will be.

As we saw in the previous chapter many fathers choose golf and grog over spending time with their kids. They are the deserter dads, derelict in their duties. They are the ones who should be at the front of the line to step up. They are the ones that single mums and the public condemn – and with some justification I believe.

But if we think in terms of internal, psychological barriers that dads create for themselves, then perhaps the biggest impediment to rewarding fatherhood is not the golf course or the neighbourhood pub. It is the office.

Make no mistake about it. There is a direct relationship between how much time a father spends at the office and how much time he spends at home looking after his own kids. Fathers who work late at the office cannot be at home to helping their daughters with homework, or their sons with their soccer skills.

But there's a dangerous difference between spending too much time in the office and too much time on the golf course. Dads who golf all the time *know* they are not getting the job done as parents. They know that their leisure comes at the expense of an overworked spouse and kids who do not get enough 'quality time' with their fathers. These dads are villains and deep down inside they know it.

Spending a lot of time at the office, on the other hand, is rather more insidious. These dads 'labour' under the delusion that they are being good dads by providing for their families. It gives them a justification, an excuse if you like, for spending so much time away from their kids. The association of fatherhood with the breadwinning role in the family household is a strong one that spans decades, no, centuries. It has seduced fathers into believing that career success equates to being a good dad. The delusion persists right up to the end, until truth is revealed in a sad and sudden realisation.

'Nobody ever goes to their deathbed wishing they had spent more time in the office.' That's how the old saying goes. But that's not quite right, is it? The saying should be 'No *man* ever goes to their deathbed wishing they had spent more time in the office.' Men have generally been the ones to experience this lament because it is they who have spent all that time in the office in the first place.

Harry Chapin's song 'Cat's in the cradle' is perhaps the best cultural representation of the deathbed paradox. The song follows the life of a father who is too busy with work to spend time with his growing boy. Each verse captures the father and son at different ages with the consistent theme that dad chooses the office over his son's request to play. In the final verse of the song, the father is an old man who has realised the errors of his ways, but when he calls to ask about his grandchildren, his son is too busy with work to talk.

Chapin's lyric was anticipated by some 60 years in a 1914 poem by Morris Rosenfeld:

> I have a little boy at home . . .
> But seldom, seldom do I see
> My child in heaven's light . . .
> Ere dawn my labor drives me forth;
> 'Tis night when I am free;
> A stranger am I to my child;
> And strange my child to me.

And so it goes; and so it goes.

What is it that men die wishing for? Mostly for time with friends, and above all, like the protagonist in *Cat's in the cradle*, with family. And while family of origin (parents and siblings) is important, in the hierarchy of family, the family of creation – and specifically children – are the people most precious to us. What men know, or perhaps come to learn after it is too late, is that what they miss through the pursuit of career success is their relationships with their own family, their parents, siblings, spouse and, above all, children.

How is it possible for men to make such a catastrophic misallocation of their time on earth? Well, to understand this we must cover at least two issues. The first stems from an assumption that fathers must *choose* between spending their time at the office versus being with their kids. If these two activities could be combined, the paradox would not exist. Although *going* to work may seem like the most natural thing in the world to many of us, there is nothing inherently natural about it.

Priorities quiz

Do you have the right priorities as a dad? Take the following quiz and find out.

Multiple choice

Consider the last few Saturday afternoons. Did you spend them:

- at work? *(1 mark)*
- at the pub with your mates? *(-4 marks)*
- actively engaged in a sport or hobby alone or with your mates? *(1 mark)*
- at home with your kids? *(1 mark)*
- actively engaged in a sport or hobby with your kids? *(4 marks)*

When you first come home from work at night do you:

- grab a beer from the fridge, sit on the sofa, and flick on the TV? *(0 marks)*
- continue working on the report for the meeting tomorrow morning? *(1 mark)*
- talk with your kids about their day and yours? *(2 marks)*
- help your kids with their homework? *(2 marks)*

If your child has a sporting match at 9 am on a Saturday morning, do you:

- go to work *(1 mark)*
- sleep in and let the missus take them? *(-2 marks)*
- go to the match with your missus? *(1 mark)*
- go to the match and let your missus sleep in? *(2 marks)*
- go to the match an hour early because you're the coach? *(4 marks)*

Short answer

What are the names of your children's school teachers? *(2 points per child)*

What shoe size do each of your children wear? *(2 points per child)*

What are the names of your children's best friends? *(1 point per friend)*

What is the name of your family GP? *(2 points)*

Interpreting your score

20+: Congratulations! You'll go to your deathbed knowing that you've lived a life well spent raising your children to be happy, healthy, successful adults.

11–19: You probably live a balanced life, where your career and your role as a father mean a lot to you.

5–10: Plenty of room for improvement. There's still time to get your priorities in order.

0–1: You're going to be the guy on his deathbed questioning his priorities.

We will need to explore how a combination of macroeconomic developments affecting the production of goods and services, and the policies and assumptions of the private and public organisations that sell those goods and services, have forced parents, but predominantly fathers, to leave their children on a daily basis in pursuit of household income.

Second, the deathbed paradox ultimately stems from fathers misconstruing the value of parenthood versus career success. Mind you, there is no correct answer here. We can't say that men overvalue work or undervalue parenthood in any absolute sense; but we must at least try to explain why men seem to overvalue work while they are passing through life compared to when they are at the end of it, and underestimate the value of being a dad as the years pass compared to when they have run out of years. We'll explore the factors that lead to this (mis)perception of value.

Why do fathers go to work?

Why do dads go to work? Why don't they *stay* to work? Why do fathers have to choose between leaving for the office and staying at home with their kids? Where did the idea of *going* to work come from? Not in the general sense of working, obviously fathers need to do that; but in the sense of a specialised job that a person leaves home in the morning to do for seven–eight hours a day before returning in the evening with money in the form of a salary payment.

Johann Bachofen, a 19th-century sociologist and anthropologist, once proposed that women initially held the power in what were universally matriarchical societies, due to their ability to give birth. This 'mother right' gave them greater status and influence in key decisions affecting the living community.

He concluded that two things changed. First, men began creating and controlling the public institutions of government, commerce and religion while women stayed at home and looked after the kids, and second, mating practices moved away from unfettered promiscuity to monogamy, largely due to the influence of religious institutions, allowing for far greater paternal certainty. Men had a better idea of which kids were theirs and which were not, although as we'll see later on, never complete certainty. Both developments shifted power and status to men, resulting in the 'modern' patriarchical societies of today.

Great little theory. The trouble is that Bachofen was wrong about most of this stuff. There is virtually no archaeological evidence of ancient matriarchies for one thing, and existing data cast serious doubt on a universal transition from promiscuity to monogamy. But an interesting idea following from Bachofen's theory is the separation of the private and public spheres of a society. The former refers to the home and the latter to the outside world.

Specifically, the public sphere comprises business, politics, education, religion, military, policing and security, whereas the private sphere entails activities and functions within the household, cooking, cleaning, financial management, child care, and many other household roles and activities.[1]

Many aspects of contemporary Australian society reflect this fundamental separation, and more importantly, that men tend to occupy the public sphere whereas women tend to occupy the private. The notion that fathers are breadwinners and mothers are homemakers is so ingrained in Australian culture that almost half of the family households with infants and toddlers have a father who works full time in the office and a mother who works full time in the home. Less than one percent of these households have a mother who works full time in the office and a father who works full time at home.[2]

---

1   Ortner & Whitehead 1981, 7.
2   Baxter & Smart 2010, 97.

This still leaves roughly half the households with mums and dads who work inside and outside of the home, but even when this is the case, fathers still devote more hours to their careers than mothers do, and mothers spend more time doing housework than fathers do.[3] How did this state of affairs come about? What created the separation between private and public spheres of society, and why did men leave the family household while women stayed home?

The conventional explanation is that it began with the Industrial Revolution. Prior to this, fathers stayed home in agrarian economies, often mentoring their children to prepare them to work on the farm. In these days, a man was very much the king of his castle. Father sure knew best.

But in addition to pollution, danger and monotony, the Industrial Revolution brought with it a separation of the workplace from the domicile. Labourers had to leave their homes to *go* to work. Since there were plenty of negative stereotypes casting women as weak, frail and generally unfit for the rigours of the modern industrial workplace, it was generally men who went off to work while women stayed home to look after the household.[4]

This explains the separation of men and women and the emergence of distinct public and private spheres of life, but not why women now face discrimination in the public sphere. Why is there a glass ceiling? At some point, as a consequence of the lack of participation by the other gender, the rules of the public sphere began serving the interests of men more than women, and the private sphere began serving the interests of women more than men. Whether this was deliberate or not is a, or perhaps *the*, contentious issue in all of this, but in either case we have the foundation for the glass ceiling, and the under-representation of women *and* men in various societal roles.

In the public sphere women are underrepresented as political leaders, CEOs of major corporations, Nobel Prize winners, chaired professors, senior partners of law and consulting firms, not to mention athletes that earn seven and eight figure salaries. But in the private sphere, men are underrepresented as house-spouses, stay-at-home parents, single

---

3   Craig 2005; 2006a; 2006b; Chesters et al. 2009.
4   Rothman 1978; Rotundo 1985; Petre 1998, 5; Farrell 2001; Pleck & Pleck 1997; Lamb 2004a.

parents, custodial parents and frankly people who know anything at all about how to run a household!

So the Industrial Revolution led fathers out of the home and into the factory all those years ago. But the question must be asked, why have things largely remained the same for the last half century? Is this really still necessary now where computers, internet connections, video conferencing, Skype, etc., allow most professionals to work from home as easily as from the office? Do we even *need* offices anymore?

With all the talk of 'family-friendly' policies encouraging fathers to spend more time at home looking after their kids,[5] by and large, when married couples decide to start families, the dads wind up spending more time at the office and less time at home following the birth of their child. In general, mums become the homemakers, and dads unwittingly slip into the role of family breadwinner.

Parental leave

The contract I signed with the University offers the following parental leave to ongoing full-time faculty members:

Maternity leave
Paid: 12 weeks or 24 weeks on half pay
Unpaid: up to 12 months following the birth of the child
Paternity leave
Paid: none
Unpaid: up to one week

In fairness, it is stated elsewhere in the contract that '. . . extended (unpaid) paternity leave is offered for a further period of up to 52 weeks which must be taken before the child's first birthday.' I can't help but wonder what criteria are used to determine whether a new father qualifies for more than 1 week away from work to spend with his newborn. I didn't apply for this extended leave when my daughter was born. I worked.

---

5   Cooper 2000; Halrynjo 2009; Kvande 2009.

And perhaps the most surprising thing is how little thought and systematic planning goes into these specialised gender roles in the household. Mums don't decide to become homemakers and dads don't choose to be breadwinners; it's just that, empirically speaking, this is what tends to happen when baby is born. Research tends to show that many couples begin their relationships with very egalitarian values and expectations, but inexplicably drift into the more traditional gender roles of their parents without much explicit discussion or negotiation.[6]

This is not good enough. It's time for husbands and wives to start discussing specific roles, responsibilities, values and expectations *before* they begin their families. If mums really do want to stay at home looking after their newborns, then great – this approach has a long history and a pretty good track record. But this really should be established long before pregnancy. If dads really do want to work long hours away from home in the breadwinning role, then this is certainly possible, but it should be clear to both spouses from the outset.

Then there are the trickier issues, notably when both partners want to work full time. What if mum wants to work full time while dad stays at home looking after his infant daughter? Not likely you say? All the more reason that husbands and wives need to discuss and negotiate these kinds of things explicitly before starting a family. And yet they don't.

Over the course of our nine-year marriage, my wife decided to work or stay at home with the kids three times. Each time it was her decision. When she decided to stay at home, I adjusted, by making more money. When she decided to go back to work, I adjusted again, by taking on more domestic responsibilities, and in particular, becoming the drop-off and pick-up person on school days. This meant the dinner–bath–put-the-kids-to-bed routine as well, all the while continuing to work a full-time job.

Men generally react to women – and I blame us men for this. We don't need a masculine movement – we need to become more aware of our own acquiescence, and to articulate (at least for ourselves) our wants, and to seek them. We need to be proactive not reactive. We need to examine and be clear about our boundaries. The bottom line is that

---

6   Deutsch 1999.

this was my own fault for not making the implicit explicit. I should have let my preferences be known. I should have discussed these things openly with the mother (to be).

I like staying home with the kids too. I often wondered what her reaction would have been if I came home one day and said, 'Honey, I've decided to quit work and stay at home with the kids. It's okay. You can work and earn the income for a while.' Either I would have had to become a very good parent and my wife a very good earner right away or the grounds for divorce would have been laid down much earlier.

But perhaps the most obvious reasons that wives and husbands should negotiate the allocation of labour within and outside of the household is – because they can. Your spouse will understand and care about the subtlety and complexity of your daily schedule. They'll appreciate that your kids need to get to school every morning, on time, in school uniforms, lunches packed, excursion permission forms signed. They'll know about school pick up at 3 pm, piano lessons for your daughter at 3:30, soccer training for your son at 3:45, the things on the shopping list that need to be in the fridge or pantry for that week's meals, the recent health problem requiring a visit to the GP, the dry cleaning that needs to be picked up, the birthday gift that needs to be purchased for the party this Saturday, etc., etc., etc.

They'll understand and care and adjust their schedules accordingly because they are your spouse, and of course, the other parent of your children; and if they don't care, go directly to divorce. With your spouse, you can negotiate who will do what and when, on an ongoing basis as life dictates.

Your employer will *not* care about all the roles and responsibilities that comprise your life. Organisational policies regarding the allocation of labour are more rigid than those in the household, assuming spouses take full advantage of the opportunity to negotiate roles and responsibilities. You can negotiate these things with your spouse more easily than you can with your supervisor.

Despite all the talk about flexible hours, parental leave and family-friendly environments, most of us work in a job where we are expected to turn up for work at a certain time every work day, remain in the designated place of work all day, with a short break for lunch, and continue working until 'quitting time', without a lot of freedom as to what to do when. This is the reality of going to work, and it is a rather strange reality when you stop and think about it.

It is curious that so many of the organisations that purchase labour are so rigid about when and where it must be supplied. How are parents expected to manage their complicated lives? Why not give employees goals and performance measures and let them decide when, where, and how to achieve them? Part of the answer stems from the fact that these organisations have historically been run by men, and their implicit assumption was that mothers manage households, leaving fathers free to be at work whenever needed.

Indeed, the closer you look, the more you see how the rules of professional success are stacked against families in general and mothers in particular. Not only do public and private organisations make specific demands regarding the timing of labour allocation throughout the day, week and year; they make specific demands throughout the life span, and once again, these demands seem to work against starting families in general and against the needs of mothers in particular.

As we saw in the previous chapter, many professions require a disproportionate sacrifice of time and effort during what would otherwise be childbearing years; the implicit assumption being that to 'get ahead' an individual must sacrifice time at home to time in the office during their 20s and 30s, typical childbearing and childrearing years.

So, institutional buyers of labour, mostly organisations run by men, are not terribly flexible or family friendly despite politically driven protestations to the contrary. Perhaps the most extreme examples of this rigid, recalcitrant attitude are professional sports organisations that dock the pay of male athletes who have the audacity to attend the birth of their children rather than playing in a match. Some teams have even gone so far as to trade players to another team for choosing the role of father over the role of professional athlete.[7]

Family households must work around the demands of the workplace, so fathers and mothers had better start negotiating who will do what when with the remainder of their time. Simply drifting into traditional breadwinner and homemaker roles, respectively, can result in

---

7   Levine 2000, 224–25.

a lot of conflict and resentment, and fewer perceived options for both mums *and* dads.

The (self-imposed?) burden of breadwinning

The relegation of mothers to the private sphere has not been good for womankind. We've heard an awful lot about that. But how good has confinement to the public sphere really been for men? This brings us to the second big question. The deathbed paradox implies that dads undervalue parenthood and overvalue their careers while their lives are passing compared to when they realise life is coming to an end. Why is this? What factors lead men to reassess their priorities very late in life? One such factor is the time frame being considered for any allocation of time.[8]

To see how this works, consider the following question. Right now, would you rather (a) change a soiled nappy, or (b) eat a gourmet meal? Did you answer (b)? Lucky guess. New parents are more likely to be doing (a), whereas couples who delay having children get to do (b). Score one for staying childless. Would you rather spend the upcoming weekend (a) looking after your sick child, or (b) skiing in Thredbo with your spouse? Score another for remaining childless.

Let's try another question. Over the last ten years of your life, which activity has been more rewarding (a) raising your children, or (b) advancing your career? Promotions are great, but watching your daughter graduate from high school is better. Score one for becoming a parent. I think you get the picture here. As the time frame shifts from the immediate future to the collective past, being a parent increases in value and having a career decreases. This is where the deathbed paradox comes from. When one is nearer to the end of one's life than the beginning, the collective past becomes more prominent than the future in assessing one's life because not much future is left.

Another factor in the deathbed paradox is the self-concept – how a person defines their identity. The essential idea is that men derive self-worth from the breadwinner role but not in the role of being a nur-

---

8   Trope & Liberman 2003.

turing parent. Indeed, research suggests a positive correlation between fathers' assessments of their breadwinning prowess and their motivation and perceived ability as nurturers; a father who is a failure at bringing home the bacon is also likely to see himself as a failure when it comes to raising his children.[9]

This idea is also reflected in research comparing the priorities of mothers and fathers. Fathers simply have career success higher on the list. At the extreme, fathers come to view time spent nurturing their own children as 'wasted time' that should have been spent at the office earning more money.[10] And fathers often engage in self-destructive behaviours because of this narrow focus. Long hours, unhealthy diets, lack of exercise and lack of sleep all follow from this single-minded pursuit of career success. Why haven't fathers learned to define their self-concepts in terms of raising their children?

In many ways, art mirrors social science. In Frank Capra's classic movie *It's a wonderful life*, the protagonist, George Bailey, is about to commit suicide. Why? He doesn't have enough money to cover a loan and he and his family are about to be put out in the streets by the evil banker Mr Potter. George Bailey is going to kill himself because he has failed as the breadwinner of the house. He has no self-worth.

It is only when Clarence, his guardian angel, shows how the world will turn out without George around, how George's love and caring for family and friends has virtually sustained the entire community of Bedford Falls, that he discovers, well, that it's a wonderful life. In the post-industrial community of Bedford Falls, a man's financial worth is what defines him. His worth as a nurturer can only be established via divine intervention.

George Bailey was lucky. Clarence saved him from committing suicide. In the play *Death of a salesman*, Arthur Miller's protagonist Willy Loman wasn't so fortunate. After more than 30 years, he was fired from his job as a salesman, a position that defined who he was and how he approached life. Faced with no job prospects and no way to earn a living, Willy inevitably settled on the natural solution. The only way for Willy to regain his self-esteem is to 'earn' money via a life insurance

---

9   Christiansen & Palkovitz 2001; Baxter & Smart 2010, 146, 148.
10   Walzer 1996, 221–22.

policy. Suicide is seen by Willy as the only chance he has to fulfil his responsibility as a husband and father.

Willy Loman is, admittedly, an extreme case of over-commitment to the breadwinner role, but sometimes it is the extreme example that best illustrates the underlying phenomenon (and I'm just guessing that this is what Arthur Miller had in mind). I'm no Freudian psychologist, but I have a sneaking suspicion that all fathers, deep down in their psyche, have an unconscious fear that they will lose the love of their family if they lose their job.

Sound absurd? Research consistently shows a positive correlation between the unemployment rate and the divorce rate, with the latter usually lagged behind the former by one to three years or so.[11] Research also shows that 'financial problems' is a frequently cited reason for divorce.[12]

Other studies have challenged the notion that single mother families emerge because fathers choose to leave in order to sow their seeds elsewhere. If this were the case, men of higher social status should be more likely to leave the family home. After all, they'd be the ones in the best position to sow their seeds elsewhere. But this is not the case. Research shows that fathers from lower socioeconomic strata are more likely to be 'relieved' of their duties as fathers; and unemployed fathers are especially likely to be *kicked out* of the family home.[13]

Research also indicates that economic conditions affect how involved fathers are in raising their children. Recessions are associated with more involved fathering, whereas economic booms correlate with less time spent with the kids. Apparently, the best way for an unemployed father to avoid being divorced is to become the go-to guy at home with the kids.[14] Perhaps George Bailey, Willy Loman, and fathers everywhere are justified in defining their self-worth solely in terms of breadwinning. Failure to do so may result in removal from the family.

And yet, in this new age of highly involved, nurturing and, frankly, feminised fathering, the traditional breadwinning role has been marginalised and even denigrated.[15] It is assumed to be 'normal' for fathers

---

11   Doiron & Mendolia 2012.
12   Kitson 1992.
13   Lancaster 1989; Boroughs et al. 1992.
14   Casper & O'Connell 1998.

to earn money, often an 'invisible' contribution to the wellbeing of children. On average, Australian fathers provide roughly 70 percent of the household income, though this percentage varies depending on the age of the youngest child.[16] Mothers are most decidedly not happy with this percentage; the breadwinning role of fathers has been challenged by women seeking equal status and pay in the workplace. Bringing home the bacon sure ain't what it used to be.

A bad day at the office is still better . . .

But having painted a picture of fathers as poor blokes who have to shoulder the financial burden of the family household like so many Atlases, we might examine what men actually do at work for purposes of painting a slightly different picture. Perhaps the paternal obsession with the office has less to do with the responsibility of providing for the family and more to do with the glory of achievement.

A disgruntled mother once quipped that a bad day at the office is still better than a good day at home looking after the kids. This, of course, was a play on all those sayings that a bad day fishing, skiing, sailing, (insert your favourite hobby here) is still better than a good day at work. The juxtaposition conveys the sentiment that the work mothers have traditionally done at home is much harder than what men have traditionally done at the office.

We have many aspects of popular culture that convey and reinforce this notion. Movies like *Mr Mom*, *Three men and a baby*, *Daddy Day Care*, and *Kindergarten cop* depict men who, after years of success in the rough and tumble world of career men, fall to pieces looking after young children. The gender politics are fairly unmistakeable.

So, was this disgruntled mother correct? Of course not. A bad day at the office is most certainly *not* better than a good day at home looking after the kids. Indeed, there's no difference on average; 'average' being the key word in that last phrase. On average life in the private and public spheres is equally (un)enjoyable. It is a matter of variances not averages. The variance of emotional experiences looking after the kids

15   Christiansen & Palkovitz 2001.
16   Baxter & Smart 2010, 95, 141.

is far greater than what happens in the office. The highs are higher, but unfortunately, the lows are lower.

Nothing that has ever happened or will ever happen at work will match the joy my daughter and I experienced the first time she did a poo in the toilet. I taught her that, and it's one of my greatest accomplishments, partly because we had so many miscues along the way. The little poos in the corner, on the stairs, in the bathtub, ugh, made the ultimate success that much better. Nothing in my career comes close.

However, I also remember the time she vomited on me, herself and her entire bedroom. Just as I had finished cleaning the whole mess, washing and dressing her, and then lastly, washing and dressing myself, she vomited all over everything again! It was two in the morning. I did the only sane, rational thing a father could do at that point. I put my fist through the door, slumped to the ground and started crying. This made her cry too. There we were, both covered in vomit, crying like little babies. She, of course, was a baby. No excuse for me.

The sentiment that professional labour is better than domestic labour is wrong, at least in terms of difficulty and emotional experience. But it may be right on the money when it comes to how society *values* the two kinds of work. Success in the public sphere comes with promotions, a company car, a six-figure salary, explicit recognition from supervisors, you name it. A top CEO makes $1,500,000 per year, is featured in business magazines and other specialised media, and gets to tell 12,850 employees what to do. A successful parent simply gets his four-year-old to eat her vegetables at dinner, is told by other parents that their little Johnny did this one year ago, and I'm still not sure how that rates overall in the parenting stakes.

Mothers have traditionally done 'invisible' work around the house, stuff that is barely noticed by the beneficiaries, much less acknowledged and explicitly rewarded. I've come to appreciate this as a single father. I do hundreds of little things every day for my family and get 98 percent of them right. The sad thing is that I only tend to hear about the two percent that I mess up, from my kids, from school administrators, from other parents, from friends and colleagues, and of course, from complete strangers. As a professor, I consider 98 percent on an exam a brilliant result. When it comes to parenting I do not feel very brilliant.

It is this lack of appreciation and undervaluation of domestic labour that leads women to lament about gender inequity in domestic and professional labour. If labour in the private sphere was more highly valued, perhaps men would be the ones doing the complaining; just a speculation. But this is not likely to eventuate.

Indeed, anthropological research examining multiple cultures over multiple periods of history suggests that as the division between the public and private spheres increases and becomes more explicit in a society, women are more likely to participate solely in the private sphere, and lose power and status as a consequence.[17] This is a general pattern. Career success equates with power.

Parallel notions of 'invisible' work

Women have coined the phrase 'invisible work' to describe the domestic labour that they disproportionately do. It took me many years to fully grasp the wisdom underlying this metaphor. 'Why is it invisible?' I used to wonder – until I became a single father. Do my kids not see that I am working myself to the point of exhaustion to make their lives run smoothly? Of course they don't. They're kids!

Many a night I would fall asleep on the sofa following the dinner clean up, only to be awakened by one of my kids saying 'Daddy, I think it's time for us to go to bed now.' It was as if I had been pushed through the invisible ectoplasm separating the world of people who could not see the invisible work going on around them from the world of people who did the invisible work – kind of like the scene in the movie *Field of dreams* where the evil brother-in-law can suddenly see all the baseball players that Kevin Costner has been obsessed by for much of the movie.

And once I could suddenly see all this invisible work going on, the transformation made me kind of angry. Angry at the, now, 'others' who could not see all the invisible work I was doing. But the anger wasn't directed at everybody in the other world. My eight-year-old and four-year-old were completely exempt. Indeed, I wasn't angry at any children for not noticing. Some of them, hopefully all of them, would begin to notice as they got older, I consoled myself.

---

17   Sunday 1981.

I wasn't really angry at childless adults in the other world either. They began to seem more like kids to me; older, with more sophisticated toys, perhaps, but still completely self-absorbed like any other children. And, of course, there weren't any mothers in the other world. They were all doing the invisible work with me on the other side.

By and large, it was the fathers in the other world who were really annoying me. But how could this be? I'm a father! I certainly wasn't mad at myself. Then it hit me. This isn't about gender at all. This is about who looks after the family and who doesn't. It just happens to be the case that mothers have typically been the homemakers, but it doesn't have to be this way. I was a male homemaker and I was infuriated with parents who shunned the homemaker role, who didn't seem to be doing much of this work; and those parents have traditionally been fathers.

So what have fathers traditionally done? They've been the breadwinners and this is also 'invisible' in a way. Not because nobody notices. Society is set up to notice and provide accolades for professional success. But men have traditionally left the home to earn money. This money is electronically transferred from the organisational account where the man works to the household account on a fortnightly basis, where it is then spent by household members who are not breadwinners. Sounds kind of invisible to me.

What I ultimately realised is that I was now both homemaker and breadwinner for my single parent household, and that I would be doing a lot of invisible work from now on. Of course, single mothers have been covering this territory for decades now.

So, rather than suggesting that the breadwinning role is a burden to those poor fathers who must carry this load, we might instead cast bringing home the bacon as a glory-seeking expedition in the public sphere, where success is accorded ample doses of acclaim, prestige, power, recognition, and heaps of cold, hard cash. Fathers *choose* to spend their lives in the office because of the status that career success gives them; but if this is the case, then why the paradox? Why do all the rewards of professional achievement fade into irrelevance near the end of one's life?

When I was five years old my parents gave me a children's book about a young adult ant that is determined to climb to the top of a huge mountain of ants. Up and up he goes as the story progresses, crossing paths with several ant characters on their way *down* the hill. One ant looks exhausted, another frustrated, another lost and bewildered. 'Did you make it to the top?' he asks each one enthusiastically, even hopefully, but each one gives some kind of an excuse for why he has failed in his attempt. Indeed, it is the explanations for the failure to make it to the top that largely comprise the short story.

The insect protagonist ages as the pages pass, finally making it to the top of the ant hill where he discovers that there is nothing at the top. No reward, no surprise, no source of wisdom, no vestal virgins – nothing. Perhaps not surprisingly, all the ant characters are male. I have desperately tried to find this book because of the wisdom of its underlying message, to no avail.

Perhaps near the end of their lives fathers discover that there is nothing at the top. That all their career accomplishments amount to meaningless numbers on a bank account and job titles and awards and congratulations – all of which are not even physical enough to gather dust. The things that really matter were right there in front of them all along, moving then and still moving, physical and not gathering any dust. How could he have missed this treasure, like diamonds buried just below the surface. Family matters more than anything else, and the only way a dad can truly fulfil his purpose in life is by being around his kids.

Breaking free

But some fathers are able to break free of this internal shackle, this self-imposed mindset that prevents them from fully realising the beauty of parenthood. I've talked with many single dads, stay-at-home dads, and many very, very involved married dads who just happen to work full time. Their stories convey specific themes, and have a certain consistency about them. Breaking free involves making a set of psychological adjustments.

The epiphanies that take fathers out of the breadwinning mindset come from different sources; difficulties at work; arguments with the mothers; experiences with their children; and just plain mental and emotional exhaustion. One father I talked to discussed the grind at work, and the effect it was having on his role as a husband and father.

> Six days a week just 12 hours per day. So, I left home and went to work, worked, came home. We were there till 6 o'clock every day. By the time I got home it was 7 o'clock at night. And I had to leave for work at 7 am every morning. There was no free time, morning or evening five days a week and on Saturday I got, you know, two or three hours before it was bed time and bath time for the kids.

For another dad, it was seeing his three sons in poor health for an extended period that sounded the alarm bell.

> There was one winter where … there was only about one week in three months where all three children were in day care when they were supposed to be. There was always one sick or another – and that was probably the first inkling that said 'well, you've got to really reassess what you're doing'.

Underlying these breakthroughs is the encouraging realisation that men and women, husbands and wives, fathers and mothers can renegotiate the gender roles that society encourages. The 'encouragement' is very strong, but there is no reason that fathers need to drift into the breadwinner role, or that mothers are more natural as homemakers. These simple, and hopelessly outdated, gender stereotypes can and should be challenged. Sometimes they will work but other times they will create problems, perhaps for both spouses. In these cases, roles within the family should be explicitly reconsidered. One stay-at-home father put it rather succinctly.

> We just sat there and said 'This isn't working. Our lifestyle is killing us. How can we renegotiate this?'

The solution in his case was that his spouse continued to work full-time while he pursued contract work that allowed him to remain home looking after his kids.

Being an involved father is the ultimate decision, whether one is a single father, a stay-at-home father, or a working father who has become the go-to parent at home. One father put it this way.

> We made a lifestyle decision, we decided that time is more important than money at the moment. We sold our house. We rent. We live on a wage of $800 a week. And we're happy. In fact we've never been happier. We earn less money than we've ever earned in our life. And we've never been happier.

For many fathers, breaking free involves an explicit realisation and rejection of the father as breadwinner stereotype. One stay-at-home dad had this to say:

> Social stereotypes say, 'You're a male. You work five or six days week. You work hard. You pay off a home. And 25 years from now, 30 years from now you have a home.' That's the way it's done. The Australian dream. I'm only a year and a half into the Australian dream and it sucks.

The interesting thing is that the fathers who do break through seem to be able to anticipate the collective past in evaluating their day-to-day decisions. For example, one stay-at-home father explained his decision to give up the breadwinning role:

> It's [rejecting] this mentality that 'we're slowly getting ahead and in 40 years' time we will be ahead.' Yes, but in 40 years time your life will be over. You will be 65 years old and when you look back and think what do you have to show for it? 'Wow, we've got four walls and a roof.' Whoop-de-do. I don't want to turn around when I'm 65 and go 'Gee I wish I'd spent more time at home with the girls.'

It's the ability to anticipate himself as an older man that allows him to avoid the deathbed paradox.

Running through these epiphanies is a rejection of more material wealth as a life goal. These fathers decided that having a nicer house, or driving a nicer car, or having a bigger income wasn't as important as popular culture often makes it out to be.

So, work 12 hours a day . . . It was a case of just going 'No. Let's sell the house. Do we really, really need to own our own home at this stage in our lives?' And we thought about it 'No, we don't.' Do I need to be a partner in this business at this time? No I don't.

I don't want to seem carefree or blasé – I am not. I am very conscious of, you know, we need to set ourselves up for 20 years' time and I don't want to be broke and living out of a shack in 20 years' time. But five years is not going to matter in the scheme of things. And in 20 years' time from now I'm not going to look back and go 'Gee I'm glad I worked for those five years and paid off 15 thousand dollars more of the home'.

But it's not that easy to break free. Fathers trying to change their priorities often meet opposition from relatives, friends and strangers just as mothers meet opposition from similar sources when they place their infant children in child care so they can return to their pursuit of a career. The problem for these trailblazing fathers is that the rest of the world is still stuck in traditional gender stereotypes. Friends, family members and complete strangers may not immediately 'get' a man's decision to give up his career to become a full-time, stay-at-home father, or even to cut back on his career goals to spend more time with his kids.[18]

And perhaps one of the most confronting experiences for stay-at-home fathers married to career-oriented mothers is the realisation that traditional gender roles have completely reversed. He has unwittingly become the 'nag' who constantly feels undervalued and resentful; and she becomes the out-of-touch parent who doesn't see all the invisible work being done on her behalf. One stay-at-home dad rather sarcastically described it this way.

I'd do the kids' food, she wouldn't be home . . . she was allergic to vacuum cleaners in a psychological sense. I would always be the one who did that . . . we'd share the cleaning of the house over the weekends – I just did more. I was carrying too much of it. And she felt frozen out from it . . . you totally reverse roles. She felt frozen out of

---

18   Deutsch 1999.

what she could give. She felt that domain, the domestic domain, was being denied to her.

Work–life balance as a women's issue?

There was a time that I was on the narrow, one-way train to professional success at all costs. I was still a relatively young professor working my way to becoming the next dean. The career progression is fairly straightforward here. First you become a dean, then a pro-vice-chancellor, then a deputy-vice-chancellor, and finally a vice-chancellor, or if you are a North American, a university president. As a young professor I'd set myself up to be a pretty strong internal candidate for the dean position, and in the back of my mind, I was thinking I could make it all the way to the top. Vice-Chancellor! Wow!

Then my wife said she wanted a divorce. The shift in priorities occurred almost instantaneously. My daughter was only two at the time, and I'd heard the stories of divorced fathers being reduced to glorified uncles that see their kids only every other weekend, especially if their ex-wives remarry, which virtually ensures that the stepfather becomes the psychological father of the young children. No way that was happening to my children, no way that was happening to me.

I immediately resigned as associate dean (that'd be the step below dean if you're keeping track of the career ladder), and planned my strategy for retaining at least 50 percent custody of my kids. This meant that I effectively dropped out of public administrative life around the university.

I did get 50 percent custody of my kids, but when I returned to work as just a mild-mannered, run-of-the mill professor, the reactions from colleagues were strange. Male colleagues came right out and said it: 'What are you doing with your life, mate? You were headed straight to the top.' One actually suggested that perhaps I was not up to the task after all, and had simply dropped out of the running due to a lack of confidence.

My female colleagues were somewhat more tactful, but the message was the same. 'How are you?' or 'Are you alright?' was their tacit way of expressing that the divorce must still be affecting me emotionally, otherwise I'd be pushing my way back up the corporate ladder.

Nobody seemed ready to believe that I had just made a conscious decision to pull back on my professional ambitions to become a more involved, better connected father. It seems that with all the talk of work–life balance around the university and in Australia in general, when confronted with a father who had actually opted for this lifestyle, people just couldn't understand the decision in those simple terms.

And even the most supporting friends and family with the very best of intentions may find the transition to domestic life difficult to comprehend.

You know, I think a lot of people they'll sort of look at you, or they'll listen to what I say and they go, 'Wow, I'd love to be able to do that.' And they just can't let go of the social guidelines that we have. 'No, no, no. You have to have a highly paid five-days-a-week job.' They couldn't – they just couldn't do the whole sea change. Which is what we've sort of done. We've done a bit of a sea change with our lifestyle.

Indeed, fathers are already so narrowly defined in terms of providing financial resources for their families that complete strangers can question any man who ostensibly fails to fulfil this responsibility. As a single father, I had to deal with domestic responsibilities inside the 'normal' Monday–Friday, nine-to-five work week.

I often experienced a distinct feeling of being 'out of place' when I was shopping, playing with my kids in a park, talking to neighbours over the fence while doing the wash, etc. There was an implicit, and sometimes explicit, need to justify my presence.[19] The reason is, of course, obvious – fathers who aren't at work violate the traditional male stereotype. What could this strange man possibly be doing on a weekday afternoon in the park? Up to no good I'll bet.

---

19   The department store episode from the opening chapter being an exceptionally pointed example.

But consider this. Do the same stereotypes that place men at work on a Monday afternoon implicitly assume that women should be the ones in the department store buying children's clothing, the one's dropping them off and picking them up from school, the one's changing nappies and cleaning up vomit? Is this just another indirect way of re-inforcing the stereotype that 'a woman's place is in the home'? Shouldn't women be just as outraged that fathers performing the simple household task of buying clothing for their children are treated as potential criminals? Is this a part of the glass ceiling?

That's the big question. Part of helping women, and especially mothers, to break through the glass ceiling may involve encouraging fathers to break free of the breadwinning mindset. Gender stereotypes cut in both directions and influence roles and responsibilities in the public and private spheres. But in the next chapter we'll talk about what these new age fathers are really getting themselves into when they break free and make a commitment to raising their children. As we'll see, it ain't all beer and skittles!

The toughest job you'll ever love!

What makes you a man is not the ability to have a child but the courage to raise one.

Barack Obama

To be a university academic takes about ten years of study or more at university level. To be a general medical practitioner requires about six years or more of study. To get most kinds of professional jobs requires at least three to four years of university level education. To drive a car requires passing of tests and 100–200 hours of practice.

To earn the title of dad, no degree, diploma, license nor permit is required.

To be an engaged father however, requires an enormous amount of time and energy. An investment which will earn no credentials, no qualifications, and no letters after your name. And a reasonable possibility of little to no thanks too!

How could dad resist the joys of parenthood! How can a cooing, smiling baby do anything but melt a human's heart – regardless of whether that human heart is male or female?

Well, there is an alternative view that a baby is little more than an eating-crying-vomiting-peeing-pooping machine which can demand attention at any time of the day or night. Like a Tamagotchi, only more complicated. Oh, and more real too!

Given the mechanistic input–output nature of this view, it is very possibly one that was originally advanced by a man. And while we're discussing inputs and outputs, I might issue a little warning to any dads-to-be – the frequency and volume of poop coming out of your baby will seem wholly out of proportion to the volume of mashed peas going in. Get used to this now.

Regardless of where the input–output description originated, it does remind us that there are both challenges and rewards in rearing children. Opting out avoids the challenges – but also misses the rewards. Moreover, it would be most disappointing if the parenting task was divided along gender lines simply because mothers have their eyes on the rewards and fathers look only at the challenges. Aside from the outcomes both good and bad, men, it seems, ought to be shouldering their share of the responsibilities.

During a rather crucial event in Ancient Greek history, Crito argued with Socrates who indicated a willingness to accept the death sentence that had been passed against him. In this argument, Crito made the statement 'No man should bring children into the world who is unwilling to persevere to the end in their nurture and education.'[1]

Socrates rejected Crito's argument and chose to drink the poison-cup of hemlock, but I very seriously doubt that he opted for death to get out of changing some dirty nappies. Fathers who absent themselves from childcare responsibilities are more likely to be facing the fairway on the par four, 14th hole of their favourite golf course than death by poisoning. Hardly a poignant example of adhering to a moral principle or a civic duty. Choosing to be an absent father by holding the view that 'It's not my job' is a cop-out, pure and simple.

So what is the real reason that so many men do not step up? Perhaps he is absent because he has no interest, that he simply does not like the parenthood role. But if this is the case, one wonders why the man contributed to a child at all, and it opens the man to criticism – and justifiably so.

But maybe he just does not realise what he is missing. I'm talking about those men who are interested, but still fail to step up. Why would

---

1 Plato, 5th/4th century BC.

a father who does have at least some interest in getting involved with childrearing, not step up to the role? And what can be done about that?

No man's land

The stereotype that it is not the man's job to raise the children has been driven back over recent years – and rightly so. However, the stereotype hangs on in a number of tenacious ways which may prevent men from stepping up.

Most men express a willingness to be more involved in caring for the children – if money were no object.[2] The sense that money is a constraint may be his perception, but it almost certainly does not help that many others hold a similar view. That is, the pressure against his involvement is not necessarily that *he* harbours this stereotype, but that *others* harbour it! Men who do try to get involved in raising their own children find that there is often a tension with their spouse, their employer, their colleagues, their friends, and sometimes even with their own children!

Reflecting this challenge, there is a presumption by at least some that fathering is somehow a threat to masculinity. I was asked recently by a journalist how taking on the task of being a full-time parent might have challenged my masculinity. On being asked the question, my first response was 'I don't care what others think!' My second response was 'Huh?' I was at a loss to see how being an active father might be perceived to reflect negatively on masculinity. I do not think I have ever engaged in any activity that I thought was more masculine than being a father.

What else makes a man feel masculine? Fighting? Working? Each reflects man's capacity to protect and provide for his family, but it is hard to beat the hands-on experience of direct involvement with one's own children. The interesting point is that the question exists at all. The question of whether hands on fathering threatens masculinity perpetuates a stereotype, in particular, that of the man as breadwinner.

---

2   Armour 2007.

The martyrdom delusion

How does a mother or father determine what is the 'fair' amount of work to do inside and outside of the household? There are, of course, many answers to this question, but at least one is suggested by the behaviour of their same-sex parent. Sons are likely to think 'what did my father do around the house?' Daughters will ask themselves 'How much money did mum earn when I was growing up?'[3]

The answers to these questions are likely to be 'I'm doing way more!' Sons think back to their fathers, who did much less around the house, and give themselves a congratulatory pat on the back for being so progressive and egalitarian compared to dear old dad. Daughters remember mothers who had nothing in the way of careers and take pride in their ability to run a family household and still get that promotion to a senior management position.

However, this mindset ignores the role of technology today in transforming public and private labour for both men and women. Can anybody remember what work was like before computers? What did people do? If the network is down these days, work comes to a standstill in many cases. Chances are your father's job was more physically exhausting than sitting in front of a computer all day. And back then, your mum wrung clothes in a wringer, hung clothes on a line, washed dishes by hand, baked cakes from scratch, to name a few examples.

But it, nevertheless, *seems* like we do more than our parents did because today's mothers and fathers do labour in both the domestic and professional spheres of society, whereas our parents were more likely to operate exclusively in one or the other.

The real danger is when we extend this way of thinking to our spouses. Parenting is, I suspect, a bit like riding a tandem bike or paddling a two-person canoe. We always feel like we're giving more than the other person. That's the martyrdom delusion, when each spouse comes to believe that they are making a far greater contri-

---

3   Deutsch 1999, 90–92.

> bution to the overall well-being of the family. This is a dangerous mindset. Treacherous waters lie ahead!

Split the parents, double the work

When I became a single parent, I suddenly found I had to juggle the responsibilities in the office and at home. In short, I discovered role-conflict. Generally, it is mothers that have informed the world about the role conflict arising from working and parenting full time – an indication that women have spent more effort, and been more success-ful, diversifying into both worlds than men. This same problem will of course confront men who seek to diversify in a similar way, albeit in the other direction – from the office into the home.

And all this juggling of roles and responsibilities is hard work! Re-search suggests that it will stress you out and grind you down. That's right. The role conflict created by being a full-time parent and a full-time employee can lead to depression in the long run.[4] Is there a resolu-tion? Is parenting ultimately a task that overwhelms any that take it on?

Not likely. This simply flies in the face of evolution. I mean, what is the purpose of human existence, you know, the grand principle that seems to guide virtually all life on earth? I'd say it has something to do with reproduction, or more precisely, replicating our genetic material, and having babies is how we humans do it. How could fulfilling our grand purpose possibly be depressing? If anything, our genes would make it more psychologically painful not to reproduce, and there is evidence that women who do not have children are more depressed than women who do, holding many other happiness factors constant.[5]

So raising children must be psychologically rewarding in order for the whole game of evolution to work. There must however, be other variables at work as studies show that parents are more stressed out relative to non-parents. We covered one such factor in the previous chapter when we considered the deathbed paradox. Some activities seem much more attractive when you consider the collective past rather

---

4   Thompson 1995; Deem 1996; Areni 2008.
5   Essock & McGuire 1989; Lyubomirsky & Boehm 2010.

than the immediate future, and parenting may be one of those activities.

When you think of all the things you have to do in a single day taking care of a three-year-old and a one-year-old, being an involved parent can seem like a mind-boggling, impossible task. But seeing each child graduate from primary school, and knowing that you've played a major role in that accomplishment, is more rewarding than darned near anything else I can think of right now as a possible point of comparison. So the time frame being considered has a lot to do with how being a parent rates compared to other uses of time.[6]

Another important variable is the family status of the parents being surveyed. A closer examination of the research findings reveals that it is primarily single parents and parents living in non-traditional households who tend to be less happy than childless adults. When it comes to good, old-fashioned, Ward and June Cleaver–type parents living in the same household as their children, there is no consistent difference in happiness between parents and non-parents.[7]

So it seems to be the case that divorce and other unusual or unanticipated circumstances can make parenting a real pain in the butt and psyche. Being a single parent does indeed seem to make one less happy. Why might this be the case? Well, for one thing most single parents have experienced the death of their spouse, or gone through a divorce, neither of which is very nice. But another fairly obvious factor stems directly from the economic law of supply and demand. Single parent households have only half the supply of labour to devote to raising children compared to cohabiting couples.

Research suggests that single mothers are more likely to experience depression and role conflict,[8] but I suspect that it's really single *parents* that experience it, it's just that single dads are a mere blip on the demographic radar screen. As a single dad I spent many an evening exhausted to the point of despair, wondering how I was going to keep this up until my daughter left for college – 12 years later! So, being a single parent creates role conflict, and conflict results in stress, and stress leads

---

6   Trope & Liberman 2003.
7   Evenson & Simon 2005.
8   Gill & Davidson 2001.

to unhappiness. Does this mean that single parents are less happy than other demographic categories? Well, yes, sort of.

But even a married mother who works full time is likely to experience role conflict and stress because her husband doesn't do anywhere near 50 percent of the childcare labour. And as long as we're comparing single and married parents, let's not forget that in other cultures extended families are the norm. Mix in some grandparents and a couple of aunts and uncles, and the amount of parenting that has to be done by each adult is divided a number of ways in the household. In economic terms, the supply of parenting labour (in the broad sense of the word) is far greater in extended families. So, the amount of childcare labour a parent has to do depends very much on the demographics of the specific household.

So what if single mums and dads do more parenting work than other mums and dads? Why should this make them less happy? Aren't kids wonderful? Don't they bring great joy? Well, yes, up to a point. But no matter how much you like to do something, eventually you get sick of it. You want to switch to something else. Think of any activity you choose to engage in when you have a period of 'free' time. It could be a hobby, reading a good book, spending time with a romantic partner or family or friends. No matter what it is, you eventually change activities. If this were not the case, each of us would pursue our favourite activity *all the time*! But we don't. When we get bored or tired, we switch to something else. Variety is the spice of life.

But what if you were forced to persist? To keep going long after you became bored with the activity? The activity would become unenjoyable. Playing a musical instrument might initially be a fun hobby, unless you are made to take lessons four hours a day, five days a week, in which case it might become drudgery. Many a budding musician or athlete has eventually become turned off by their instrument or sport for exactly this reason – too much practice! Well, parenting as an activity is no different. It *is* wonderful, perhaps the ultimate enjoyable pastime, but like any other activity, only up to a point. Pushed beyond that point, a parent no longer finds it enjoyable.

This is what is going on when we hear an exasperated parent talking about how drained and exhausted they are after a difficult weekend looking after children. One stay-at-home dad conveyed the following:

The only thing that used to really send me – it still does send me absolutely spare – is when the children woke up sick and you've got to rearrange your life. That sends me ballistic. I feel put upon . . .

This father adores spending time with his three sons, and probably enjoys looking after them when they're ill. I must admit that I feel most like a father when one or both of my kids are sick. When I soothe them and reassure them that everything will be alright; when I bring down their fever with a damp cloth on the forehead and a little dose of medicine; when I read them a story, or two, or three . . .; when I tuck them into bed and tell them I'll be in to check on them later. That's when I feel most like a dad. But if I have to take care of sick kids for as long as this dad did, forget it! I'd go ballistic too!

Put another way, we humans may not be perfectly cut out for the nuclear family as a childcare arrangement, especially if one parent is away all the time earning to feed and house the family. And in this vein, single parent homes may be a particularly bad option. The extended family, with its large pool of adults available to take on short shifts of parenting duties may be more consistent with our evolutionary history as primates travelling in multi-family social groups.

Consistent with this explanation, research shows that mothers in extended families are relatively happy compared to their childless counterparts. Also, mothers in nuclear families who have frequent contact with adult relatives are less prone to symptoms of depression.[9] So, whether it is an actual extended family, or a quasi-extended family, when adult relatives in separate households help out from time to time, parents, and particularly mothers, seem to benefit psychologically.

Also consistent with this explanation is the obvious fact that raising human offspring is really, really hard, compared to darned near every other living species. The demand for human parenting labour is simply higher to start with. A direct comparison of humans with other species indicates that we've adopted a 'quality over quantity' strategy for reproduction. Instead of fertilising thousands of eggs and hoping that some

---

9   Depression epidemiology: study data from the University of Montreal update knowledge of depression epidemiology, *Mental Health Weekly Digest*, 29 May 2008, 445.

small percentage survives to reproductive age, we humans do things basically one at a time.

Even compared to other primates, humans still emphasise quality over quantity. Fewer offspring are born to women than to female bonobos, chimpanzees, gorillas, orangutans, gibbons, howler monkeys, and, well, you get the picture.[10] And the nurturing period for human offspring is longer than for any other primate. In short, raising a single human from birth to adulthood takes a lot of time and effort.

But the pay-off is obvious. Adolescent humans are excellent little survival machines, and with good parenting they are far more likely to survive to adulthood.[11] For non-primate mammals, roughly ten percent of offspring survive to adulthood. For most non-human primates, the percentage increases to 25 percent.[12] For primitive hunting and gathering societies, the figure jumps to over 50 percent.[13] In developing countries, the figure moves to 70–95 percent, and in post-industrial Western countries it exceeds 99 percent.[14]

So, in an evolutionary sense, all the effort that goes into parenting appears to pay off, and if anything, the investment in nurturing is increasing. Two of the most interesting trends in rich, Western countries are fewer children per household and the increasingly older age at which children leave their parents' household. The idea of a 30-something, only child still living with her parents is not the anomaly it would have been 30 years ago. Here is the quality over quantity strategy taken to its ultimate extreme – you raise one child your entire life!

The point being that any culture that 'invents' the two-parent nuclear family, faces an obvious risk of putting a great deal of pressure on those two parents. From this perspective, single parents seem positively heroic.

Funny I don't always feel that way.

---

10   Lancaster 1989.
11   Dawkins 1976.
12   However, bonobos, orangutans and gorillas do surprisingly well, with survival rates of 73 percent, 73 percent, and 67 percent, respectively (see Volk & Atkinson 2013).
13   Lancaster 1989, 65.
14   Volk & Atkinson 2013.

A Western sweat shop – single parenting

So you think parenting is tough. But you want to up the ante? You want discipline, challenge, excitement? Go ahead, be the parent, but go it alone. Get up at six in the morning, regardless of how late you were up working on the latest project at work. Pack lunch; get the kids out of bed; set their clothes for them; put on the coffee; make breakfast; clean up after breakfast; shower; shave; get dressed; and take something out of the freezer for dinner. And that's the easy bit!

Actually getting the kids from home to school is the hard bit. Dropping two children off to school on the way to work would seem like one of the simplest tasks you could imagine, but in fact it involves a rather complicated mental calculus weighing the advantages and disadvantages of various options, with the stakes on each day quite a bit higher than one would expect.

My children go to a public school where they are expected to be in the 'line up' at precisely 9 am every weekday morning. There is a large, no, *monumental*, premium for being on time, and the penalty for tardiness, in the form of guilt, would make Dostoevsky's *Crime and punishment* seem like a Dr Seuss book. Signing in your child late, after all the grades in the line-up have proceeded to their respective classrooms, is always met with an avoidance of eye contact and a subtle shaking of the head of the women in the reception window. And if you accumulate too many late arrivals in a term, you receive a letter reprimanding you for being too consistently tardy. In essence, parents are marked along with their children.

And I don't even like to think about how my kids feel wandering into class five minutes late and presenting their 'late cards' to their teachers. Did they face the ridicule and scorn of their peers? I could almost hear the voice of Nelson Muntz from *The Simpsons* series saying 'Ha, ha – [insert name of child here]'s late again!' My own personal version of this guilt was probably triggered one morning when I overheard a conversation between two sweet little girls in my son's class. One of them looked up at me and said 'That's the late kid's dad'. Needless to say, I was immediately and simultaneously consumed by guilt, shame and mortification.

> The point of all this being that dropping my kids off to school on a storming day involves assessing complex trade-offs between three negative outcomes (1) a parking ticket for $185, (2) getting caught in the rain on the way to and from the school, and of course, (3) the guilt trip associated with being late. There are clues for weighing the relative likelihood of success for each option every morning. For example, keeping an eye out for the green vests of the Parking Rangers is an obvious tactic. I've even enlisted my kids in this exercise. My seven-year-old knows to tell daddy if she sees one of the 'green men'.
>
> Then, of course, there is the task of gauging the severity of the rain by the visual pattern and noise levels of the rain drops on the wind screen. But my point is that even the seemingly simplest of parenting tasks, requires thought, and thought requires energy, and expending energy every day on a moment by moment basis is exhausting.
>
> The benefits? The daily pleasure of taking the children one step further. Note to self: try to find someone else to share the job – and the pleasure!

The stay-at-home dad is still sufficiently unusual that he gathers a lot of media attention. What is interesting is how people try to make sense of this unusual situation.

People often assume that the decision is driven by an economic imperative, and in at least some situations, it is the case that she earns more than he. For instance, Trey Burley is a stay-at-home dad who maintains the Daddy Mojo blog and explains that this was the decision he and his wife took.[15]

Another father explained his decision to me this way:

At the time Karen had the higher wage, right? But if Karen left, there was going to be a greater hit, in inverted commas, to our lifestyle. I can tread water, advance a bit and I'll get back to where I want to be. I know I'll always be a couple of steps behind than if I had stayed at it. But at the end of the day that's the way that I looked at it.

---

15 Mojo 2013.

However, even with this explanation, a man can detect that there is an implied insult. Men are meant to earn more – and in fact, the widely cited pay gap makes many question this claim. As Nigel Marsh notes, a man who does not earn any income has a lot of explaining to do, even to women he hardly even knows.

> Although I don't like to think of myself as a 'keeping up with the Joneses' type of person, I was worried about my old friends' reaction to my unemployment. After 20 years in an office career, it wasn't a simple task to divorce my self-worth from my job. . . . Although everyone seemed incredibly supportive of my choice not to go back to work, I couldn't help suspecting that many of them (especially the women) were simply being polite and had already translated 'decided to take a year off' into 'poor bastard can't find a job'.[16]

So dads that take care of kids become the target of snarly gibes about not having a job, leaving the mother to do the work, and so forth.

> It was a surprising like, 'Oh, wow. Really? You stay at home with the kids?' . . . Yeah, it's like, 'Oh okay. Yeah, I know a couple of people who do that.' And they are like – everyone, at first – the first thing everyone assumes is, is that my wife must have a high paying job.

What the stay-at-home dads can tell other dads is that parenting is a real job. Trey Burley has the subheading to his blog 'A parenting site on family, life, and poop culture.' A stay-at-home dad I talked to had this to say:

> Yeah. It's about going 'Hey, I did a great job today.' They'll never grasp the concept that my girls are really happy and we had a wonderful day today therefore I did a great job. They don't think of it as a job. That's the one that gets a lot of blokes – in answer to your question, some of the guys get it, some don't. Looking after the kids is a job. Some don't get that looking after the kids is a job.

---

16   Marsh 2007, 62–63.

'Where's the instruction manual for this thing?'

So in fairness, parenting *is* a really tough job. Just ask any mother! The word 'mother' is virtually synonymous with dedication to childrearing.

And if mother means all this, then the term 'single mother' takes this to another dimension. A mother who is trying to raise children, while also keeping the house, working, and without a partner is one of the most striking modern images of a battler worthy of admiration and compassion.

The word 'father' – whether referring to single fathers or otherwise – does not evoke anything like this kind of effort and sacrifice; and justifiably, perhaps, given their apparent willingness to put childrearing into the 'too hard' basket.

Why is raising a baby seen as so different from other man-projects? I mean, it's fiddly, the details can be annoying, and he will certainly get his hands dirty (covered in poop to be more precise), and yet the chaos that takes place in the workshop will produce something magnificent. In fact, a child is a better project than most because it keeps on developing. The child is always growing, changing, and at some point, she/he is very likely to take on a mind of her/his own.

The difference between being a dad and other man-projects is, of course, that you will not always be in control of the situation. For dads wanting to change their ways and get down and dirty with some hands-on parenting – keep this in mind. As much as you may want there to be one, there is no instruction manual for raising children. It ain't like changing an oil filter or building a deck in the backyard. You can't just follow the steps correctly and come out with the perfect result.

 Don't even kid yourself – things will go awry! Something as simple as a feed can turn into a mess that will take you an hour to clean up. You will have to learn to accept that your wife may be several streets ahead of you on the parenting superhighway, and she can be your best source of information when things go haywire.

This is not as obvious a point as you might think because most men have a built in reluctance to ask for help. It is reasonable therefore to expect that they will be equally reluctant to ask for parenting advice. To lack competence can be ego-threatening for some men. Get over it! When in doubt ask your wife for help.

But a word of warning to the mums – only offer advice if he asks! As we'll see in the next chapter, mums need to learn to fight that urge to carefully observe every little thing dads do in order to identify and correct 'mistakes'. This is *not* the way to proceed. If you catch yourself doing it – stop! He will not appreciate your 'advice' if it comes in the form of unsolicited criticism.

Dad can also learn from mum's example as well as her advice. And it is not only in terms of how to care for the children, but also how to pursue other productive activities outside the home.

Mums have shown men that child care can be accommodated alongside other achievements – even in defiance of stereotyping and bias. Rather than just showing him how to care for the child, mums have shown dads that being a parent can be accomplished along with other achievements, and even in the face of people doubting their capacity to do so.

The migration of mothers to the workplace offers two lessons for dads. One is to offer a kind of invitation to dads to participate more on the domestic front. It may be implicit, but it is clearly there – the children cannot raise themselves, or if they do, there could be some negative consequences. The second lesson is showing dads the way of defying 'invisible' barriers that might prevent his involvement in the home domain.

So if the man isn't always willing to take advice, is he at least willing to make mistakes? There is something about the nature of childrearing that is fundamentally different from the stereotypical male challenges of arduous journeys (Odysseus in the *Odyssey*), dangerous feats (Heracles in the *Bibliotheca*), and using power tools (Tim Taylor in *Home improvement*). The implications of making a mistake can take on an entirely different dimension.

Imagine someone who is about to jump from a plane with a parachute on their back for the first time. What they feel is fear – a fear that things could go terribly wrong. And if something goes wrong, he (or she) is in serious trouble.

However, the fear in a challenge like skydiving – and like many of the challenges that men do like to tackle – is of a personal nature. That is, 'If I get this wrong, I might be damaged.' The fear in the challenge of childrearing is quite different: 'If I get this wrong, my child could be damaged.'

Perhaps the greatest terror I have ever experienced is when my then two-year-old son learned to open the front door. I'd left it unlocked. He must have reached up, turned the knob (no doubt after observing me and other adults doing the same thing), and decided to go for a little walk around the neighbourhood. I was busy making dinner, and when I took a break to check on him I saw the open front door from the other end of the hallway. Terror! Panic!

I went running up and down the two nearest streets screaming his name at the top of my lungs while calling '000' on my mobile phone. I found him about 100 metres away from the front door while in the midst of an hysterical rant with an incredibly patient and understanding police officer. It is a fear I will never forget.

For a man to feel this kind of fear is a step in the right direction. It means that he has realised that there is someone out there that is more important than he is! An important step towards manhood is the shift from seeing himself as the centre of the universe to seeing himself as an infinitesimal and integral element of the universe.

You will get it wrong – and that's okay

It might be useful to realise that you are going to get it wrong! There is no such thing as perfect parenting. It is an ideal that like the Hollywood marriage is often an unrealistic ideal. The danger is that many parents try to achieve this – and of course fail.

Set up to be a good parent; leave the perfect parent to fairytale films.

A friend of mine described how she was so worried about damaging her daughter psychologically. She worried about telling her off too fiercely, she worried about denying her too much, she worried about being too generous to her, she worried about a lot of stuff.

In particular, my friend worried that one day, her daughter would end up in psychological counselling over some trauma that had been created by the mother.

In my blunt masculine way, I tried to allay her fears:

'You know, your daughter may well end up in counselling one day. And of one thing you can be certain: she *will* blame you. However, the event or trauma for which you are responsible will most likely be one that you have not even considered, don't remember or frankly doubt. Despite that, it will be real to your daughter, it will be the reason she is in counselling, and there's nothing you can do to stop it.'

Such a feeling is shared by both mothers and fathers, and for rather a long time. For instance, Silas Marner is an often-forgotten model of single fatherhood created by novelist George Eliot (pen name of Mary Anne Evans) in 1861.[17] He is typically remembered as a miser – and so he was – until he became the adoptive parent for a young toddler that found her way into his home as her drug-addicted mother died in the cold nearby.

Eliot's novel celebrates his fathering of the child. However, like all parents, he faced the problem of delineating right from wrong for

---

17   For full text of the book, see the Gutenberg Project (http://www.gutenberg.org/files/550/550-h/550-h.htm). The 1994 film *A simple twist of fate* written by and featuring Steve Martin is adapted from this book.

his adoptive daughter Eppie. Marner expresses exactly this fear of punishing his very young adopted daughter for misbehaviour.

Of course, universal themes like the difficulties of a single father raising an adopted daughter tend to reappear in popular culture throughout the ages. The year 2013 gives us the animated motion picture *Despicable me 2*, where reformed super-villain Gru struggles to navigate the treacherous strait between discipline and femininity in raising his three adopted daughters, Margo, Edith and Agnes.

Baby steps

Antenatal classes are not exactly tailored to the needs of fathers-to-be. More on that in the next chapter. In these classes, I learned that many people have an opinion on how to raise a child, the opinions and information are complex, complicated and surprisingly to me at the time, apparently even conflicting and contradictory.

Sitting in the final session, I remember the most useful piece of advice that was given to us by the trainer. In recapping the course, she pointed out that we had learned a lot, and while this may have provided some information that reduced our lack of knowing, it may have created additional fear around the notion of too much information – and she was right. She had a solution. She said: 'You have to do what you feel is right.' This was, I thought, a great insight. Being a dad is pretty straightforward. You just do it, one step at a time.

Of course, being a 'dad' is quite different from being a father. Becoming a father is about basic biology, 'just the sperm'. Dad, however, is an honorific title for someone who fills the boots, who sees 'fatherhood' as important. And for all that mums can do, she cannot fill the boots of dad. And dad has to learn how to parent just the same way that mum does: hours of on-the-job training. The job that does not buy bread to put into tummies, but one that changes lives. What, exactly, do dads provide, what is fatherhood? Here's Jessica Hagy's take.[18]

---

18   Hagy 2008.

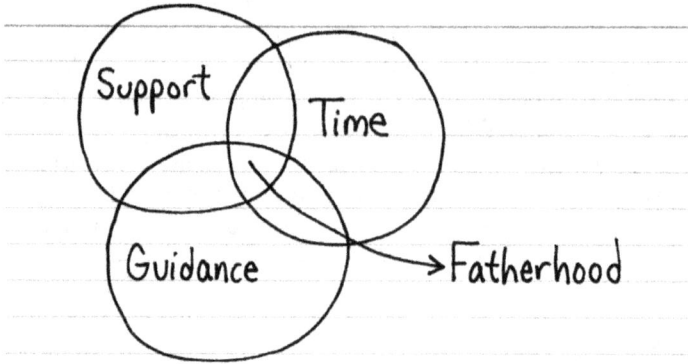

(1) Support, (2) time and (3) guidance are a great start. Of course, dads provide more than this. Let's add a few circles to this diagram.

(4) Discipline – Perhaps one of the most feared threats from my mum as I was growing up was 'Wait till your father gets home.' I used to think of my dad as very fair. I realise now that it was because when he got involved, I *really* had been very bad. Mum dealt with misdemeanours, dad dealt with felonies. Mum was a magistrate. Dad was a Supreme Court judge.[19]

(5) Freedom – My dad let me do things that mum would not allow me to do. 'Go ahead, climb that high tree.' And yes, sometimes with consequences such as a broken arm that both he and I would have to explain to mum with very red faces. But I thank him for that. Without dad, I would not have had as much freedom.

(6) Resilience – The world is a tough place. You don't get things just because you want them. Sometimes you have to fight for them. And the world is going to knock you on your bum from time to time. Get up. Have another go. And you may still fail. Dad may be the strong, silent type, and yet even in this, he can help instil the important quality of resilience in his children.

---

19 Blair & Lichter 1991.

(7) Inspiration – Yes, mums offer inspiration, but in the world of creativity, two heads are better than one, and dads can provide another whole different head full of imagination, dreams, goals and visions.

(8) Protection – While crossing Momma-bear will certainly evoke a protective response, one thing that men generally have going for them is they can pack some punch into protection. Something about the male in many mammal species is his ability to protect his family from danger. Men have this instinct too. Somewhere in the reptilian part of the brain lies the hardwired program – mess with my child and I will hurt you!

(9) Love – My kids are the centre of my world. I cannot imagine life without them, and I can't possibly remember why I thought my career, favourite sports teams, car, mobile phone, favourite rock bands, watch, clothes, and entertainment centre were so important to me. They all seem more trivial now.

(10) Money – Getting money is as important as lactating from the point of view that they both fill bellies with food. It may be wrong and even the product of a sexist world, but men by and large seem well adapted to bring home the bacon. However, this should not be his only or major contribution – that's why it is #10 in the list. In fact, if mum's better at earning money than dad, then the ideal role-specialisation for the family may be well worth re-viewing!

Dads do all these things – eventually. But it's a cumulative effect over time. On a moment by moment basis we're not always sure what we're doing or why we're doing it. It's very much a 'learn-as-you-go' process. It's, dare I say it, intuitive, and yes dads do have intuition when it comes to child care.

The birth of my son is all a bit of a blur. I remember all the things that happened – or at least I think I do – but more like someone looking at photographs than remembering being there. The birth of a baby is a bit like a first-timer's bungee jump; an emotional, physical and psychological rush. A kind of overload with so much data flowing in that all that is left later are some more historical markers of what happened over time without a sense of how I was feeling when it all happened.

But then there is the time when the emotions began to come back into focus and the reality of impending responsibilities of parenthood began to drop into place. The first one was when the hospital said we could go. I am not sure if they said we *could* go, or we *ought* to go. I do remember feeling very nervous about the prospect of driving away and thereby taking on the full responsibility of caring for our brand new child.

I drove the car around to the front door of the hospital so that the mother, carrying our son, would not have to walk too far. As we strapped him into his baby-seat for the first time, I had an overwhelming sense of how important my role as father and protector was. I would be driving the car – and while I'm a very safe driver – I felt extra cautious as today I would be driving my first-born child, my son and heir, and all of those silly ideas.

As I attached the seatbelts, I checked and rechecked that they were secure. Again, the notion of a first-time bungee jumper comes to mind – better check the safety equipment one last time!

The mother of my son is also a good driver, but we did tend to follow the stereotypical norm whereby when we went out together, I, the male, drove. In this particular instance, there seemed to be some reason to this rhyme. The mother had recently delivered a baby – by emergency caesarean section as it happened – and therefore, it was the role of the other partner, the male to step up.

In effect, I was very conscious of this – even if stereotyped, I chose consciously. The mother clucked over whether our baby was safe. It was my role to make sure, and then call an end to the stalling. It was time to go home. Not like at the hospital where we could press a button to call someone to help. We now had to go it alone.

Of course, it was all a little over the top. The drive from the hospital to our home was just two kilometres. But the weight of parenthood was present – all due to the presence of extra two kilos of a healthy pink baby swaddled and strapped into a baby-capsule which if the advertising is to be believed, would probably protect the child in the event of any number of cataclysmic events including mere stupidity on my part.

Being the father meant for me protecting the child not only for the child's sake, not only for my sake, but for the mother's sake as well. Talk about serving multiple masters.

Like other challenges I have faced in life, it is with a great deal of pride to be able to recount having made it. Unlike so many other challenges which have been predominantly personal, this one was one that affected two other people – the mother and our child – directly.

This is the path of the father. And sure, these are just the first steps, but they are important because they were the first steps where I felt my responsibility expand beyond just myself.

The rewards

There are three clear beneficiaries from dad getting involved in helping raising the children. The first beneficiary when dad gets involved with child care is mum!

What this single dad has learned from mum is that she's right – it's a tough gig balancing both family and work. I was lucky in some respects – I shared single parenthood with the other parent. This allowed space for both mum and me to pursue other interests. From the ashes of divorce are some useful messages for parents everywhere – whether together or apart.

Dad helping out with the child care gives some time for mum to pursue other interests. As mums engaged with raising young children will tell you, there is only so much goo-ing and gah-ing and bouncing baby that a parent can do. Many mums I have met comment on how they crave some adult activity to give balance to their life. So if dad gets involved, mum gets to get some time off from the 'toughest job', and dad gets to learn to love it.

Dad getting involved gives mum some time to pursue her other interests like getting a career, making a financial contribution to the household, and so forth.

The second beneficiary is the child (or children). The child gets two loving, hands-on parents. And curiously, this appears to be a case where not only is two better than one – it works even if the two do things differently.

Research is constantly suggesting that dad's role is perhaps surprisingly important. There are host of findings that show the important influence of fathers on the cognitive and emotional development of their children.[20] We'll learn more about the specific benefits of having dad around later in 'The compleat child'.

---

20 Cabrera at al. 2007.

But perhaps the most obvious beneficiary of having dad involved in childrearing from the very beginning is dad himself. The first benefit to dad of being more involved with his kids is a sense of satisfaction. Fathers who see their contribution to the development of their child as important express more satisfaction with themselves.[21]

Dad does not go to his deathbed wishing he had spent more time with his kids. Well, he probably does – but partly because he realises the time he did spend with them was so great, and partly because he's dying and he's not going to get more time with them. At least he will not go there feeling that he completely missed out on the experience of having children.

Then there is the research showing a positive relationship between being a parent and happiness, and ironically, that there is a stronger relationship for fathers compared to mothers.[22] That's right. Becoming a father improves the emotional wellbeing of men *more* than motherhood does for women. Also, research consistently shows that the more fathers are involved in caring for their own children, the happier they are.[23] One father I talked to decided to put his career on hold in order to look after his children. He described the experience this way:

> I had this desire to do everything. So the more of everything I did, the better I felt. I might have been tired, stressed and whatever else but I felt better about myself doing that. And then you realise what you have done.

And then there is, perhaps, the ultimate benefit of being a father – you get to live longer! Yes, you read that correctly. One recent study estimates that for any given age (i.e. year of life), and controlling for many other lifestyle factors, childless men are roughly twice as likely as fathers to die. For childless women, the rate is four times as high as for mothers.[24]

One of the great pleasures of being a dad for me has been to relive my childhood through the eyes of my father. I remember my dad being more absent. I think all dads were in those days – that's 'just the way it

---

21   Ladd 2000.
22   Nelson et al. 2012.
23   Baxter & Smart 2010, 70.

was' as they say. We had a farm, so I'm not sure that he was really that absent, but he was certainly less present than mum.

However, as I raised my child, I had these flashes back to my childhood. But they were kind of bizarre because rather than being back in my shoes as a child, I was there seeing me as a child through my father's eyes.

One day, my son was sitting on my shoulders. I took him around like that a fair bit. It seemed pretty practical, he enjoyed the ride, and he sat comfortably on my shoulders. Anyway, one day I suddenly noticed something that my son tended to do. His fingers would be playing around my throat, and in particular, around my Adam's apple.

It was not the first time he had done this, but it was the time that I was suddenly cast back into my childhood. I remembered my father's Adam's apple. It was prominent – as is mine. I remember as a child, wanting to have one like that – and my mother telling me that it might happen. I had never even realised that this childhood dream had been realised – or at least, not until that day I realised my son was playing with and fascinated by my Adam's apple.

It was a weird experience. I was taken back to my old childhood, but saw it through the eyes of a father, my father perhaps, rather than through my own child's eyes.

It was – and is – a great experience. Being an active father means that I get to relive my childhood, but it is a double pleasure. I get to remember things that I have long forgotten, things that I appreciated as a child. And I get to see my son appreciate things that I too appreciated – and the additional pleasure of getting a sense of what it must have been for my father. An unfolding into fuller consciousness:

> As the child's mind was growing into knowledge, his [Silas Marner'] mind was growing into memory; as her life unfolded, his soul, long stupefied in a cold narrow prison, was unfolding too, and trembling gradually into full consciousness.[25]

---

24   Agerbo el al. 2012; Pro creation: having children prolongs life, *The Economist*, 15 December 2012. Retrieved 31 January 2014 from http://www.economist.com/news/science-and-technology/
21568362-having-children-prolongs-life-pro-creation.
25   Eliot 1861.

Part 2
Mothers letting go

Up until now it's been mainly the men who've been copping it. I've challenged fathers to become more involved in the lives of their children, and more generally, with all aspects of domestic life. I've questioned the assumptions that fathers make about how and where to spend time, and identified some of the internal, psychological barriers that prevent or limit their more active engagement with their kids.

Yet this is only half the story.

Now we must explore the external barriers to paternal involvement, which are often created against the will of fathers everywhere. As we'll see, many of these obstacles are created by mums themselves. But it goes far beyond that. Fathers receive a consistent message from multiple sources about their secondary status as parents, and the avalanche of propaganda begins from the moment of conception.

'We're pregnant!' ('No, I'm not!')

On the road to parenthood, there is perhaps no image quite as joyous as the expectant mum standing hand-in-hand with her proud partner announcing to the world at large: 'We're pregnant.' But while young couples may be keen to show how well they are sharing everything, saying 'we are pregnant' is not sharing; it is fantasy land. She is pregnant; he is not. Her tummy will get very big over the next nine months. His tummy will remain unchanged, unless of course he significantly increases his intake of beer during her pregnancy, which as it turns out, is *not* an effective way to deal with her mood swings.

When the pregnancy is announced, she will get all the congratulations. Everyone will come up and rub her tummy, smile, and say 'Congratulations! You must be so happy!' No-one will pat his John Thomas and say 'Well done.'

She is carrying the baby; he is not; it is as simple as that. And this is not a trivial point, because it reflects a fundamental principle that drives the politics of parenting at this early stage: 'her body, her choice.' It is this principle that makes the pathway to fatherhood especially difficult. Whatever obstacles a woman faces in becoming a parent, the father faces also. But a man faces even more obstacles. It is tougher for a man to be a father than a woman to be a mother.

I can practically hear you gasp at the audacity of such a statement! How can I make such a statement when it is mothers who put up with a nine-month pregnancy, complete with uncontrollable mood swings, morning sickness, and an awkward, heavy load to carry around, while fathers sit around doing nothing with that dazed, 'What's going on??' expression on their faces?

Mothers endure this only to experience sometimes excruciatingly painful labour, while fathers 'coach' them through the delivery. Yeah, I did the whole coaching thing. What a big 'help' I was! Without me there to tell her to 'Breathe honey, keep breathing', I am sure she would have stopped inhaling and suffocated right there in the delivery room. This is another part of the sharing delusion. She is giving birth; he is doing stuff all.

Then after the baby is born it is mothers who do the bulk of the childcare work while fathers go off to work during the week and play golf on the weekend. How can it possibly be the case that being a father is tougher? Perhaps a slight rewording will help.

It is tougher for a man to *become* a father. Still disagree? Consider this. Any woman who decides to become a mother can go to a sperm bank, get artificially inseminated, and have a bouncing baby nine months later. No potential father need be consulted.

Now what about a man who decides he wants to become a father? A man does not get to be a parent without the consent of a woman,[1] and the asymmetry in power and control over reproduction starts well before pregnancy. A man in search of fatherhood must pass through four gates. And the gatekeeper in all four instances is a woman.

First, a man needs a woman's consent to *contribute* to conception. His sperm need to be introduced to her egg(s). In the natural arena, he has to get her in bed, and ensure that no contraception is being used.

Second, he must then hope that he was the *only* one invited to contribute or that he is able to beat out the competition.[2] Here, the gender stereotypes do not hold. Get this – women can be promiscuous too!

Third, he needs her consent to actually have the baby. Here the principle of 'her body, her choice' is embodied in law. If she decides to abort the pregnancy, there is nothing he can do about it.

Finally, even if she gives birth, she can put the baby up for adoption without him even knowing about it.

---

1 Townsend 2002; Goldscheider & Kaufman 2006.
2 See Robin Baker's *Sperm wars* (1996) for a fascinating account of the ways that men and women consciously and unconsciously manoeuvre to become parents.

Let's examine how his need for her consent guides and shapes parenthood, both hers and his. We will begin long before junior has even been conceived, starting with the first hurdle – the consent to have sex without contraception.

Princesses, don't kiss just any frog!

Women are beautiful! Absolutely beautiful – and attractive in a very, very carnal way! I've been obsessed with their beauty from puberty to the point at which I typed the last word in this sentence. I cannot imagine a world without women, and I am sure I would not want to go on living without them.

After that massive infusion of testosterone in my early teens, the single greatest purpose in my life became how to make women attracted to me enough to want to have sex with me. This little obsession is hard work! Don't women have to work for sex too? Well, maybe a little, but not as much. If there is a gender stereotype that is largely consistent with the available evidence, it is the perpetually horny male.

Research has established that testosterone is directly linked to sex drive. Inject a male rat with a big dose of the stuff and he'll hump anything that moves, female or male. If you pump enough into a female rat, she'll start humping like a male! What a great little hormone! In humans, a man, or woman, who loses the ability to produce testosterone, will lose interest in sex. But in general men have 20 times as much of the stuff coursing through their veins.[3]

And this stronger sex drive translates into a greater willingness to have sex, with anyone, anywhere. Men are more eager and willing to have sex than women in virtually any situation.[4] Men and women enjoy sex with steady romantic partners about equally. On a scale of one (no pleasure at all) to five (extreme pleasure) both women and men rate sex with their regular lovers in the 4.5–5 range. However, this is where the similarity ends. When asked about having sex with attractive acquaintances or strangers, women's ratings dropped to the 1–1.5 range of the scale. And men? You guessed it. Still in the 4.5–5 range!

---

3   Moir & Jessel 1991, 103.
4   Ellis et al. 2008, 924.

> ### She really does have a headache
>
> That men have a stronger sex drive than women has no doubt led to marital conflicts from time to time. The stereotypical excuse for a wife not wanting to have sex with her husband is that she has a headache. As it turns out, women do have headaches more frequently than men.[5] However, it also turns out that one of the best non-pharmaceutical cures for a headache can be sex.[6] Go figure!

Women are more likely to report being 'in love' with their first sexual partner and with sexual partners in general, whereas men like sex with just about anybody they are attracted to. The nature of the relationship is entirely irrelevant.[7] What's love got to do with it? Nothing if you're Tina Turner or the typical man.

It's hardly surprising then that men express more positive attitudes towards premarital sex, sex with multiple partners, casual sex, and sex of just about any kind, even masturbation.[8] And when women do have sex, they don't like to admit it. Women tend to under-report the number of sexual partners they've had; men, you guessed it again, tend to over-report.[9]

In general then, women have much more stringent criteria for who they will and won't have sex with, and underlying all this is perhaps the most basic sex difference of all, the one we began this chapter with. Women can have babies; men can't. How does this lead to many of the attitudes described above? Consider the notion of fecundity distributions, that is, the range in the number of offspring that can be produced by males and females in a given population. Simply put, the range is much narrower for females.

In many animal populations, most males produce no offspring at all, with a small percentage of 'alpha' males fathering a large number of progeny. Hence, overall the fecundity distribution stretches from zero

---

5   Ellis et al. 2008, 938.
6   Carson-DeWitt 2009; Cox 2008.
7   Moir & Jessel 1991, 109.
8   Ellis et al. 2008, 484, 631.
9   Ellis et al. 2008, 720–21.

to those large numbers produced by the alpha males. In short, a small number of males are winners, while many are losers. Things are not so extreme for humans, but the same basic principle holds.

The maximum number of babies born to a woman is 69, with 67 surviving infancy. The mother was a Mrs Vassilyev.[10] This number would seem to be pretty close to the maximum potential. If each birth was a single birth, that's the equivalent of 52 straight years of being pregnant. In fairness, *all* of Mrs Vassilyev's children were born in a series multiple births over a 40-year period (1725–1765). So let's set the maximum potential for females at 70 children just so we have a nice, round number.

What's the maximum potential for males? According to multiple sources, the top male in our derby, Moulay Ismaïl Ibn Sharif, the last Sharifan Emperor of Morocco, produced 888 babies from a harem of over 1000 women. But even this number seems well below a man's maximum potential. Since a male orgasm only takes a couple of minutes, it represents a minimal amount of work relative to the woman's nine months gestation, not to mention lactation to follow. Okay, we have to allow the man some recovery time, but even with recovery time taken into account, a man could produce far more than 888 babies in a lifetime.[11]

Put simply, if a woman wants to have sex, she can. Men have to work for it.[12] In a typical nightclub on a given night, virtually every man will be looking for sex then and there; and I do mean there, in the nightclub, if necessary. Only a subset of the women will be looking for immediate sex, but virtually every one of them that wants a sexual partner will succeed in finding one. Put another way, if a woman wants sex, the odds are in her favour. If a man wants sex, the odds are against him.

---

10   See http://en.wikipedia.org/wiki/Feodor_Vassilyev, also discussed in more detail by Clay 1989.

11   Smith 2007, 88.

12   Kendrick 1989, 5–24.

What was that all about?

Sex! It was all that I thought about in my late teens and 20s. From the perspective of 30 years later, it is fascinating to reminisce – and to wonder – 'What was that all about?'

For good or for bad, I was a young adult in the 80s. Premarital sex was publicly still a 'no-no'. Privately of course, it was a different matter, as it has been throughout history.

The desire of a young man is a difficult thing to quench. My favourite memory is of a girlfriend who was happy to kiss and cuddle, but was always rather more cagey about sex. Actually, I say 'always' but as is so often the case, that was not strictly correct. She was 'always' reluctant except for one or two days every four weeks! I would live for those few days every four weeks.

It is curious to me that her infrequent sexual urges were accepted, while my constant sexual urges were dismissed as base and crass. Who, exactly, was setting the norms here? As has been well established in business and negotiations, the one with least need for the other party holds the power. Or to put it a little more colourfully perhaps: it is true that it takes two to tango; but the one who can unilaterally leave the dance floor holds the key to the dance.

Despite the insatiable drive I felt to have sex, I was not in a hurry to have a baby. I therefore broached the idea of my buying and having condoms available. Curiously, my girlfriend would have none of that. To obtain and carry condoms she felt implied that we were going to have sex; hard to argue with her on that. She was resolute, and I, the partner without the power, would comply. So once a month, when she would feel the urge, our kissing and cuddling would take on a little more urgency, she would pull me on top of her and we would end up having sex.

To add to all this excitement, my girlfriend's father was a judge. And the timing for her urge nearly always fell on Sunday night, the night we would dine with her father and the family. So after dinner, we would caper off to her childhood bedroom to kiss and cuddle which would eventually evolve to having sex on her single bed – with her father wandering the hallway calling to her and asking why she did not want to come and watch television!

Sex was a constant pre-occupation for me as a young adult. The female's power to limit sexual access was a major frustration to be negotiated along with the mores of society and many other obstacles – such as fathers who are judges strolling the hall just metres away!

Having said all that, the whole mating game can't be much of a picnic for women either. They're supposed to sit and wait for some jerk to come up to them, invariably with the worst pick-up line imaginable. Men, here's some advice for you – drop the stupid pick-up lines and avoid calling her 'baby' at all costs. She won't think you're cool. She'll think you're a loser; and you are.

Just smile and say 'hi'. If she smiles and says 'hi' back, tell her your name and start a normal conversation. And for goodness sake women, even if he is a jerk, or you're uninterested for any other reason, be nice about it. No need to knock his ego in the dirt. Remember, it took some courage to say hello in the first place.

Even if our hypothetical father to be has managed to get laid, there's still the figurative and literal barrier known as contraception. His sperm requires a clear thoroughfare to her egg for the party to begin.

But before we go any further, it must be acknowledged that, while it's difficult to have a baby without a bit of sperm, you don't really need a man – or at least, not in the flesh. You can go to a gamete supermarket and place an order for some sperm. Then a white-coated doctor using a microscope can tease it, freeze it, and if it pleases the women, use a number of artificial approaches for getting one of the wrigglers to weasel into her egg. Certainly helpful if you can't conceive any other way; but to choose this route for convenience seems a little bizarre. Call me old-fashioned, but I can't imagine opting out of the charm and intimacy of the natural option!

We've commoditised the male gamete to the point where sperm banks are not much more than a retail shop, but not so the female gamete. Imagine our would-be father rocking up to a clinic and demanding an ovum and a uterus? The market in this respect is much less developed. Human ova can be harvested, but still a uterus is needed. Admittedly some women have agreed to lease out their uterus when they act as 'surrogate' mothers. The woman's involvement relative to the man's then is very much in-the-flesh.

Beyond the physical limitations, the very thought of allowing a man to initiate all this on his own as a single parent is repugnant to many, and already there have been moves to make the purchase of harvested ova illegal under any circumstance.[13] So the asymmetry between motherhood and fatherhood is already apparent in contemporary attitudes and policies towards male and female gametes.

But back to our hypothetical prospective father-to-be, who is now having sex, but is not sure whether his sperm have on-ramp access to the reproductive super highway.

Contraception inception

In the 1980s, I was travelling around Australia conducting marketing research for Ansell, a global manufacturer of 'protective solutions'. The research comprised of small discussion groups ('focus groups') and was addressing the topic of condom usage. The client was particularly interested in how heterosexual couples negotiated the use of condoms, and how the onset, timing and frequency of sex is negotiated in new and / or casual relationships.

To facilitate the discussion, we piled a vast array of different brands of condoms in the middle of the table at which participants were seated. As I travelled from one focus group location to another, I lived in fear of my briefcase falling open or being inspected at an airport security check.

The groups were segregated because we reasoned that putting men and women together to discuss sex-related topics might be embarrassing or might lead some people to lie about their actual behaviour. It seemed reasonable accordingly, that the group's facilitator be the same sex as the group. I was therefore facilitating only groups of males.

However, I realised that there might be some value if some of the groups were facilitated by an other-sex facilitator. When I facilitated some of the women's groups, I learned some things that had not emerged in the men's groups.

From the men's groups, I learned that negotiating condom usage was very tricky. There are two major motivations for using condoms:

---

13   Cohen 2012.

one is for contraception, the other is for protection from sexually transmitted diseases.

For him, this negotiation is tricky. When he raises the topic of condoms, she might think he is implying she has a disease or he has a disease or that she is 'easy'. For her, the negotiation is more straightforward as I learned moderating the female groups. Her request for condoms for protection against conception is perfectly legitimate and no-one's sexual health or behaviour is impugned.

Condoms are an imperfect form of contraception in many ways, but do offer some protection against sexually transmitted diseases. The negotiation for using condoms is arguably easier for her than him, but the ultimate contraception asymmetry is seen in the combined oral contraceptive pill (COCP) developed in the late 1940s and 1950s.

> Said a well-meaning mother to her daughter: 'The best contraceptive is an oral contraceptive. Just say "No".'

To be sure, the history of the pill is populated by a good number of women. Edris Rice-Wray Carson[14] was a particularly important contributor being involved in important early clinical work. Other women played critical roles encouraging, supporting and facilitating (including financially) the development of the pill: e.g., Margaret Sanger, Katharine McCormick.

However, while women were involved, most of the scientific development was undertaken by men: Russell Marker, Gregory Pincus, Min Chueh Chang, John Rock, Carl Djerassi, Luis Miramontes, George Rosenkranz, and Frank Colton to name a few.[15]

Curiously, some women were quite vocal in complaining *after* the COCP was released for public consumption in 1957 in the US. Barbara Seaman published a book called *The doctor's case against the pill* in 1969. Senator Gaylord Nelson launched Senate hearings in 1970 to deal with the issue. Alice Wolfsen and other feminists became incensed at the hearings as it was only men that presented evidence.

---

14 See http://en.wikipedia.org/wiki/Edris_Rice-Wray [Accessed 31 January 2014].
15 See http://en.wikipedia.org/wiki/Combined_oral_contraceptive_pill [Accessed 31 January 2014].

Despite these early concerns, the pill is widely distributed today. Like many medications, it has associated risks and benefits. However, it is difficult to imagine that women would permit the pill to be removed from sale in today's era.

The pill provides good contraception. From the women's focus groups I learned that, more importantly, it gives control to women. Whereas the rhythm method and condoms require more active participation from both parties, the pill requires no participation from the man. Indeed, the man need not even know that she is taking an oral contraceptive.

There is some talk about an oral contraceptive for men. A male contraceptive pill would, of course, allow men at least the power of veto. If the male contraceptive pill works, then the man – without informing the woman – can ensure that she does not have a child with him as the father. It does not, however, give him the choice and the power to have her become a parent to a child without her knowledge. Or rather, biology would eventually and inevitably reveal who the mother is.

So as we can see getting that first form of consent is no small feat if you're a man. If you've gotten laid, congratulations to you! But even if your gametes are working fine, and there are no pills, condoms, IUDs, or diaphragms to deal with, you've still got three more hurdles to clear.

Let's proceed to number two – establishing that you're the only sexual partner she's having unprotected sex with at the moment. No matter how often you contribute your seed, if you're not handcuffed or otherwise shackled to her, you have no way of knowing whether *her* baby is *yours*.

The folly of patriarchy

There is nothing that quite smacks of the power of patriarchy as patrilineal mapping. That is, giving children the surname of their father rather than their mother. What were our forefathers thinking? *For* fathers, no doubt. Men were looking after their own interests, effectively treating their wives and children as property. But matrilineal mapping would have been a much safer bet for knowing the true lineage of every child, and this perhaps explains why maternal uncles in many cultures serve as a primary role model to children.

The royal families are a varied lot, and I am willing to bet that there are a fair number of queens that gave birth to children whose sire was not the Sire. I daresay that the emergence of DNA evidence in recent times will do much to undo any idealistic notion of patriarchal lineage. Imagine finding out that the patriarchal lines of monarchy are a lot patchier than history and hegemony would have us believe! Ironically, if we had chosen matrilineal mapping, we could have known at least one side of our ancestry with certainty. Instead, we chose to trace parentage through the father, the one side about which there can always be some doubt.

The real junior

For all the advantages that there might be to being a man, a man cannot give birth to a baby. Okay, maybe in the movies. Arnold Schwarzenegger famously gave birth in the movie *Junior*. But that's just Hollywood, right? Not exactly. Thomas Beatie has given birth to three children to date.[16] However, this 'exception' most decidedly establishes the rule. Thomas was originally named Tracey. He was born a girl. She decided to have gender reassignment surgery and is now officially a man.

So, men may have the power in saying who the father is in *official* terms, but in *real* terms, the truth about parentage lies almost entirely with the mother. It is this parental certainty that gives her, not him, a strong degree of control over reproduction. She holds the power in her hands, or more specifically, in her womb.

The simple reality is that men and women are *not* equal when it comes to reproduction. Officially men dominate women by giving his name to their offspring, but the reality of parentage is quite different, as captured by this old Irish joke.

An Irish lass comes home fearful of something she must tell her father.

---

16   Pous 2001.

'Fother, t'ere's sometin' oi need to tell ya. Oi tink tat oi'm pregnant.'

The daughter sighs in relief having made her admission. Her father smiles at her.

'Roight you are dortor of moine. But are ya shore dat it's yoars?'

Of course, it is the father who must determine whether the baby is his, and this fundamental asymmetry gives women certain advantages at the negotiation table when it comes to reproduction. Information is power it is said. Women hold particularly privileged information when it comes to conception.

To be sure, a man must have contributed. No human child can be born without a contribution of a man. Even if the man's contribution, a sperm cell, organic and natural, was snap-frozen at harvesting, defrosted, and subsequently hand-delivered to the awaiting egg cell.

It is the woman, fecund and fertilised who can be rightly called a mother. She carries the egg cell fertilised by a sperm cell – called a blastocyte, initially – and later elevated to zygote status.

She can be sure that it is her egg. But the man that can be rightly called the father? Heaven alone knows. Close behind heaven is the mother who, under natural insemination procedures, has the best chance of knowing who the father is, especially if she's restricted her sexual exploits to one partner for an extended interval.

Contrast her knowledge of who versus when. *When* the mother comes to realise that she is pregnant can vary enormously. However, she is going to realise at some point if the pregnancy runs to term.

Some women claim to know or feel conception at the exact moment that the sperm fertilises the egg. Even if that intuition fails her, there is the missed period to signal the beginning of a new life. And if that signal fails to offer sufficient notice, eventually her swelling belly will make apparent what is going on inside.

It is difficult for a woman to not realise that she is pregnant. At some point, the baby will be out of the amniotic bag. However, hard as this is to believe, there have been cases of women who have delivered babies without even realising that they were pregnant. Albeit rare, this raises an interesting query. If the pregnancy can be invisible to the mother, then how much effort is needed to conceal it from others?

There was an era when 'ill-conceived' babies, that is, pregnancies in under-age and/or unmarried women were concealed from an entire community. So it is entirely conceivable (pun intended) that a woman could conceal her pregnancy from the father.

In contrast with women, men's knowledge about a conception is very limited. He may not even know that a woman is pregnant let alone what man impregnated her. His understanding is necessarily based on what the woman tells him combined with his skills in detecting signs and piecing together a story. It is rather ironic then that men are oft-times criticised for their poor performance at reading hints or clues.[17]

The mother's parentage can never be doubted. A father's parentage can only rarely be described as certain. She is the gatekeeper being the

---

17   Hall 1978; Klein & Hodges 2001.

only one with any real access to this fact. And this assumes she is both willing and able to say who the father is. The flipside is a man who is made the father without having made any biological contribution to the child.

Daddy deception – 'Who's your daddy?'

> It's a wise child that knows their own father.
>
> Chris Holden

Who's your daddy? Who knows? And you may be cuckoo to think it's yours!

The potential for a man to conceive without his knowledge is so complete as to defy counting. So what's the big deal? This has been going on for millennia. Some men even find the idea of being a father without responsibilities appealing. It certainly must be admitted that 'sowing your oats' is a strategy that is only available to men.

In general, nature affords men the 'advantage' of leaving the women holding the babies as it were, but with this comes the disadvantage of never knowing whether they are fathers for sure. Women on the other hand, know with complete certainty that a baby is theirs, but with this comes the potential disadvantage of having to raise it without his help.

However, not satisfied with allowing nature to run without constraint, human culture has generally imposed a number of rules or guidelines or norms on how the two sexes play together in the reproduction game – and in particular, how child care will be managed.[18] In most human cultures, men are expected to be responsible for their offspring. And women can demand that be the case – sanctioned and reinforced by law in many countries.

So he can't easily leave her holding the baby anymore. But what about *his* disadvantage – not knowing if he is the father? What has

---

18 Helen Fisher, in her book *Why we love*, argues that men and women are biologically tuned to remain together for about four years which matches the period when a young child is most helpless. That is, biology has apparently favoured men and women who at least stick together for four years after having a child.

culture done to correct this injustice? Not much. The current legal environment allows a woman to commit a rather cruel deception. She has the power to name as the father a man who is not.

Cuckolding isn't new. For as many millennia as men have been 'sowing their oats,' women have been convincing men to raise children who are hers but not his. It is also widespread in the animal kingdom with biologists noting that monogamy is rare rather than common.[19]

It is often popularly claimed that about 30 percent of children have been fathered by someone other than the man they thought to be their father.[20] However, these are figures from contested cases of paternity.[21] That is, DNA testing was conducted because the father already had some suspicions. Still, the fact that his suspicions were justified in 30 percent of these cases is disturbing.

No-one knows the rate of paternity fraud in the general population. A paper in the respected journal *Science* reports one molecular geneticist who says that US labs screening for inherited disease expect to find about 10 percent of children tested are fathered by someone other than the one thought to be their dad.[22]

One paper found and examined 17 studies that provide enough information to be able to identify paternity fraud.[23] The authors found that the estimates range from 0.8 percent to 30 percent with a median value of 3.7 percent. So it seems reasonable to assume that the actual rate of paternity fraud is between three percent and five percent.

Reasonable? Reasonable that up to one in 20 children have been fathered by someone other than the person they call 'dad.' Maybe we need to revisit the definition of reasonable.

Even more disturbing is the fact that in Australia and many other countries in the world, the courts formally recognise the difficulty of

---

19   See Morell 1998.
20   For example, http://www.rense.com/general51/chsup.htm [Accessed 31 January 2014].
21   Bellis et al. 2005; see also http://en.wikipedia.org/wiki/Paternity_fraud and http://www.mens-rights.net/law/paternityfraud.htm for balanced accounts, and realistic assessments of the statistics available [Accessed 31 January 2014].
22   Morell 1998.
23   The authors actually use the term 'paternity discrepancy' to acknowledge that the father may not match due to adoption, artificial insemination, abandonment, etc., possibly unknown, possibly concealed. For details, see Bellis et al. 2005.

identifying the father – and bypass the problem by 'presumption of paternity.' For instance, the *Family Law Act* in Australia states that if a woman cohabited with a man to whom she was not married during a period of 44 weeks to 22 weeks before the birth of a child, then that man is presumed to be the father.

What if she cohabited with a number of men during that period – sequentially or serially? I don't know, but I do know that a lot of money would have to be paid to lawyers by a man trying to defend himself against this draconian presumption. Moreover, if cuckolding or paternity fraud is about resources, I might hazard a guess at which one she would choose to identify as the father. My money is on the one with the money. And the money goes to the lawyer and the mother.

Mums need to know their rights

Dear Ann Landers: . . . My 21-year old sister is three months pregnant. She has had several miserable relationships and despises men, but she wants a family . . . When dad asked if she knew who the father was, she said, 'Of course, I picked him out . . . he thought I was on the pill.' (Sam)

Dear Sam: . . . She needs to know that the baby's father is legally responsible for child support, even though she deceived him . . .

Moreover, any man that identifies himself in writing as the child's father is presumed to be the father. Even if he later denies it and even if DNA testing proves that he is not. The lesson to be learned here is, if you say you want to be a father, you better damn well mean it! The courts appear to be rather curiously disinterested in what may or may not eventuate in DNA testing. And the consequence is that many a presumed father must go on supporting children that are not his own.

Is it possible to change the legal environment to prevent this injustice? Yes. How hard would it be to require hospitals to conduct DNA tests to establish paternity? Wouldn't this eliminate a lot of the nonsense that ensues when parents divorce? Am I out of line here?

Having said that, I'll happily admit that there is a certain hypocrisy in men who, having found out years later that they are not the biological fathers of their ex-wives' children, suddenly want to be compensated for previous childcare payments. The results of paternity tests should not allow a man to give up his responsibility to his children.

I have a nine-year-old daughter that I adore. I raised her as a married parent until she was three, and she has lived with me 50 percent of the time since my ex-wife and I divorced. Now suppose I found out that her biological father was some bloke my wife met at a conference in Singapore, and that he was a 'one night stand' in the classic mould. If I tried to rescind my childcare payments in this scenario, much less to demand compensation for previous childcare payments, I would be a heartless, cruel, unloving brute.

This would create financial distress for my ex-wife, and therefore, emotional stress for my little girl. Nor in this case should I be absolved from future child support payments. I am psychologically and emotionally that little girl's father and I would be an absolute moral monster for wanting to save a few quid by not supporting her.

All the men's groups who are arguing that an ex-husband should be able to seek compensation for previous childcare payments in any case where DNA tests prove he is not the father should stop for a moment and consider the hypocrisy of this position. These same men's groups whine and moan about how unfair it is when ex-wives take their children away from their ex-husbands after divorce, breaking a vital emotional bond between father and child, which does irreversible psychological harm. Fathers are vital in the emotional lives their children and mothers should not be able to unilaterally destroy this relationship after a divorce, so the argument goes.

That is, until an ex-husband finds out that he is not the biological father. Then the emotional welfare of the child suddenly doesn't count. Here they argue that, not only should the father be able to stop the childcare payments, but he should be entitled to damages in the range of $50,000 to $250,000, depending on how long he's been paying.

The fact that this would financially cripple the mother, and create emotional stress for the children is now apparently irrelevant. So men need to lighten up on the whole DNA testing thing entitling ex-husbands to compensation. It's about kids, not dads. Unless . . .

Let's change my scenario a bit. Let us say my divorce from my wife occurred three months after the birth of my daughter, and that I had been relegated to supervised visitation 'every other weekend', as sought in court by my ex-wife.

Moreover, let's assume that my ex-wife's new husband-to-be moved in two weeks after I moved out, and a DNA test showed him to be the biological father three years later! In this scenario, the motive for deception is more obvious, an instant divorce followed by an instant marriage.

In addition, my relationship with my 'daughter' would be more tenuous than her relationship with the biological father, three months versus three years. Moreover, my ex-wife actively sought to limit my contact with the child, and both she and her new husband would have a clear financial motive to deceive me.

In short, I'm clearly being used by the biological mother and father as a source of income for a child that is not mine, either in the biological or the emotional sense. In this scenario my demand for financial compensation seems more justified.

Are these 'exceptional circumstances'? I think not. In situations where the mother's motive to deceive is transparent, the child's emotional attachment to the cuckolded father is marginal due to childcare arrangements sought by the mother, and the biological father (or any new partner of the ex-wife) benefits from the child support payments, the ex-husband should be able to seek damages.

In situations where the mother's motive is tenuous or speculative, the emotional attachment of the child to the cuckolded father is vital, and there is no new 'partner' who also benefits from the child support payments, the courts should not allow such an action. Once again, it seems like the courts have ignored a reasonable middle ground that elevates the rights and status of fathers without impinging on the rights of mothers.

Reality check

I can still remember when she told me that she was pregnant. It was not exactly something that I was hoping for. It was a 'surprise', an accident. How funny to think of conception as an accident. Best accident that ever happened to me, but unintended or not, she was pregnant; missed period, tender breasts, positive pregnancy test. Not much more evidence was needed. So she announced to me that she was pregnant, and asked 'What shall we do about it?'

What indeed? I needed a day to ponder this.

We were together, but not married. We had not envisioned marriage, much less having babies. Our relationship to this point had been a very tempestuous sort of event. Sort of more like a rollercoaster – short rides with some ups and downs and even some loops. But more importantly, lots of getting off the ride altogether and walking away, then coming back later for another go around. I loved the woman, but I did not love the ride.

My thoughts about having children had always been positive, but closely followed by the condition of 'not right now.' Yeah, I'll have them one day, just not sure when. I realised that I was somehow waiting for the right moment to come along, waiting for a spare 18 years to appear on my diary which could be dedicated to having and raising a child. And of course, that was silly.

There was never going to be an ideal time to plan for the 18 year interlude that was required to have a child. Even if I could say that I was ready, there was no way that I could plan what would play out in those 18 years. I decided that this was a 'suck it and see' kind of life event. It may go well, it may go badly, but 'for better or worse,' I would be committed.

Having thought for 24 hours, I returned to my girlfriend and said the following.

I've thought about it – the pregnancy. What I would like is to go ahead. I know this is a weird thing to say, but I am prepared to care for this child even if you did not want it. That is, if you will deliver the child, I would be willing to care for the child on my own – if you were not interested.

Bizarre. In so many ways – but especially this way. We tend to assume that mums are the ones who decide whether to have the babies, and leave dads the option of staying or leaving. Here I was reversing the roles; and yet, deep down inside I knew the decision was really not mine to make. But that was what I wanted.

So if a man's girlfriend, partner, wife is pregnant and he is sure he is the sire, well done! But with two barriers passed, now his access to fatherhood depends on whether she wants to have the baby – or to abort.

Roe v Wade – either way, the man is up S*** Creek

> If women have the right to choose if they become parents, men
> [should] have that right too. There is a connection between legalizing
> abortion for women and ending of paternity suits for men. Giving
> men their own choices would not deny choices to women. It would
> only eliminate their expectation of having those choices financed by
> men.

Karen DeCrow (former president of NOW)[24]

Roe vs Wade is remarkable both for the nature of the case, and for the
lack of interest of Roe (real name Norma McCorvey) in the case itself.
She was an unreliable witness first claiming her pregnancy was the result of rape, and later recanting the claim. By the time the case came
to the Supreme Court, Norma McCorvey had already had the child.
Nevertheless, she became a cause célèbre for the issue of abortion on
demand.

It is even more remarkable although rarely acknowledged, that
the power women won through this case was granted through those
who are so often seen as limiting women's rights. This case and the
judgment emerged through the male-dominated legal institution. The
ruling opinion was delivered by a set of male judges.

Despite the judgment which gave women the right to abortion on
demand, the issue is one that is debated on an ongoing basis, even
among women. On one hand are those who defend the foetus' 'right-
to-life' and on the other are those who defend the mother's 'right-to-
choice.'

Perhaps not surprisingly, research suggests that women are more
extreme in their attitudes toward abortion. Women pro-lifers are most
adamant that abortion should be illegal, and pro-choice women are
most resolute that it should be legal. Men, whether they are pro-life or
pro-choice, tend to sit on the fence relative to women, which makes a

---

24   Retrieved on 3 March 2014 from http://www.people.ubr.com/
historical-figures/by-first-name/k/karen-decrow/karen-decrow-quotes/
if-women-have-the.aspx.

great deal of sense when you consider which gender is most directly affected.

But that does not mean that the other gender is unaffected. One stakeholder, the individual that is essential for this circumstance to arise, is not even invited to the battle. Where is the father? Imagine a mass gathering of men, complete with posters, bull horns, and pamphlets arguing for their right to choose whether to have a baby. It's absurd.

The rights of the father are simply non-existent. Even if he wants to defend the rights of the foetus over the mother as noted by a (male) Supreme Court justice:

> A father's interest in having a child – perhaps his only child – may be unmatched by any other interest in his life . . . It is truly surprising that . . . the State must assign a greater value to a mother's decision to cut off a potential human life by abortion than to a father's decision to let it mature into a live child.[25]

The Supreme Court justice is not alone in his opinion. Research suggests that a majority of men and women believe that a father should be informed that his partner is considering an abortion, that he should be invited to participate in this decision, and in the case of married respondents, that he should have a right to veto her abortion decision.

I have no delusions about any of this research. There is no way that a man is ever going to have the right to block an abortion requested by his partner; nor should he have that right. Her body, her choice must be the guiding principle here. But is there a middle ground that hasn't been fully explored?

Should hospitals and abortion clinics be required to set a two-week 'cooling off' period for any woman requesting an abortion? Should the clinic enquire about the contact details of the suspected father (remember, fathers can only be suspected not established)? If the clinic receives those details, should it be required to contact the suspected father?[26]

Somewhere in between denying fathers any rights at all and forcing a woman to have a baby she does not want there is room for policies

---

25 Supreme Court justice Byron White, *Planned Parenthood v Danforth*, cited by Parker 2008, 54.
26 Farrell 2001, 130–35.

and procedures that acknowledge the man's role in reproduction. Do these proposals violate the woman's privacy? Yes. But when we consider the stakes, this seems like a meagre price to pay. In the US alone, for example, the number of foetuses aborted *each year* is more than double the number of American military deaths in all US wars.[27]

The issue is particularly perplexing when it is realised that, although the woman alone decides whether or not to carry the foetus, the man who has no role in the decision can be required to pay for support of that child, even if she deliberately deceived him about her ability to become pregnant. Even if she tells him that she is medically incapable of conceiving, on the pill, or wearing a diaphragm, if she becomes pregnant and has the child, he is responsible for approximately 20 years of child support payments.

What's yours is yours and what's mine is yours to give away

But at least if the mother decides to have the baby, our hypothetical father will at least be able to see his child, right? Well, not necessarily as it happens. In fact, even while there is a lot of social pressure nowadays for men to be present in the birthing suite along with the mum[28] – mum does have the power of veto over this. This is not unreasonable, but it goes further. She gets to make a lot of choices going forward from the birth in which the father gets no say. Indeed, he may not even know what is and what is not happening.

We do not make an unwilling mother raise a child. Very reasonable. Equally, we do not make an unwilling father raise the child either. Well, that's not quite right. We are happy to make an unwilling father contribute financially to the child's upbringing as noted earlier, but no, we do not make him raise the child any more than the mother.

The obvious bit that is missed is that while we generously allow unwilling parents off the hook of raising the child, her vote trumps his. Specifically, we do not even allow a willing father to raise the child. Why not?

---

27   Farrell 2001, 235.
28   Cannold 2013.

The father is the other parent, the first one who should be considered if the mother decides to abandon the children to adoption. But it doesn't work like that. Welcome to the fourth and final gate of fatherhood. She can immediately put the child up for adoption without him having the opportunity to intervene.

In the rather frightening and media-worthy case of baby Richard,[29] the father knew that his estranged girlfriend was pregnant. When he contacted her after hearing that the baby was born, he was informed that the child had died in childbirth.

However, 57 days after the child had been born, he heard that the child was still alive – and had been given up for adoption by the mother. He then proceeded to contest – through the legal system in the US – for the right to custody of the child. After four years, he won. But the media circus turned his win into a loss.

The return of the child to the father was a televised event. As can be well imagined, the young boy of four was in tears as he was torn from the only people that he had ever known as caregivers. The image and story was emotionally wrenching.

The father was clearly identified as a villain, and perhaps rightly so. Was he really thinking about the welfare of his son at this point? Shouldn't the obvious emotional distress of the four-year-old boy have persuaded him that this was not the best option? But was the father the real villain?

The media was doing its job and selling a newsworthy story, but in so doing they overlooked the real crime. The real crime was that the father had to fight to win custody of his own child for so long when the mother did not want the child.

Due process takes its time, and it is undoubtedly difficult to allow a child to be removed from an adoptive family. But it is equally difficult to allow that a father has to fight for four years for the right to raise his own son as in the case of baby Richard.

Once again there must be some middle ground between allowing a woman to put a baby up for adoption without the father knowing a thing and forcing her to raise a child she does not want. Should adoption agencies also be required to set a two-week 'cooling off' period?

---

29 See http://en.wikipedia.org/wiki/Baby_Richard_case [Accessed 31 January 2013].

Should the agency be required to ask about the contact details of the suspected father (again, fathers can only be suspected not established)? If the agency obtains those details, should it be required to contact the suspected father?

It must be acknowledged that these proposals violate the woman's privacy. In this instance, we dads are happy to accept second-class status. That is, biological fathers may be given fewer rights than biological mothers, but shouldn't they come before complete strangers who have registered with an adoption agency?

Perhaps biological fathers must earn their second-class status, or otherwise risk being relegated to the third option for raising their own children, behind the adoption agency as has been suggested by some researchers. They might do this by being involved in the 'prenatal life' of their unborn child.[30] For instance, I used to read Dr Seuss books to my unborn son, while resting a microphone on my wife's tummy.

Another approach involves making a financial investment in his unborn baby's future. Establishing a college fund prior to birth is one way to do this. Purchasing a crib or baby clothes is another. All of these prenatal investments seem like good ideas, provided the expecting mother grants permission for these kinds of gestures. If she decides to keep him out of the loop, it is not clear how he would earn his right to be an active father.

Moreover, making fathers earn their right to become a parent, prior to the birth of their child, might actually give prospective mothers who do not want a man around an incentive to intentionally deceive him about the pregnancy. After all, if he doesn't know she is pregnant, he cannot possibly make the kind of prenatal contributions that would grant him subsequent parental rights. We now begin to see how it is that fathers who want to be involved in the raising of their child need consent from the mother.

---

30   Shanley 2001, 64.

Are fathers even necessary?

The cause celebre in the US has been the brave women who decide to be mothers without having a man involved, and especially the 'choice mothers' or single mothers by choice. Books have been written celebrating the 'new American family',[31] with the focus on supporting those women raising children alone. Rather less focus has been given to the children themselves.

There are so many options for wannabe mothers, and while they may need some things men have to offer, they are offered almost *à la carte* the contributions that they want from the man.

The first thing the mother definitely needs is sperm. Men may not be needed in the flesh, but they are needed for their seed. But a woman does not need to be linked to the man who gave his seed. She can separate from him at any point if she tires of him. Or she can seek to be inseminated through one-night stands and casual relationship. Or in our modern retail world, she can just place an order at the sperm shop and be artificially inseminated.

Anything else that a man has to offer to the mother is less essential. Mothers typically need financial and material resources to raise a child. If she has enough herself, or others around her (family, friends – male and female) can provide these resources, then no problem. For those women not so fortunately placed, governments, while reluctant to provide resources directly, will actively help the mother collect from a man identified as the father. He may be the biological father, or maybe not. Neither the mother nor the government are especially motivated to explore further.

So, the striking part of this account of the mother's needs is that a man is not very important beyond his sperm. Now it may sound like the woman holds all the cards with respect to becoming a parent. But I would argue that all this comes at a very great cost to all women.

---

31   E.g., Choosing single motherhood: the thinking woman's guide, Mikki Morrissette (http://www.choosingsinglemotherhood.com/ [Accessed 11 September 2013]), *Single mothers by choice: a guidebook for single women who are considering or have chosen motherhood*, Jane Mattes; *The complete single mother*, Andrea Engber and Leah Klungness; *The single mothers survival guide*, Patrice Karst.

These 'advantages' reinforce the old-fashioned, outdated stereotype that 'a woman's place is in the home', that women should be 'barefoot and pregnant', that for a woman, becoming a mother is of primary importance, and everything else, like having a successful career, is secondary. And you need not take my word for it; women have been making this exact point for decades.[32]

Gender stereotypes never operate in isolation. They pervade culture. If we're going to eliminate the 'woman as homemaker' and 'man as breadwinner' stereotypes, we better start early, before the birth of the first child. Remember, that is when research suggests that egalitarian gender roles in the family home start to polarise into the homemaker and breadwinner stereotypes.[33] And as we'll see in the following chapter, the asymmetry between mothers and fathers only gets worse as the children grow up.

---

32 Eyer 1991, 9.
33 Areni 2014.

The second parent

She is the incidental, the inessential as opposed to the essential. He is
the Subject, he is the Absolute – she is the Other.

Simone de Beauvoir [1949] 1972, 2

That women have been treated as second-class citizens is a shameful
history which has received justified criticism from a long line of women, perhaps most notably Simone de Beauvoir who offered the observation that women were the Second Sex in a book of the same name.

That men can be treated as second-class citizens in the home is not
generally acknowledged – in fact it is barely even considered. However,
it follows as a fairly 'natural' extension from the obstacles that stand in
the way of a man who wants to father a child (as discussed in the last
chapter) to a man who wants to be involved as a father.

The mother's involvement during the period of gestation is a necessity of nature. However, once established, the predominance of the
mother can be difficult to shift after the birth of the baby. Many men report the experience of being 'overlooked' once a baby is born.[1] At some
levels, this is understandable as the mother recovers and turns her attention to the child. Moreover, to the extent that this is about his own
diluted sense of self-importance, he just needs to get over it. However,

---

1   Dye [1998] 2011.

this exclusion can have a more disappointing element, which is that the father's eagerness to get involved can be thoroughly quashed – or simply disregarded.

This is unfortunate, especially as the man must overcome his rather tenuous link to parenthood relative to the mother in order to step into the role of active parent. Given man's supposed lack of intuition, his detachment from feeling, it is ironic that a man who chooses to engage with a child as a parent – based on little more than trust and feelings – must sometimes fight the mother for that right. If a man steps up to care for a child (in whatever way he can), he should be commended, not condemned. The mother's commitment is founded in her physically birthing the child; the father's commitment is based on a nebulous connection of little more than faith and love.

The concern here is less with dad's ego, and more with his involvement with his children. By letting the man be a little more involved, three parties benefit – dad of course, mum because she gets help, and above all, their children. In the following, I explore the ways that men wanting to be engaged as parents are marginalised by mothers, markets, media and society in general.

Lactation – milking it for all it is worth?

Why is it that when it comes to the idea of childrearing, mothers tend to be seen as primary and fathers as secondary? An obvious answer is that the difference is inherent in nature. That only women can bear and birth babies is obvious. But this does not necessarily extend to a 'natural' superiority of women in parenting tasks than men.

There seems to be a school of thought that says mothers are the primary carers of newborns and that fathers do not really start to get involved until the children are older.[2] But as intuitive as this may sound, it is at odds with research suggesting that fathers are equally effective at caring for infants, but struggle more with toddlers.[3] Is this because men are more helpless than mums in handling the terrible two-year old who has learned so proficiently to say 'no'? Are men simply not suited to the

---

2   Rotundo 1985.
3   Averett et al. 2005.

task of caring for a young child by nature? Is it simply that they lack the practice and experience?

What is the reason why a woman is naturally more qualified than the man to care for a child post-delivery? Perhaps there is no *single* reason; perhaps there are *two* – mammary glands.

Should breasts be considered evidence that mothers are better at caring for newborns? Breastfeeding obviously offers physical nutrition to the child, but it also provides the mother with considerable physical and emotional access to the baby. The potential downside is that this practice – important as it is – can indirectly influence the access of the father.[4]

Should breasts be an obvious indication that mothers are better at caring for newborns?

In this thoroughly modern era, mothers quite clearly make choices about whether they will breastfeed or not. A choice that is challenged it must be admitted. On one hand, there are the 'breastfeeding Nazis' I heard about during an antenatal session who deplore any mother that does not breastfeed. These breastfeeding zealots try to limit women's choice to breastfeed by suggesting that formula milk is like AIDS![5]

---

4   Miller 2010.

Meanwhile, on the other hand, there is the prudishness of the public that can make public breastfeeding difficult for young mothers. While this seems more tolerated nowadays, the latent prudishness was clearly revealed by the widespread horror expressed in response to a recent cover of *Time* magazine (May 2012) featuring a photograph of a 26-year-old mother breastfeeding her adopted three-year-old son.

Regardless of the pressures, women do get to choose whether to breastfeed, and for how long. The key point to note is that while the woman has choice about whether to breastfeed and for how long, the man's role in the decision is at best advisory, and at worst, a rather ridiculous joke.

That breastfeeding might be viewed as a burden is of course not new and is reflected in norms about how long to breastfeed. In times past, wealthy mothers were able to absolve themselves of any need to breastfeed their children by handing them over to wet nurses.

Regardless of the option chosen (formula milk or wet nurse), a modern mother takes charge of feeding decisions by virtue of nature having given her breasts – even if she is not using them. It is curious that a woman can retain the 'natural' right to take primary responsibility for feeding a newborn because she has breasts – even if she chooses not to use them.

In this way, breastfeeding – or simply the potential to breastfeed – can become another small step in the general marginalisation of fatherhood relative to motherhood; but it need not be this way. There are many ways that daddy can be given a more central role in the feeding routine from the very start.

The simplest way to get dad involved from the very beginning, without fundamentally changing the breastfeeding experience for mum, is to have him do the burping afterward. I am reminded of how in some cultures, burping is a sign of appreciation. And of course, burping (and farting) are so stereotypically associated with men, it seems an extraordinarily apt way for dads to be involved. Baby then associates both daddy and mummy with the feeding, a very nice part of early life. She provides the tucker; he provides that feel-good, get-the-air-out thing afterwards.

---

5   Murray 2012.

Dads will of course need to get over any phobia about getting a little vomit on themselves. Given the stereotype again of men 'going bush' without even thinking of a shower or soap for days on end, he should be well prepared for the next few years which will take his exposure to vomit, urine, excrement, and other nasties to a new level. He will of course get used to it, to the point where he will put on a shirt for work in the morning, notice a little vomit stain on the shoulder, and say 'Who cares!' and wear it anyway. As psychologists have pointed out, exposure is a great way to reach desensitisation. Horror and disgust at the sight, smell, or contact with bodily fluids will soon disappear. Trust me on this. Been there, done that.

There are options for involving fathers more directly in the feeding, but they are – as has been noted – very much in the hands of the mother. So for those wanting more involvement from daddy without giving up all the health benefits of breast milk, there is the option of expressing breast milk, although I am of course completely unqualified to comment on how pleasant this experience is for the mother. Nonetheless, it does allow daddy to feed his baby breast milk without actually having direct access to a breast.

Another option for involving daddy directly in feeding is infant formula. Now I know that infant formula is not nearly as good as that medical wonder, breast milk. The research is pretty clear about this,[6] but it is a pretty decent option if mummy is unable or unwilling to breastfeed or express breast milk.[7] The upside is that mummy and daddy can be involved in feeding on a more or less equal basis.

Slippery little sucker

While bottle-feeding may allow the father to get a little more directly involved, feeding – as any parent will tell you – is a tricky game.

My daughter was ten weeks old when her mother received an offer of a one-week, all expenses paid trip to Melbourne for the second week of the Australian Open. A sweet little deal, no doubt!

---

6 See, for example, Cunningham et al.1991; Raisler et al. 1999; Pardo-Crespo R et al. 2004.
7 Oddy 2001; Todd 2003; Penttila 2005.

To allow for this to happen, I took a week off from work to look after the little one and her brother. The problem however, was that my daughter had received nothing but breast milk up until that point, leaving us just over a week to wean her. One week in which we learned that even a wordless baby can wield a world of power.

My wife continued to breastfeed during the day, but expressed one bottle of breast milk as well. After I came home from work, she would go out and leave me to give the baby the last feed of the day from the bottle.

Well, that little girl had the stubbornness of 100 mules! (Still does actually!) No way she was having anything to do with that bottle! Hour after hour she would resist, wailing away in the process. My wife would return late in the evening to a screaming baby and an exhausted, stressed out, and completely defeated husband.

I even tried cutting a hole in my shirt and sticking the rubber nipple out where my breast would be – if I had breasts. No dice. In the end my wife did not go to the Australian Open.

The problem, as it turns out, was twofold. We were asking our little girl to switch from flesh to rubber and from mummy to daddy, in retrospect, perhaps a little too much for a ten-week-old.

So one word of advice I would give to parents opting for this route is to have mummy wean the newborn from the breast. Once mummy establishes the rubber nipple as a darn good option, it will be much easier for daddy to do the feeding.

From lactation in which women clearly have a natural advantage relative to men (regardless of whether they actually breastfeed or not), there is a tendency to marginalise fathers on the basis that mothers are 'naturally' better at caring for newborns. Perhaps because mothers are thought to empathise better and are better at decoding nonverbal communications[8] which is pretty much all an infant has in their communication repertoire. But the evidence of female superiority in empathy is context-specific and is probably an extension of experience.

---

8   Hall 1978; Klein & Hodges 2001; Toussaint & Web 2005.

That is, if mothers already spend more time around young children than fathers, guess what? They become better at reading the facial expressions, intonations, and gestures of children. My wife wasn't a naturally better parent when my son was an infant she just had more experience reacting to his signals. Research suggests that this is a common experience of new fathers, always playing 'catch up' when it comes to reading their baby's signals correctly; and when daddies are involved in child care from the very outset, they develop a 'paternal instinct' every bit as sensitive to the nonverbal signals of their infant children.[9]

Besides, empathy is not the only skill one needs to be a successful parent. Empathy is just one of the many things a parent should have in order to be successful. If mothers are naturally better parents than fathers, this would mean there is evidence that women are better at most or all of the things that parents need to be successful. There is no scientific evidence to support such a claim, for one thing, because we still do not know what exactly children need from their parents in order to be psychologically healthy. We have a list, but not an exhaustive one. There are many things that physicians and psychologists have not yet discovered. Moreover, children's needs are individual.

And even if we could make an absolute scientific claim that women do possess more of the skills necessary to be good parents, does that still mean we should deprive children of the skills and corresponding benefits that their fathers possess? As we'll see in 'The compleat child', research has uncovered several intellectual, emotional, and behavioural benefits of fathers spending time with their babies.

The gender stereotypes that link mothers to infant care seize on a few generic biological and psychological differences between men and women, and use them to justify why there are so many stay-at-home mothers and so few stay-at-home fathers. This is way too simple a solution, especially when we consider the stakes – psychologically and physically healthy children.

---

9   Lamb 1997b; Levine 2000; Miller 2010, 375.

Permission to be a parent

Another contributing factor to the establishment of the norm of father as 'second parent' is likely the early separation of the father from his child. Mums may begin calling the shots based on the knowledge they have accumulated about baby's needs – knowledge they may have inadvertently prevented dads from acquiring firsthand. Without firsthand knowledge, the fathers must accept the guidance of the mother as expert – which is fine, but then we get a father who simply does as he is told. Mums become the de facto supervisors of child care; dads are reduced to being simple labourers.[10]

I was keen for this not to happen when my son was young. So while he was young, just three months old, I made sure that I spent one day with him every week. I wanted this time to be his and my time.

Very quickly I discovered that there was a complicating factor – his mother. On the first or second occasion, she was elsewhere in the house, and as he cried, she would holler at me. 'He wants his nappy changed' or 'He wants a bottle' or 'He's tired, he needs to be put down for a sleep'. This, it turns out, is a fairly common experience for fathers – taking orders from their wives who, nevertheless, expect them to do the actual work;[11] sort of like, dare I say it, being a personal assistant in the home.

I objected to this, and the following week I explained that this was our time – just my son and me. The solution that I proposed to her was that, either she leave the house for the day, or he and I were going to leave the house. This was our time together, our time to learn to communicate with one another. I objected to her assumption that somehow, she, a first-time mother, knew more about raising the child than me. My work allows me to work at home, and as a first-time father, I had spent almost as much time with the baby as her. Sure, she carried the child and breastfed him – but I challenged whether she had the monopoly on understanding his needs.

Dads see things differently from mums. This is not automatically bad. In fact it can be a good thing. Just before our separation, my son's mother had been keen for us to practise 'controlled crying'. I did not

---

10   Baxter & Smart 2010, 6.
11   Levine 2000, 170.

have a strong desire to support this practice, but I did not state this. She argued that it was needed so that she and I could spend time together. The irony is perfect. Months later she leaves the family home because she cannot stand spending time with me. The upside was that after we had parted, I very quickly decided to dispense with the practice. I much preferred holding my son to calm him as I put him to sleep. In fact, it remains a very fond memory of having my son fall asleep on my chest as I held him.

The point is that sometimes mothers can be their own worst enemies when it comes to getting their spouses to do more with young children, and around the house in general. Mums probably *do* know how to do things better at this point, but their insistence on having things done 'their way' may inadvertently give their spouses an 'out' for not doing their fair share.[12]

Research backs these anecdotes up rather convincingly, showing for example, that maternal attitudes predict paternal involvement in caring for infants. Which attitudes? Whether mum thinks dad is motivated, whether she thinks he is any good, and whether she believes that women are naturally superior as parents. Mothers who reported that their husbands were not very motivated and not very good at child care, and who believed that fathers were naturally inferior as parents wound up doing more of the child care on their own.[13] Surprise, surprise!

But this may not be a power play at all. Mums may not like calling the shots at all. At the end of the day, maternal 'gatekeeping' may have more to do with fear. Mothers love their children and fear for their safety and wellbeing. Trusting their little angels to anybody else is fraught with danger – even if that somebody else is her children's father. Mums may inadvertently lock dads out of many parenting roles and responsibilities due to the simple fear that something will go wrong. How to get over this little dilemma? Here's a tip for the dads – demonstrate your competence as a parent in front of your wives as often as possible. Put her at ease. Ask her if you can do things like changing your newborn's nappy, with her in a 'supervisory' role of course. After a few monitoring sessions she'll see that you are good at it, putting her at ease, and giving you greater scope to be a dad. Just a thought.

---

12   Baxter & Smart 2010, 7.
13   Beitel & Parke 1998; Allen & Hawkins 1999.

Where to start in encouraging men to become more than second-class parents? There are so many possibilities, but one promising opportunity is right from the beginning of fatherhood – the birth of his first child.

The Royal Prince Alfred Hospital in Sydney has a Women and Babies unit. Flinders Private Hospital in Adelaide opts for the more traditional Maternity Ward. The Royal Darwin Hospital offers Maternal and Child Health services. Sandrington Hospital in Victoria has a Women's and Children's Health department.

Many hospitals go one step further, devoting the entire facility to women's health, including of course, a prominent ward for having babies. So, for example, the Royal Brisbane and Women's Hospital includes a Women's and Newborn unit; and the Royal Women's hospital in Victoria advertises itself as 'Australia's largest specialist hospital dedicated to improving the health of women of all ages and newborn babies.'[14]

Why not refer to these units as, say, 'Birthing Centres'? Why the explicit reference to mothers but not fathers? Well, there's one rather obvious reason – the mother is the only actual patient. In most rich, Western democracies we've come to expect that childbirth will go smoothly with no complications, but it's not a guarantee. Indeed in many parts of the world the mortality rates of women giving birth are still shockingly high,[15] so it's a good thing to bring mothers into hospitals just to be safe.

But naming hospitals and wards after mothers and their children may have the insidious, if almost certainly unintended, effect of reinforcing the notion that babies are to be cared for by mothers, not fathers, who are left unrecognised. Am I just being pedantic here? Is this much ado about nothing? Perhaps, but consider this.

The Department of Health organises playgroups for new mothers, helping them to create networks of support in their new role as a parent. Nothing like that exists for new fathers. Government education programs for new parents are, in effect, programs for new mothers, focusing on things like proper breastfeeding and postnatal exercise

---

14 The Royal Women's Hospital, http://www.thewomens.org.au/ [Accessed 11 September 2013].
15   Caldwell et al. 2007.

programs.[16] This omission is all the more surprising given research indicating that education programs for new fathers actually work, making them more sensitive and accurate in interpreting the behaviours of their infant children.[17] Many hospitals do not even bother to collect the father's details for their hospitals records or the birth certificate! One conversation proceeded as follows:

> Nurse: 'Mother's name?'
> Father: (Gives his wife's full name)
> Nurse: 'Child's name?'
> Father: (Gives his newborn child's full name)
> (Pause)
> Father: 'Don't you have another question?'
> Nurse: 'No, that'll be all.'
> Father: 'What about the father's name?'
> Nurse: 'How do we know you're the father?'[18]

Encouraging stuff! A thousand-mile journey begins with one step, and this is the first step! Makes me feel like a particularly unequal partner in the whole parenting gig! It is all the more surprising that hospitals engage in such practices given research indicating that women want their partners to be present and involved during the birthing process and that most men want to be involved in any way they can.[19] In this sense maternity wards don't seem to be very user friendly.

Still think this is nitpicking? Ponder this. In one hospital nurses were trained to explicitly greet the men who accompanied an expecting mother to the maternity ward. This simple act increased paternity establishment from 18 percent to 60 percent.[20] Assuming that establishing paternity may be vaguely important from the newborn's perspective, maybe these little slights against fathers are not as inconsequential as we think. Moreover, research suggests that fathers who are involved early stay involved as their children get older.[21] A simple greeting in the

---

16 Petre 1998, 4; Baxter & Smart 2010, 151; Fletcher et al. 2011.
17 Magill-Evans et al. 2007.
18 Levine 2000, 200.
19 Bozett 1985.
20 Farrell 2001, 110.

maternity ward is just one step that could lead toward a devoted dad for life – or if omitted, could set him off on a much more travelled, if more criticised, path.

So from the very beginning of the newborn's life, society is already inadvertently reinforcing the notion that fathers are peripheral to starting a family, and not all mothers are happy about this, feeling, quite justifiably, that it is the beginning of an inequitable division of childcare labour for the next 15 years or so.[22] If dads are unrecognised, or deliberately excluded, from the very beginning, they may come to accept this as their normal status, leading to absentee status during much of the first year of the baby's existence.

Dads in ads, mums in marketing!

I imagine there is still resistance to the idea that men are being treated as 'second parents'. It is perhaps hard to imagine because men dominate in most domains. But in matters of family, well, the picture is very different. For example, one article reviewing academic research on parent–child relationships found that roughly half of the studies examined both fathers and mothers; so far, so good. But in studies examining only a single parent, the vast majority focused on mothers (98 percent).[23] Apparently, even academic research on parent–child relationships can't help but exhibit the very same bias so prevalent elsewhere in society.

Men are not particularly well recognised in markets for baby products. In fact, men are very much cast as the 'second parent' in such markets – despite the fact that the vast majority of the companies that market these products are run by men. I am just guessing that these CEOs may not have changed a lot of nappies, done a lot of laundry, prepared a lot of family meals, etc.; this is just a guess, however.

But by the time a father begins buying things like prams, baby food, nappies and cribs, the marketplace is driving home the message that a man's place is not in the home. To get a better feel for the range of this communication, consider some research I conducted in my role as a

21 Baxter & Smart 2010, 47.
22 Eyer 1991.
23 Phares & Compas 1992; Hosley & Montemayor 1997.

single father. Supermarket shelves give a pretty clear indication of how the marketplace views childcare responsibilities in the home. In order to examine gender stereotypes in action, I noted the packaging of the product categories typically associated with taking care of children and the associated domestic labour.

There were a lot of product categories fitting this general description, but I finally settled on three super categories: cleaning, food preparation, and care of young children. This is essentially what the homemaker of the house does, they eliminate dangerous microbes by keeping the household clean, they prepare food for the family, and they take care of children.

Then I looked at the front of the package of any product fitting one of these labels and noted whether it featured (a) a woman alone, (b) a woman with a child, (c) a man alone, or (d) a man with a child. Any other package image was not counted. I literally carried a scoring sheet around with me while I filled my shopping cart with the family groceries.

For cleaning products, seven featured a woman alone, six featured a woman with a child (all laundry products), and one featured a man alone. The lone male was depicted on a spray starch product, you know, for ironing cotton clothes to eliminate wrinkles. The cartoon male on the package was wearing a sharp, indeed nicely ironed, dress shirt. The package, in essence, was saying to each wife 'Use this product on your husband's dress shirts, so he will look really spiffy in the office, and get that promotion that the two of you want so much!' Did I mention that the men who run these companies probably don't do the family laundry on a regular basis?

Arguably then, all 14 cleaning packages were 'gendered' as female. What about child care products? Once again we get a clean sweep. All 13 products fell into just one category – women with children. The cooking products were only slightly less skewed; 14 featured a woman only, three featured a woman with a child, one featured a man only, and two featured a man with a child.

So, like hospitals, supermarkets convey the same message: women are nurturers; men are not. And like the nurse in the maternity ward, the supermarket environment may invite women to assert their 'natural' superiority in all matters parenting. One anonymous woman approached me in a supermarket just after I had spoken to my son. I speak to him only in French. She approached to criticise me for speaking to him in a foreign language, saying 'We live in Australia, we speak Australian' (um, I think it is called English, but she was on a roll, and there was no way I was going to stop her with this trivial piece of linguistic reality). I chose to move on.

In addition to product packaging and imagery, marketers also convey the message that dads are incompetent parents via advertising – dolts, jerks and schmucks according to one blogger[24] who explains that each serves a different role. One television ad for the Sony Cyber-Shot camera depicts the father of the family as a horse's backside – literally. Every scene shows other family members interacting with the back end of a horse, which is meant to represent the father.

Okay. So there are subtler approaches. Can dads change a nappy? Apparently not. A recent ad for Huggies puts the product to the ultimate test. And what *is* the ultimate test? Five straight hours with daddy after a big feed; and why is this test *ultimate*? Because daddy cannot change the nappy, of course, so the nappy better be able to hold a lot of pee!

Homework? Not much better. One ad for an internet supplier shows a father looking over his pre-teen daughter's shoulder as she works on a school report. He comments, naively enough, that the website she is viewing on her computer looks 'encyclopaedia-ish.' She replies that 'It *is* an encyclopaedia, no "ish" ', in a rather dismissive way. So it is pretty clear that the daughter doesn't respect her own father, but it gets better, or worse depending on your perspective.

Mum appears in the doorway asking her husband whether he is looking after the dog as he is supposed to do. He points to the dog lying on the floor and nods in the affirmative. But the daughter has clearly had enough of her father's unwanted presence, so she gives her mum the 'Please get him out of here' look, to which the mother asks her husband to leave. When he suggests that he is helping his daughter with her homework, his wife yells at him, ordering him to leave! Ouch!

What about cleaning? Here we go from mildly demoralising to completely absurd. An ad for a toilet cleaner shows fathers and sons apologising with rather guilty looks on their faces. One after an-

24   Parker R 2013.

other saying 'I'm sorry', 'I didn't mean it', you get the picture. The female voiceover makes it clear that this ad is directed at women. Suddenly the epiphany – these dads are apologising for peeing all over the place, and the ad is based on the assumption that the mothers of the world will be the ones cleaning the misses!!! An ad that manages to denigrate dads *and* condescend to mums! Fantastic!

We'll leave the best solution to Dr Karl (Kruszelnicki), Father of the Year in 2003. His research showed that the toilet lid should be shut when you flush. Otherwise a plume of bacteria and water erupt from the bowl. So, whether you lift the seat or not, everyone should close the lid when finished.[25]

Media beat-down

It is not just marketers that make a mockery of masculine parenting. The portrayal of all things paternal in television *programs* is even worse.[26] One cable channel features a two-hour block of cartoons, which present satires of the American family. The three fathers are idiots. That they are stupider than their wives goes without saying. No, they are stupider than their daughters. Indeed, the intelligence ranking in all three programs is fairly consistent: mothers are smarter than daughters, who are smarter than brothers, who are smarter than fathers.[27]

Put another way, all three cartoons are implicitly based on the premise that women are smarter than men, and women get smarter as they age, whereas men apparently get stupider. Even the family pets are smarter than the fathers. It would be tempting to say that these fathers were depicted as incompetent nincompoops, but the typical incompetent nincompoop would seem like a Nobel Prize–winning physicist compared to these dads.

Of course, all this can easily be dismissed with the simple argument that these programs are satires, comedies; none of this is meant to be

25 Retrieved 3 February 2014 from http://www.abc.net.au/science/articles/2004/07/01/1143577.htm.
26 The surviving dads of ads. *Brandweek*, 12 November 2007.
27 Ambramovitch 1997.

taken seriously! They're cartoons for goodness sake! Good point. But more systematic research based on content analyses of family-based television programs furthers the point. Fathers are consistently depicted as less competent parents than mothers.[28] The TV message is clear – mothers are saints and fathers are imbeciles.

What about more serious programming like, for example, the evening news? Research suggests a similar pattern of bias. Men disproportionately make headlines as perpetrators, whereas women tend to make headlines as victims.[29] This basic bias extends into the parenting realm, where mums are either victims of an oppressive system or heroes fighting oppression. Interestingly, the single mums depicted as heroes often, in fact, break the law.

My personal favourite would have to be the story on CNN (29 March 2009) about women in prison in Kabul, Afghanistan.[30] The mothers interviewed were convicted of crimes ranging from heroin trafficking and possession of a car bomb, to serial murder. All claimed to be innocent – nothing surprising there. The most common story told by criminals is that they did not do it.

However, a number of the women admitted the crime but blamed others and were accordingly portrayed as victims. One blamed members of her church who recruited her as a drug mule, a convicted (attempted) suicide bomber claimed she was drugged, kidnapped and woke up wearing an explosive vest, and a serial killer (27 victims) blamed her lover.

The CNN story was obviously sympathetic because, in this case, the politics of gender perfectly coincided with the agenda of the Obama administration ('Those barbarians in Afghanistan! Look what they do to their women! We must commit more troops to rectifying this appalling situation and rescue these women!').

And just in case the victimisation was not sufficient in recruiting sympathy, the story showed that the women were raising their innocent children in jail with them. The 'prison' was American-funded, and the

28   Butsch 1992.
29   Pritchard & Hughes 1997; Friedman 2008.
30   Afghanistan's most dangerous? (2009). Video report, CNN, Afghanistan, 30 March. Retrieved 11 September 2013 from http://www.edition.cnn.com/video/?/ video/world/2009/03/30/abawi.afghan.women.convicts.cnn.

rooms looked more like family suites at a Best Western than prison cells. Even the serial murderer enjoyed this arrangement.

Now let's just reverse the genders here, as a kind of thought experiment. Imagine a male inmate convicted of heroin trafficking, possession of a car bomb, or serial murder. Imagine he claims he is innocent. Nothing too hard to handle there – no-one on the inside is willing to admit their guilt. However, let us imagine these men were to say that they were victims – set up by their wives and other women who were the real guilty parties. Are we getting any sympathy yet? Of course not, the idea is preposterous.

But we can go even one step further in our inexorable march towards complete absurdity. Let us suppose a suspected serial killer is a father. Are we going to turn his prison cell into a suite so he can raise his children? Even more ridiculous you say? Right, and now the clincher, imagine an imprisoned father, convicted of serial murder, raising his children in his prison cell/two-bedroom suite – without the mother present at all! He gets the kids in prison; she gets little or no access. The reality is that incarcerated fathers rarely if ever get to see their children, and that the custodial mothers often prevent contact 'for the good of the children'.[31]

Before you dismiss the potential influence of these media depictions, consider the current debate on the ideal 'body image' for women. Here the argument is that the beautiful female models featured in magazines and on television are far thinner than the general female population, and this creates unrealistic expectations for teenage girls and young adult women. These women then engage in a self-destructive pursuit of the ideal bodies they see in mass media.

Just seeing lots of thin models in magazines makes women depressed, makes them want to chuck up their last meal, and in some cases, makes them want to give up food for good. If women can be induced to depression, bulimia, and anorexia nervosa by photos of beautiful women, is it really such a leap of faith to say that news stories depicting fathers as incompetent fools or dangerous criminals might influence societal attitudes about paternity? Which is the more credible source here, CNN or *Cosmopolitan*?

---

31 Arditti et al. 2005.

Come fly the not-so-friendly skies

Media stories also report on how the world sees men – and the picture is not pretty.[32] In general, people seem very quick to believe that a father is a potential child abuser. How pervasive is this tendency? Many airlines will not allow an unaccompanied minor to be seated next to a man, even if he is a father. Mirko Fischer was asked to change seats with his wife, who was pregnant and had asked for an aisle seat for more comfort. The problem? This left Mr Fischer seated next to an unaccompanied minor, which was a no, no according to company policy, so Ms Fischer had to switch to the middle seat before the plane could take off.

Mr Fischer sued on the basis of sex discrimination, and was awarded £2161 in court costs and £750 in damages. BA subsequently changed its seating policy. In turns out that Mr Fischer was not alone. Boris Johnson, the mayor of London, was also asked to switch seats on a BA flight, even though he was seated with his own children! One of his kids had to switch seats with him to occupy a seat next to an unaccompanied minor. Qantas and Air New Zealand have admitted to having similar policies in the past.

Now regardless of the assumptions and good intent on which this policy is, no doubt, based, it is patently absurd. An airline flight is the last place a pervert would be able to molest a child. In a plane? 10,000 metres above the earth? Toilets the size of matchboxes, and uniformed flight attendants endlessly circulating about the cabin? So the policy is asinine on the face of it. But the implication is obvious. Men can't be trusted. Even a father of four young children is deemed, by his gender alone, to be more of a risk than a single, childless woman with a nose ring and a rather unusual tooth to tattoo ratio. He is a potential molester; she is not.

---

32 Jamieson 2010; Shah 2010.

Raising good daddies

While some may draw a parallel between hubbies and bubbies, such comparison is generally negative. But there is a way in which it is valid: fathers have to learn to be a parent – just as a baby has to learn to be an adult. And mothers are no different although this seems often overlooked.

Mothers and fathers are not born but made. And just as childbirth brings a woman to motherhood, the same experience has much potential – and much of it unfortunately lost – to bring a man to fatherhood. So, Mum, how about a little support? Next time he bothers to lift a finger, to do any little thing at all no matter how trivial, tell him he did a good job. Even if he did not get it exactly right, lie a little. Psychology 101 tells us that if you encourage him, he will be more likely to do it again in the near future – and he *will* get better! *Of course* he will get better! It is not rocket science.

Any way you approach it you will find that your man will get better at housework over time. A little practice and a little encouragement can go a long, long way. But here is the catch, the better he gets, the more he will do things *his* way. Not the way you would. Let it go! Your reward will be more time to do the things that you want to do, whether it's working toward that big promotion or a two-week vacation in Europe.

So let dad do things his way. It is often trivial, and it might even lead to a good outcome. My wife used to insist that tea towels be hung full length on the clothes line with pegs in the corners, whereas I tended to fold the tea towels over the line in the middle. My argument was simple – the towels would dry more quickly and we fold them down the middle anyway when we use them. She did not agree with me, but allows this barbaric practice when I do the laundry. The net result? I do more laundry.

Here's another laundry example – yeah, I do a lot of laundry – like most parents. When the bath towels came off the clothes line, my wife used to fold them into quarters before putting them in the linen closet. One day she noticed me folding them in thirds, then in half before putting them in the closet. Befuddled, she asked why I engaged in this peculiar practice. I noted that when we hang the towels in the bathroom we always hide the edges by folding them in thirds. I reasoned it was easier if they were already stored that way, and we would not have the crease down the middle when we first hang them. She now folds them the same way that I do.

How about an open-minded discussion about different approaches to typical domestic responsibilities? One stay-at-home father I interviewed talked about his different approach to disciplining his two girls. He and his wife had switched breadwinner and homemaker roles when his younger daughter turned three. His wife tended to be more lenient with her children, picking her battles when it came to discipline; but daddy was having none of it. His approach was more rigid, disciplined, and absolute. 'No' meant 'no' – always!

This difference in parenting styles led to a discussion between husband and wife about which approach was better. His approach had the advantage of conveying a clear and consistent message – always do what daddy says – but at the cost of teaching his daughters about which things are more important than others, and learning about contingencies ('Sometimes this is all right, other times it's not').

Her approach offered the advantage of teaching the girls about contingencies and priorities, but at the expense of obedience. Both daughters tended to question mummy and disobey her. In the end, both parents decided to maintain their parenting approach and tolerate its limitations. If mummy has to tolerate more disobedience, so be it; and if daddy has to explain contingencies more often, that is just fine too! Imagine that! A husband and wife sitting down and discussing strategies and tactics for raising their own children!

So mums and dads can discuss and negotiate things when they disagree as to how to raise their children and run their household, but this, as it turns out, is only part of the problem if you are a dad. A father needing permission to parent from his wife is one thing, but when complete strangers intervene to correct poor parenting practices, things have gone a little too far. This happens regularly in the life of a father, and the intervening 'experts' are almost always women, even those without children of their own. I could recount dozens of examples here, but the publisher has set a page limit, so I will keep it brief.

On a visit to a theme park in Orlando, Florida I was waiting in a queue to order dinner. I had already asked my kids to behave when I heard my little one shriek. As I turned around she was hitting her brother, playfully rather than brutally, but nevertheless hitting him. I quickly grabbed her and reminded her that I had just asked her to behave, and then the most extraordinary thing happened. A woman, standing about three metres away, who was talking on her mobile phone during this incident, interrupted her conversation to say 'He [my son] hit her first. He's the problem.' I looked up and smiled and said, 'Thanks, I'll handle the parenting from here.' But she persisted. 'He hit her first!' This time I did not smile and repeated that I would handle the parenting.

It is difficult to imagine a man lecturing a mother in this same way. The 'helpful' woman interrupted a conversation on the phone to advise me of the appropriate action. I do not think this woman was crazy. Quite the opposite, she was behaving in a way that is normalised. She felt perfectly entitled to assess the situation and then intrude upon my interaction with my children in order to correct me. The incident reflects a stereotyped norm where women are presumed to be the better parent, and men to be less 'qualified.' Should a father have to justify himself to a female stranger? Should a female stranger presume to intervene if the father is – in her opinion – not coping?

Mr Mum and the masculine mystique

But perhaps the biggest enemy of fathers trying to establish equal status in the parenting realm is not mothers, marketers, mass media, or maternity wards. It is fathers themselves! Research often shows that mothers rate the parenting skills of their husbands higher than the fathers rate themselves. Is this just the 'feigned incompetence' ploy from another deadbeat dad? Not likely. Even very involved fathers rate their skills negatively.[33] Men, if we are not going to step up and assert our competence as parents, we can hardly whinge about mothers, strangers, mass media depictions, and society in general. It is time to put up or shut up!

Fathers undermine their own status as parents by denigrating their own ability to care for their children. As a result, dads are not always allowed to do things the way they see fit, even when they do possess the skills and motivation to become the go-to guy at home. But the

---

33 Deutsch 1999, 192–94; Baxter & Smart 2010, 58.

confident dads, who gain permission not only from their spouses, but also from strangers with opinions on good parenting practice, do get very good. At this point, they might expect some recognition for their unique contributions to parenting. Do not hold your breath, dad. It is also likely that good fathers are assimilated into the bosom of motherhood and ascribed with maternal characteristics.

There are many subtle ways in which one gender can be 'assimilated' into the 'other side.' An obvious and often discussed instance of this is when a woman succeeds in the professional realm, and she is denigrated as 'acting like a man'. Leading business women are essentially 'masculinised' by their male colleagues and subordinates. And these unfair stereotypes of female leaders are often decidedly negative. Terms like 'bitch', 'bull [dyke]', and 'butch' are muttered by men under their breath to disparage a successful woman who acts 'too much like a man'.

But this same basic bias can work against a man who 'succeeds' in the domestic realm, and once again dads may be their own worst enemies here. It is astounding how many involved fathers describe themselves as 'second mummies', as if they cannot or dare not recognise any unique advantages they might bring to the parenting table.[34] One stay-at-home dad was delighted to receive a Mother's Day card from a female friend, though perhaps not surprisingly, his wife, who worked full time, was not impressed.[35]

Here's another example. My son was invited to the birthday party of a school mate. You know how these things usually work. The parents drop off the kids and then have the option of staying for wine, nibbles, and other grown-up activities while, in another room, the kids eat chocolate cake and other sweets that will keep them up until 3 am the next morning. As an empirical observation over the years, more mums drop off kids than dads, and mums are far more likely to stay for wine and nibbles than dads. Generally the topic for conversation is kids and the joys and perils of raising them. I decided to stay. I was the only dad.

As per standard protocol the wine did, indeed, flow, and the mums got progressively less reticent in conversation. While we talked about wine tourism at one end of the table I kept tuning in to the conversation

---

34   Deutsch 1999, 235.
35   Bryant 2001, 58–59.

at the other end, where three or four mums were discussing how in-adequate their husbands were in the parenting department. The gener-alisations were quite abundant! 'Men can't do this. Men can't do that.' I was gradually withdrawing from my conversation to listen to what increasingly sounded like unbridled ranting. Finally, one of the mums said that men are simply not equipped to spend more than two or three hours at a time with young children.

At this point the entire table went silent, as it was apparent that I was listening intently to the conversation at the other end of the table, and that I was not entirely in agreement with the general sentiment of the forum. I have raised my two children as a single parent while they lived with me 50 percent or more of the time since my daughter was two. Clearly this has required my spending considerably more than two or three hours at a time with my young children. This fact was known by the mothers at the table including the one who had made this last unfounded generalisation. She brushed it off by saying 'Oh you don't count. You're not like our men!'

I did not say anything at the time, not wanting to ruin the festive occasion that had prevailed to that point. But I did mention this to a female colleague the following Monday. This colleague is highly intelli-gent, has a PhD, has published in a number of high-ranking journals, and would certainly consider herself a staunch feminist. Her reply was that I had been 'paid the highest compliment' by the birthday party mums. 'They considered you one of them,' she smiled.

And keep in mind that the birthday party mums talked about men with me present from the start – but only latterly became aware of my presence when they realised that I was an apparent contradiction to what they were saying. Just imagine – this will take only a second – if a bunch of men at a business meeting stood around busting their chops about women, what a woman present would say. Imagine a man mak-ing a similar derogatory comment about women in the presence of five or six of them.

Successful women in the professional realm are, on average, every bit as feminine as women who conform to some chauvinistic man's ex-pectation of how they should behave. Being professionally successful does not make them less feminine, and there is little doubt that profes-sional women have been unfairly forced to do things a man's way in the office due to policies, guidelines, and good old-fashioned coercion.

But fathers are often forced to do things a mother's way for largely the same reason, because traditional gender stereotypes ascribe competence and authority in various realms of society on largely arbitrary grounds. Perhaps the important difference is that women have done a commendable job in articulating how traditional gender stereotypes have impeded them from pursuing various paths through life. All we are saying is that men who not only participate in the domestic realm, but actually succeed in it, should receive a fair and unbiased assessment of their parenting skills.

And even when fathers do succeed in becoming good parents, stay-at-home and single dads may pay a price. We may be emasculated, and while women may view this feminisation of fathers as being the ultimate compliment, we do not; no more than a woman likes to be masculinised for succeeding professionally. For every 'bitch' who runs a major corporation, there is a 'wimp' who stays home to raise the kids while his wife brings home the bacon.

Not only are these gender stereotypes ridiculous, they are not in the best interests of women who are trying to shatter the glass ceiling. They link women to child care, and more generally the homemaker role. There are only so many hours in the day. If she is changing nappies or making dinner, that is time not devoted to her career.

And as a single father who *has* changed nappies, and *does* make dinner, but is also actively pursuing a career, I may be a bigger ally to mothers than is immediately apparent. Imagine the following scenario. A single father has invited some single male friends over to watch the big football game. He has arranged for all the necessary party favours, beer and pretzels, beer, pretzels, and of course, beer and pretzels. Not a single word is spoken as the four men, one single dad and three single men, thoroughly enjoy the first half of the game . . . until, that is, until the dad's four-year-old daughter comes screaming into the room with blood flowing from her right knee.

The dad springs into action, first taking his daughter to another room so his friends can continue enjoying the game, then immediately sympathising with his daughter. 'Yes, it *is* a big boo boo. I'll bet it stings, doesn't it? I remember I had a boo boo like that, and it really hurt. We better put some medicine on it. That's alright, it doesn't have to be the burny kind. We'll put the other medicine on it.' After the plaster is finally in place, he sends her back out to play in the backyard with a little kiss on the side of her cheek.

Now he returns to his friends to watch the game just before half time. 'Where were you? You missed the rest of the half!'

'My little one got a raspberry on her knee.'

'Ouch!'

'Yeah, that's why the crying was so loud. It kind of scares her.'

'What'd you do?'

'Well, the most important thing is sympathy, you know, telling her that you understand that it hurts and that she's a brave girl. That's actually more important than treating the wound. It's the emotional wound not the physical wound that matters.'

'Oh.'

'So what happened while I was away?'

'Right! The Panthers scored on a beautiful . . .'

Lesson learned. Mothers, if your goal really is to change the attitudes and behaviour of men, let us single and stay-at-home dads show our male brethren the way. As one stay-at-home dad put it 'I've had my mates ask "What's the way you've done it? I want to do it like this". And a lot of them say "I want to be a dad like you are"'.

We are their potential role models, and that makes us your potential allies. Encourage our efforts. Discourage public institutions and others that treat us as second-rate parents. Together, we can change the way men and women view motherhood and fatherhood. The choice is yours.

Weekend warriors

Part 2 of *The other glass ceiling* has largely painted a picture of what it is like being a father in the postmodern world – from a father's perspective. This may seem rather obvious – to talk about fatherhood from the perspective of a father – but it is surprising how often depictions of fatherhood in popular culture stem from the imaginations of women or childless men. But let's also be clear about what Part 2 of this book is not. It is not the male insurgence in the war of the sexes to win the title of biggest victim. It's not a big whinge. That's a no-win game, and one that everyone would do well to leave well alone.

Here, I join the dots to complete some elements that are often overlooked or ignored, to allow a different perspective to be developed. And in so doing, offer the flipside of the 'glass ceiling' argument – a flipside that can offer to complement the push for more recognition, acknowledgement and equal opportunity for women in the male-dominated public sphere. The argument is simple. Sexism harms in both directions. Attitudes and stereotypes that limit one sex in certain domains are paralleled by the limits on the other sex in other domains.

In the opening chapter – 'Deadbeat dads' – we depicted fathers, and especially, divorced fathers, as being a far less than reliable bunch, and to some extent this is true. But as soon as we – meaning men, women, and society in general – start accepting the stereotype that fathers are not very dependable parents, or at least not as dependable as mothers, that notion pervades other aspects of life, with perhaps unintended consequences.

In this chapter we'll consider one of those domains. What happens when fathers, particularly divorced fathers, have made the commitment to become the very best parents they can be? What if, after divorce, they actually strive to be better parents than their ex-spouses (gasp!). Does the world welcome their efforts with open arms? This chapter shows the other side of the same coin – fathers who are held back by the stereotype of the 'deadbeat' dad. The title of this chapter, 'Weekend warriors', stems from the all too familiar child custody 'arrangement' following divorce. He gets to see he kids every other weekend – if he's lucky!

The consequences for society of fathers being relegated to 'second' parents are not good. Mothers can be trapped into childrearing and feel locked out of the public sphere and pursuing a career. Children miss out on arguably the most important male role models in their lives. And fathers? Well, they will miss their children.

The elements that contribute to the father becoming removed from child care are numerous. They can include dad's failure to step up, and mum's reluctance to let go. However, regardless of the reasons, the distance of the father from his children becomes a real problem if the big 'D' word arrives. And I am not talking about death here but divorce. Ironically, a child whose father dies suffers less emotionally than a child whose father is absented through divorce.[1]

Divorce is of course a disaster zone and inevitably, there will be loss, hurt and suffering. Separation hurts both sides of the separating couple. My interest here is in the hurts that are suffered by fathers. (In the next chapter I'll discuss some of the ways that children of divorces suffer).

Moreover, while stereotypes (of deadbeat dads and struggling single mums) may be invoked as contributing factors, the real issue here is how social institutions shape the outcomes. Society at large has taken a curious turn toward rejecting paternal input, and even normalizing the notion of children being raised in single mother households.

---

1 Compared to children from homes disrupted by death, children from divorced homes have more psychological problems (Emery 1988). See also McCann 2000, 10.

I say society, but really it is government departments and judiciaries which behave in a way that reinforce gender stereotypes that are often rejected in other contexts.

An employer that denies a promotion to a qualified woman because 'she'll just resign in a few years anyway to start a family' has broken the law and should be rightly punished for doing so; but a court that awards sole or primary custody of the children to the mother after divorce, even though the father seeks equal custody, is essentially reinforcing the same prejudiced gender stereotype – that women are primarily caregivers, homemakers, wives and mothers.

Father's Day cards

Several Councils in Scotland banned thousands of primary school children from making Father's Day cards 'for fear of embarrassing classmates who live with single mothers'. The initiative was adopted 'in the interests of sensitivity' to the growing number of single parent homes. Of course, nobody bothered to ask why all these single-parent homes had mothers and not fathers in the first place. The making of Mother's Day cards in these schools continued unabated.[2]

Here, I explore the story of the weekend warriors, the way that dads in divorce lose more than a partner, more than money, but possibly their children too. All because of the operation of and reinforcement of stereotypes that see dad as a breadwinner and not a caregiver.

Stormy weather ahead

Long-term forecasts are fraught with problems as boating and outdoor people know. That there will be storms is certain. When they will occur and what damage they will bring is unknown. The same is true for long-term forecasts for marriages. There will be squalls, storms and tempests. When and how bad – who knows?

---

2 Johnson 2008.

However, based on past data, the forecast is that about 50 percent of marriages will end in divorce. The remaining marriages will end in the death of one or more of the partners. The implication is that relationship endings are never nice – but divorce can leave two people with hurt – and maybe more.[3]

But the outcomes post-divorce for men and women differ significantly. Both may suffer, indeed they are likely to, but each will suffer in very different ways.

Women are reported to suffer primarily in a financial way. One of the primary disadvantages confronting women post-divorce is that of the so-called poverty trap. Post-divorce, the woman's income tends to be significantly less than the man's. This adds a considerable strain on post-divorce mothers who also often generally have to manage the burdens of keeping the house, caring for children, etc.[4]

So what are the ways that men suffer post-divorce? One way they suffer is in being divorced when they did not want divorce! Curiously, there is a strong sex bias in the initiation of separation and divorce. About three in four separations/divorces are initiated by the female partner.[5]

Why does she leave? Perhaps because the men these women have chosen are truly intolerable. Of course, this is a pretty grim scenario implying that just under 40 percent of married men (given approximately 50 percent of marriages ultimately end in divorce, and 75 percent of divorces are initiated by women) are pretty useless. Either these men are nothing more than a couch-potatoes with Y-chromosomes, their women are picky and think they can do better elsewhere, or most likely, some combination of the two. But regardless of *why* she leaves, it seems reasonable to presume that the leaver – typically the woman – figures she will be better off without him.[6]

The experience of divorce is different for the leaver and the person left. The leaver's strategy is pre-emptive – it means the leaver, typically

---

3   Retrieved 25 February 2014 from Australian Bureau of Statistics, Marriages and Divorces, Australia, 2012 at http://www.abs.gov.au/ausstats/abs@.nsf/ Products/3310.0~2012~Chapter~Divorces?OpenDocument; Stevenson & Wolfers 2007.

4   Weston 1992.

5   Dixon & Weitzman 1982; Cancian & Meyer 1998; Brinig & Allen 2000.

the woman, has been able to prepare for the separation. The leavee, typically male, has to deal with his stuff after she has finished with hers.

Once the words, 'I want out' have been uttered, the journey of divorce begins. The first significant step in this journey is for one person in the couple to leave the family home – or in more legal language, the shared residence.[7] Curiously, and despite the fact that women are the initiating party in three out of four relationship breakups, the step away from the family home is more likely to be taken by the man.[8]

Then follows the more formal elements of separation overseen by an entourage of institutions including government agencies, lawyers, mediators, and in rare cases, courts. In separating, the couple who ironically have presumably been unable to agree on very much now need to set to and create two agreements, one covering the separation of the net assets, the other covering the custody of the children.

The statistics show that about 80 percent or more of mothers have sole custody of their children. Meanwhile, approximately 80 percent of fathers are payers of child support.[9] The net result is that most mothers will have unimpeded access to the children; most fathers have contact with the children that is controlled by and must be negotiated with the mother. And he has to pay.

Finally, there is the separation of the finances. As men have generally generated more income than women, they typically hold a greater proportion of the assets. However, a woman, even if her earning power is not equal to a man's, is generally deemed to have made an equal

---

6   See Divorce and separation. In Diversity and change in Australian Families. Australian Institute of Family Studies, pp.211, 223. Retrieved 25 February 2014 from http://www.aifs.gov.au/institute/pubs/diversity/15divorce.pdf; Brinig & Allen 2000; See also Who initiates the divorce more often, the wife or the husband? *Divorce Lawyer Source*. Retrieved 25 February 2014 from http://www.divorce-lawyer-source.com/faq/emotional/ who-initiates divorce-men-or-women.html.
7   This is the description given in more legalistic lingo. E.g., http://www.people.howstuffworks.com/divorce4.htm [Accessed 11 September 2013]
8   Mulder & Wagner 2010.
9   US Divorce Statistics. Retrieved 11 September 2013 from http://www.divorcemag.com/statistics/statsUS.shtml.

contribution in a long-term, married relationship. Accordingly, the net assets will be divided roughly, but not necessarily exactly, 50:50.[10]

Depending on the jurisdiction, the parent that wins primary custody, typically the mother, enjoys two additional financial benefits. First, the main custodian may be granted a larger share of the assets than the other parent – depending on the jurisdiction and rules operating in that jurisdiction. Second, the main custodian will be able to claim a greater share of child support from the other parent. Child support is collected by government agencies which have the authority to take the money at source.

Ironically and sadly for a parent who has less contact than they would like, the rate of child support is based on amount of contact – less contact, higher child support. That is, the person who primarily controls the contact of the non-custodial parent is . . . the custodial parent. So the custodial parent sees the children more, and benefits from more child support if the other parent sees the children less.[11]

These are of course just the statistics. Nonetheless, if you were a gambling man, then the odds on your getting divorced are even. And the odds of the man losing access to his children and having to pay ongoing child support are exceedingly high. This is the reality the man faces.

No fault but a great divide

While no-fault divorce is the guiding principle in family law in many jurisdictions around the world today, the process of separation is almost always started by one person, and this creates an enormous divide in the experience of the two parties to the relationship.

Women – as has been noted – are three times as likely to initiate divorce as men. This represents a surprising reversal of a stereotype. From as far back as Jane Austen (*Pride and prejudice*) and the Brontë sisters (e.g., *Jane Eyre*, *Wuthering Heights*) and perhaps farther, it is generally the women who are perceived to be the ones that are eager to enter a matrimonial state. Men are generally perceived to be the more reluctant

---

10 O'Neill 1992.
11 Weiss & Willis 1985; Laakso 2004; Horwitz & Lewin 2008.

party. However, once married, the picture apparently reverses. At least based on the data about who initiates divorce, it is the women who are more motivated to exit the marriage than the men!

Remarriage: I do – again!

Men are more likely to remarry than women. Younger women are more likely to get remarried than older women, but wealthier men are more likely to get remarried than less well-off men. Age isn't as strongly related to the probability of a man remarrying, and wealth isn't as strongly related to the probability of a woman remarrying. This makes sense according to evolutionary psychology. Richer men can provide more resources for offspring than poorer men, but age has very little to do with a man's reproductive success (e.g., Clint Eastwood became a dad in his late 70s). Younger women can produce more offspring than older women, making them more attractive to men; and although richer women can also provide more resources for children, a woman in that situation hardly needs a husband around. Of course, an alternative explanation is simply that women learn from their mistakes and men don't.[12]

Why then, in general, do married women want to quit and married men want to stay? In view of no-fault divorce, we can really only speculate on the antecedents and why so many women choose to leave. She says he is intolerable. He says she is intolerant. 'I didn't start it, she/he did!' Whatever the reasons, looking forward, she has presumably decided that out of marriage is better than in marriage.

Regardless of who starts it or why, what is clear is that the consequences of separation are quite different for the leaver versus the person who is left. The leaver typically experiences her pain and upset in the lead-up to the separation. The separation is therefore the leaver's resolution of the problem. However, her solution is now his problem. The 'leavee' experiences his pain and suffering in the period following separation.

---

12   Stevenson & Wolfers 2007.

While marriage is a consensual act (at least in the Western world), separation is not. It may take two to tango, but it takes only person to leave the dance floor. Marriage is about negotiation and compromise; divorce is all about unilateral decisions. Hence, divorce makes an exceedingly poor basis for subsequent negotiations.

Of course, the right to separate is equal, but the consequences are not. For the leaver, the consequences are a better life. Or at least, hopefully a better life, otherwise why do it? Despite women initiating divorce the majority of the time, the focus is generally on the difficulties faced by women post-divorce and not those of the men. Yet they both suffer, though in different ways.

Struggling mums and depressed dads

The media, press and others make much of how women struggle post-divorce. She will have to manage an independent household, feed and clothe the children, and do all this with less money and less help than she had before. Certainly this suggests that the experience for many women post-divorce is difficult. But divorce damages both sides, both the leaver and the leave. Let me unpack the losses for each sex post-divorce.

The big issue that confronts women post-divorce is the 'poverty-trap'. When one household divides into two, and the amount of income remains unchanged, then of course it is more difficult for that money to cover two households rather than one. The poverty trap focuses on this issue – that the woman has less income than the man. To some extent this reflects a much touted fact that men's incomes tend to be higher on average than women's – even now in after all these years of pushing for equality.

While I accept this as true, the notion of a 'poverty trap' is somewhat misleading as income is just one part of wealth. The other side is assets – or rather net assets. In dividing net assets, the deal that is encouraged by law and courts is one that is generally around 50:50. Deviations for relative 'contribution' may be made for short-term relationships and inheritances, but aside from that the amount will tend to be split down the middle. The exception is if there are children – then a larger share will typically go with the primary child-carer. As that is the woman the vast majority of the time, it is women who generally end up with 60 percent or more of the assets.[13]

She gets less income but more assets. Yes, the problem with assets is that they look good on the balance sheet, but may not be readily accessible. She may have the superannuation, but it is inaccessible and does not contribute to how 'well off' she is in terms of covering her expenses after the divorce.

So where income is used a measure for 'standard of living', men look better off. However, add in assets and a different picture emerges – as has been established in the academic research. The bottom line is that there are numerous ways to measure financial 'wellbeing', not to mention that the time frame in which the 'post-divorce' data are collected can vary from study to study. Hence, it is hardly surprising that different studies can draw very different conclusions about whether ex-husbands or ex-wives are worse off financially following the dissolution of a marriage.[14]

Why do we not know or hear more about this? Newspaper journalists, not burdened with issues of truth and accuracy, tend to focus more on tapping into political agendas that sell newspapers. Despite the inherent ambiguities associated with the 'poverty trap' facing single mums, it has garnished a great deal of media attention, and promulgated the widespread belief that 'women are worse off financially after a divorce'.[15] It is perhaps more accurate to say that some women suffer financially after a divorce relative to their ex-spouses, but others may wind up better off.

What about fathers? How do they fare after divorce? This has received somewhat less attention in the media. The suffering experienced by men appears to be more emotional – and accordingly less tangible. Of course, men can be held partly to blame for their emotional burden. They do tend to choose to suffer in silence – almost certainly to their own detriment. The problem is that there is little encouragement for the man to express his emotions: 'Buck up mate, you just gotta deal' is what he will likely hear – be it from his mates or his own inner voice.

---

13 Horwitz & Lewin 2008.
14 Smock et al. 1999; Bedard & Deschenes 2005; Lyons & Fisher 2006, 40; Bratberg & Tjotta 2008; de Vaus et al. 2009.
15 Farrell 2001, 240.

And in some ways, he does have to just deal with it. Yes, his problems are real. In the majority of cases, he unwillingly loses his partner, loses his home and has to go about setting up a new household, and he loses freedom of access to his kids.

Then there are the financial burdens. The man still needs to work to provide for his kids – mandated by child support if his own willingness to do so is lacking. Child support is set according to earning capacity. Accordingly, the paying parent, typically the man, cannot pull a 'sickie' even if he really is suffering from depression. Tough! Man up and get on with it!

It is little wonder that the men who are left are confronted by enormous emotional issues post-separation. The degree of the suffering is clearly reflected in the higher incidences of substance abuse, depression and suicide among divorced men compared to divorced women.[16]

So why is there so much attention on the suffering of divorced women? Men suffer too, and three times out of four, his suffering began with her decision. A little compassion towards his concerns seems justifiable. This is not a contest to see who suffers more. It is about having compassion to see the suffering of both sides.

Unhoused husband

I'm a fantastic housekeeper. Every time I leave a man, I keep his house.

Zsa Zsa Gabor

'It's over, I want you out' is how it often starts. Why does he move out? Is it because it is honourable? The right thing to do? To avoid making waves? To give her space? Who says that chivalry is dead? Or perhaps he is simply conceding that she is right. But more specifically then, he is conceding that the home is her domain, a concession that may have very legal consequences as we'll see shortly.

---

16   Yang 2000; Farrell 2001; Owen 2003; Drinking after divorce: men are more likely than women to turn to drinking after split, study says, *Huffington Post*, 20 August 2012. Retrieved 4 February 2014 from http://www.huffingtonpost.com/2012/08/20/drinking-after-divorce_n_1812235.html.

Whether chivalry or conceding the home is her domain, or both, the striking aspect of his agreement is that it hinges on sexist stereotypes – the same sexist stereotypes that are normally being so systematically eliminated in society. In divorce, the stereotypes come to the fore. He acts true to stereotype by moving out – and no-one would think to criticise him for doing so.

Who knows why the man agrees to move out, but that he does so seems to be the generally accepted norm. It is certainly what the statistics reflect. And it is what people see in the media. For instance, the TV sitcom, *The odd couple*[17] featured two divorced men sharing an apartment in NYC. Each episode began with each man being thrown out of the house by his respective spouse. He leaves his home with a resigned look on his face, the voiceover saying 'Deep down, he knew she was right'. There is no explanation offered for *why* she was right.

The subtext is that back then, the woman said 'jump', the man asked 'how high?' The more insidious element is that this seems as true today as then. If a woman decides she wants a divorce, the man must accept this and move out of the house.

The problem is that in acquiescing to her request, he is wading into strategically dangerous territory. While she may have called the end to the relationship, his physically leaving sets him up as a deserter, as the one who has abandoned his family.

Sure, talking of strategy seems far removed from the warm, fuzzy vibe of a loving home, but once one party has declared they want out, the loving home has lost its vibe.

Accordingly, the man must ask if he is moving out for her sake or his sake. Aside from the way that his action may be presented and perceived, it also has two real consequences that are more like 'sticks and stones' than name-calling. By moving out, he undermines his attachment to his own children, and he undermines any claim to occupy or make decisions about the family home.

When the man leaves the family home, he will almost certainly reduce his contact frequency and maybe the amount of time with his kids as a consequence. Divorce as we shall see almost always results in a very

---

17   Based on a movie starring Jack Lemmon as Felix Unger and Walter Matthau as Oscar Madison (1968). The television program (1970–75) featured Tony Randall as Felix and Jack Klugman as Oscar.

changed pattern of contact for the father with his children, but moving out makes it happen sooner, and can make it worse in the longer run. This is because the new form of contact that is established after his moving out is likely to have a strong influence on the legal outcome regarding the ongoing contact long after the divorce.

The second consequence of his leaving the family home is that he seriously undermines any claim he might make on the family home, which for many families represents the primary asset. Given the old adage that 'possession is 9/10ths of the law', the man may well see himself on the path of giving up any control over or occupancy of the family home. To some extent, the courts take the view that he 'abandoned' the family home – even if he responded to her call to do so.

So a word of warning – if you are the leavee (male or female), do not agree to move out without some forethought. In particular, it is not clear that you 'owe' this to the person who has chosen to end the relationship and is asking you to leave. If you are a man, and you agree to move out, be aware that this will change your contact with your children and may affect the contact you can negotiate in the longer run.

If you move out as a show of chivalry or as a concession that the house is her domain more than yours – recognise that you are being sexist and reinforcing stereotypes that are damaging to both men and women! But you might be forgiven because, as will soon become apparent, stereotyping and discrimination based on sex is rampant in post-divorce settlements.

The price of divorce

A father goes to a toy shop which features a Barbie on display in the window. He asks the sales person,

'How much for the Barbie in the window?'

The salesperson answers, 'We have a range of Barbies Sir. Which one do you want?'

'Which ones do you have?'

We have: Work-Out Barbie for $19.95, Shopping Barbie for $19.95, Beach Barbie for $19.95, Disco Barbie for $19.95, Ballerina Barbie for $19.95, Astronaut Barbie for $19.95, Skater Barbie for $19.95, and Divorced Barbie for $265.95.

The amazed father asks: 'It's what?! Why is the Divorced Barbie $265.95 and the others only $19.95?'

The annoyed salesperson rolls her eyes, sighs, and answers:

'Sir . . ., Divorced Barbie comes with: Ken's Car, Ken's House, Ken's Boat, Ken's Furniture, Ken's Computer, one of Ken's Friends, etc.'

The price of divorce is high. But if you grin, smile or laugh, you understand a point I am making here; that the price of divorce is quite different for men versus women. Barbie is obviously just a doll, and not a real, in the flesh, woman. If she were, the story would be less . . . I dunno . . . sterile. What is notably absent from Divorced Barbie's list of 'assets' is the kids.

Child care vs child support

For years, we have been told that women have had to fight for an equal right to be alongside man at the coalface. Actually women are not all that keen to work on the coalface it seems. Men are over-represented relative to women in the base and dangerous jobs (e.g., mining, sanitary services, trucking, etc.) just as they are over-represented in the board-room.

Nonetheless, for many years women have fought for, and gained the right to participate equally in the public world of professional careers. This is a positive step forward. No longer would women be defined solely in terms of their domestic roles as wives and mothers.

Imagine my surprise then when a female counsellor told me in no uncertain terms that it is the woman's role to care for the child. What?!? Um, can you repeat that?

It's true. In a counselling session with my ex in which I was trying to negotiate more time with my son, the counsellor told me 'Your job is to provide financial resources.' She endeavoured to bolster the role, and 'stroke' me with the importance of my role in supporting the health and wellbeing of my child and his mother.

I struggled however to get around this brazen appeal to stereotypes that would be considered archaic, unjust and bigoted if used in any other circumstances.

Both childrearing and breadwinning are indeed important. However, have we not just spent decades working out that these roles need not be gender-specific? Some women find that being solely a mother and wife is not enough. It becomes an imposition, an obligation, a constraint. Some men find the role of being the sole breadwinner, working nine to five away from home six days a week, and dealing with suits, meetings and budget reports all day as onerous and unpleasant. Balance is in order – for *both* parents.

So I was – and am – incensed at any presumption that men should be expected to provide financial and material support for the child post-divorce while women become custodians of the children. I am genuinely surprised that more women are not willing to argue against this kind of sexism.

Yes, it benefits single mothers who desire sole custody of their children, but at the cost of perpetuating gender stereotypes that fathers are breadwinners and mothers are homemakers, the very same stereotypes underlying the gender pay gap and the glass ceiling.

Indeed, the top-income earner – typically the male – is mandated to pay child support at a rate determined by the government. The government is unwilling to take on the burden of supporting children from a marriage where there is sufficient income for those children to be supported by the parents. This seems reasonable, but the rate of support is set to minimise claims against the government. No effort is made to make it 'easy' on the parents.

Ongoing child support is paid according to means. As men typically earn more, they pay more. He also pays more if he has less contact with his children. The more access mum has, the more dad has to pay and the less he sees his children.

And once established, child support is very inflexible. If a mother decided, post-divorce, that she wanted to earn more and contribute more financially the raising of the children, it is unlikely that anyone would dispute her right to do so, even if, in making the decision, she is sending her children to a day-care centre.

However, if a father decides that he wants to contribute more time to the raising of the children, child support does little to support this. Child support agencies will not allow his income level to drop. If he changes job or takes extended leave as he deals with the divorce, no concession will be allowed. If his income does drop for some reason, child support agencies will typically 'deem' his income to be as it was before and draw from his earnings as before.

If the divorce forces a dramatic re-evaluation of what is important in life and triggers a change of heart and a desire to be more involved in child care, institutionally, no-one cares or makes any effort to accommodate that. The net effect is that he will have more time to devote to his career following divorce, and a greater financial incentive to do so, whereas she will have less time to devote to her career unless she relies on day-care centres and other substitute forms of parental care. He is the breadwinner; she is the caregiver.

Status quo

It's interesting that wedding planning has become such a widely accepted profession. Was it that JLo movie? I have to admit that I hired one – or should I say we hired one, or should I say my wife hired one – for our wedding. I can't imagine how we would have survived the ordeal without her, and by 'her' I mean of course the wedding planner. We're still several decades, or should I say millennia, away from a world where men plan weddings, though it is an interesting fantasy that, for me, would involve far more beer, sport, and rock and roll than is currently the case in most ceremonies.

The point I will eventually get around to making is that no such profession exists for divorce planning. Planning weddings maybe complex, but divorces, with or without planning, are even more complex. What begins as an interpersonal conflict between two people sends out shockwaves that touch many other people. The tussle of two can become so fierce and grand that the cavalry and artillery in the form of government agencies and peace-brokers in the form of mediators and lawyers and judges, are often called in to help resolve the complexities.

The big issues that require resolution post-divorce are the (re)distribution of wealth and children. In line with the complexity of divorce, the two are strongly co-mingled. If there are children involved, the re-distribution of wealth depends on the arrangements made for the children.

The primary principle for resolving both the financial and child issues might be considered to be an effort to maintain the status quo. The objective is to create a situation for each party in the parting that will leave them ideally no less well off than they were within the relationship. Accordingly, net wealth will tend to be divided roughly down the middle.

Children of course cannot be cut down the middle, so the court is left in the unenviable position of having to decide where they go and when they go there. Children generally go with the parent who has had most contact with them in the past – this is the operation of 'status quo'. The non-custodial or absent parent, typically the father, is then required to contribute child support in proportion to his income and in inverse proportion to his contact. More income, more child support; less contact, more child support.

Not unreasonably, it is difficult to expect two adults going through the trauma of divorce will be able to negotiate arrangements that maintain parental contact with the children exactly as it was before the separation. So if mum has been the one most responsible for caring for the children, then the children will very likely end up going with the mum. However, it is status quo with an important caveat: it is status quo that ensures children will now spend most of their time with their primary caregiver.

The reality is that divorce necessitates enormous changes and 'status quo' is an ideal that cannot possibly be achieved. There is no sense of status quo in terms of maintaining the contact that the children had with the other parent. Even if the amount of time is maintained, the nature of that contact is likely to be substantially changed from what it was.

Yes, this is a pragmatic reality. It may not be in the best interests of the child, but is this really a bias against men? Well, it is noteworthy that while status quo supports the children going to mothers if she is the primary caregiver, this does not work in the reverse.[18] Even if the man has been the primary caregiver, and even if his claim for custody is uncontested, the likelihood of him ending up with the children is significantly less than for the mother under the same circumstances.[19]

This does seem to reflect the bias I am talking about – and in my view, it is a fairly straightforward extension from the discussion

---

18 Benatar 2012.
19 Hetherington et al. 1997; Cancian & Meyer 1998; Swinton et al. 2008.

of the father as the 'second' parent. Such is the nature of the discrimination mediated by the institutions that are involved in and guide couples through divorce. The implications for fathers are pretty clear. If he wants to be involved in parenting, he needs to get involved early. If he only improves his game once separation has been started, his efforts are likely to count for little in terms of the child custody arrangement.

Parental power plays

Power is never distributed evenly. For much of the last couple of centuries, men held enormous power in the household by virtue of their being the provider of income. In fact, in centuries past, in the event of a divorce, the children would automatically go with the father.[20] The father had the financial resources, the mother did not.

With women fighting for and winning a right to a place alongside men in the workplace, this power has been diminished. And institutions have ensured that a woman can end a marriage, keep the children

---

20   Goldberg 1997.

with her, and still be assured of access to financial resources to support 'her' family.

The problem is not about the granting of power, but rather the abuses of that power. It is the abuse that shows the pendulum has swung too far.[21] The obvious power that women hold in the post-divorce situation is that over access to the children. By being granted custody, they become the gatekeeper of the time that the children will spend with the father. If he is not interested in spending time with the children, it is easy; but if he is a devoted dad, she can serve the best interests of the children, or she can serve her own desires to hurt her ex-husband. Sadly, there are many – way too many – cases of the mother choosing the latter option. Even sadder is how ineffectual the institutions that oversee divorce are in checking this abuse.

For instance, one Australian woman brought her four daughters from their home in Italy to Australia in 2010 on the pretext of a holiday, but then never returned. For two years, she defied orders from both the Italian and Australian courts for the girls to be returned to their father. The Italian father had to come to Australia to see his daughters. But as the case dragged through the courts, appeals were scheduled, and new reports were written, he despaired of ever gaining the custody he had already been awarded and returned to Italy. Interestingly, the father reportedly gave up the fight for the children in view of their being thrust into situations that were not in their best interests emotionally or psychologically.[22]

Of course this is extreme, but not necessarily rare. One son I interviewed recounted how his mother ran off with her boss, absconding with himself and his sister. One day the father simply came home to an empty house. In the interview the son explained, 'Mum said "We're leaving. We're moving" and we were like "What?" ... Mum just made [the decision], and never told dad what was going to happen. She kind of took control over this whole thing.'

In this instance, the son made a surprise visit to his father a year later only to find him broken and depressed. A military man with a disciplined lifestyle that saw him showered, shaved, and in uniform by 6 am each day had been reduced to an unkempt borderline alcoholic.

---

21 Benatar 2012.
22 Marriner 2012.

The son, 13, and his sister, 11, made the decision to move back to live with the father, which they did from that time until leaving home at as 18-year-olds.

Less extreme examples of abusive control are even more common. For instance, one single father told of a mother who threatened legal action if a school released any information about her children to her ex-husband. As a biological parent with custody 15 percent of the time, he had a legal right to those records. However the school, not willing to take on the wrath of the mother, denied him access until he took legal action himself.[23]

Limiting and controlling access to the children is just one way that mothers can abuse the power they have over fathers. Making false allegations are another. Women make the vast majority of false allegations during divorce proceedings.[24] Talking to divorce lawyers, the man will often be informed of the real danger of allegations of domestic violence and child abuse. It happened to me. I was warned of the possibility of domestic violence claims, and I was falsely accused and investigated for molesting my son.

The ultimate power play?

One retiring Family Court judge had the mettle to go public with what is perhaps the ultimate power play in the divorce derby. Justice David Collier, who retired from Parramatta Family Court after 14 years on the bench, discussed the willingness of parents to use their children to damage each other.[25]

'If a husband and wife really get down to it in this day and age, dirt flies,' Justice Collier said. But he was quite specific about the biggest abuse in the system – mothers who make false allegations of abuse against former partners.

'When you have heard the evidence, you realise that this is a person who's so determined to win that he or she will say anything. I'm satisfied that a number of people who have appeared before me

---

23   McCann 2000, 99.
24   Farrell 2001, 79.
25   Alexander 2013.

> have known that it is one of the ways of completely shutting husbands out of the child's life.'
>
> 'It's a horrible weapon.'

Another domain where abuse is common is in names. Patrilineal tracking has meant that traditionally, children have carried the father's name. Some mothers try to change this name. I was confronted by a childcare agency that had my son listed under his mother's maiden name – even though they agreed it was not the name on the birth certificate. This battle over a name reflects how much this battle is about the parents and not about the child.

However, the real naming crime is in giving the title of 'dad' to another when the real dad is still around. The simplest form of this is for her to insist that her children call her new partner Dad. So they end up with two dads – as I remember my young son telling me when he was about five. The more extreme version, which happened to a friend of mine, is where the mother had the child call her new partner Dad, and insisted that the child refer to her biological father by his first name. The father was stripped of the title!

Perhaps this does not sound all so serious – especially encouraging the children to refer to her new partner as dad. But how is this in the best interests of the child? It may make the new partner feel important. It may please the mother to have 'replaced' the father she does not like. But what does this communicate to a little girl or boy? Mostly that the name 'dad' is meaningless, or little more than, say, 'uncle'.

Missing my children

Maybe saying that men get a raw deal post-divorce seems hollow, complaints of unequal treatment sound like so much whining. Perhaps this is true. But leaving out any issue of equality, what cannot be denied are his feelings.

I remember one time going to pick up my young son from his mother. It was handover time, it was agreed that he would come and spend some time with me. However, his mother was very reluctant to give him up this day. She hugged him tightly to her chest. With tears running down her face and crying, she said 'You will have to come and take him from me. You cannot possibly understand how hard it is to give him up.'

What?!? Did she actually mean this? Am I not forced to give up my son back to her with the same frequency and in the same intervals? I suspect it is the regular frequency and interval of switching between households that creates, or at least, exacerbates, the problem.

I was an involved father and I was lucky enough to have the flexibility to work at home. Post-divorce, I spent much less time with my son than I had before. And the nature of the contact was dramatically different. I spent a lot of time crying and missing my son.

Even when the time is more equitably shared, the missing can still be there. Nowadays, the handovers take place every Friday night. And the missing is still there. I may enjoy Friday night and Saturday on my own, but by the time Sunday rolls around, I just miss my kids. There is really nothing I want to do on my own. I spend most of these Sundays catching up at work – doing what, ironically, takes so many fathers away from their kids! The following Mondays and Tuesdays are not any better. I begin anticipating the return of my kids.

Men may not speak much about this kind of loss, or about emotional pain in general. And when they do, others may resist hearing. However, we do not have to listen very hard to hear fathers telling of their experience of missing their children post-divorce. A recent collection of separated fathers' stories reflects that many have similar feelings:

One of the strangest aspects of the profound loneliness that often goes with being a non-custodial parent is that you can be around people every minute of the day, you can be well loved and cared for by your own family, a new partner or good friends, yet you can still feel like nobody is there. You might even be fully engaged in a job that you love, but nothing comes close to healing the profound schism you feel. At its core is a mind-bending divide between your past 'me' as an engaged parent and your new 'me' as a partially or fully disengaged parent . . . The difficulty and the sense of loneliness seem to be dramatically compounded when your co-parent's actions, intentionally or incidentally, work to exclude you further.

A simple yet not uncommon illustration of this is to be told that your children do not need you any more while it is also made forcibly clear that if you are late with your child support payment all hell will surely break loose. There is a daily stress that goes with not seeing your children while being reminded continually of the need to work hard – perhaps in a job you no longer enjoy – in order to pay, what feels like, an onerous percentage of your income towards you children's care. Coupled with the emotional spiritual dilemma of your life's purpose being so thoroughly questioned, the challenge of making sense of all this aggregate stress is substantial.[26]

As we get older, we get wiser about where we devote our attention. And most of us wish we had spent more time with our family and friends. Bonnie Ware, a palliative nurse and singer made this observation in a blog that listed the five common regrets of the dying.[27] Interestingly, she made particular note that 'every male patient [she] nursed . . . missed their children's youth'.

Fathers miss their kids, and it should be understandable. Even if all that has been done is in the best interests of the child, the man suffers the loss of his children. The centrality of this emotion, this feeling of loss, is underlined and highlighted by virtually all divorced men who wish they could have more access to their children.[28]

Best interests of the child?

The argument is often made to fathers that 'it is the quality, not the quantity of time with children that counts'. But how the quantity is distributed surely affects it quality. While married, the father may only have seen his children before and after work. However, post-divorce, he is very likely to be restricted to seeing his children every second weekend and half the school holidays. Fathers get hit by a double-whammy.

---

26 Manson 2012.
27 Berry 2012; Ware nd. A book was published in 2012 that grew out of the blog post, see Ware 2012.
28 Fathers want more time with children, *News.com.au*, 30 August 2012. Retrieved 4 February 2014 from http://www.news.com.au/money/money-matters/fathers-want-more-time-with-children/story-e6frfmd9-1226461517924.

They get less time, and they get it in a very different form to what they had before.

Putting the minutes together in one block may suit the mother, but it may not suit the child or the father. Then as the father tries to make the best of the deal and engage with his children fully on the weekend, he is criticised for being a Disneyland dad! It's true! This is a frequently heard criticism of Weekend Warrior dads.

How dare a father, who due to court orders only sees his children every other weekend, try to create lasting experiences for his children by doing special things like theme parks, camping trips, sporting events, etc.?!? Who does he think he is compensating for his limited actual time with his children by creating cherished memories that retrospectively enhance his role in their lives? Actually, he sounds like a pretty smart, well-meaning dad! How else would a parent compensate for only seeing his kids two days out of every fortnight?

Political views on fatherhood

Morris Iemma's was Premier of New South Wales from 2008 to 2009. During his term, Iemma argued against the granting of rights to divorced fathers, saying 'Rather than making it better, it is actually increasing the harassment and the intimidation and prevents the mother and the child from rebuilding their lives.'

Ah, I see. Only the 'mother and the child' need rebuild their lives after a divorce.

Then Mr Iemma made a sudden and early decision to resign leaving his political home a mess. Why did he resign? Mr Iemma explained at a press conference 'I have never, ever handed in my resignation as a husband and a father. So instead today, I hand in my resignation as Premier and Member for Lakemba, and I go back to the job I cherish so much, husband, loving father, of four children and a wife.'[29]

Well Morrie, you better hope that Santina thinks you're worth keeping around now that you do not earn a crust as a major politician. Otherwise, you can kiss your 'new' job goodbye.

The greatest losers in divorce are perhaps those who were a product of that same relationship in a happier time, and whose voice is so rarely heard or heeded. The institutions say they are looking after the children's interests, but they do so under the presumption that it is better for a child to live in a divided home with one parent. This seems bizarre.

In our modern era, we have come to see widespread divorce as acceptable. Fair enough – what happens between consenting adults is their business. But to the extent that their decisions have consequences for their children, it is not so clearly acceptable. Blended families are fine, but children are increasingly leading a life alienated from one of their biological parents, more specifically, their fathers.

In Australia and New Zealand today, about one third of all children live in a home that does not include their biological father.[30] In the US this figure is 40 percent.[31] In the 1960s about ten percent of children lived away from their fathers.[32]

How is this in the best interests of the child? The strengths of a separated home or a single-parent household is that parental conflict can be minimised – but it is not necessarily in the best interests of the child. It is the next best alternative because the parents are unable to establish an effective co-parenting model. And at least part of that problem is that institutions simply do not encourage that.

Shared residence is an option which Australia approached, and then rejected. It is noteworthy that the move away was not based on any notable failure of the presumption of shared parenting, but the claims that it would fail. Yet a recent summary of the academic research on shared residency cites numerous studies showing a variety of positive effects on children and parents.[33]

Yes, there is resistance to these ideas. But it appears to come mostly from those defending the mother's right to be free of the man she has

29 Morris Iemma quits politics to be husband and father. *The Daily Telegraph*, 5 September 2008. Retrieved 27 February 2014 from
http://www.dailytelegraph.com.au/
morris-iemma-quits-politics-to-be-husband-and-father/
story-e6frewor-1111117403219.
30 McCann 2000, 6.
31 Chira 1994.
32 Livingston & Parker 2011.
33 Nielsen 2011.

chosen to divorce. It is not a best option; it is a next-best option. It may protect the mother; but rarely if ever can be claimed to be the best arrangement for a child.

The irony is that what I am saying is the flipside of the glass ceiling argument. Just as business prospers by having women engaging in the workplace, raising children surely benefits from having the involvement of men. A society that acknowledges this problem and addresses it will have children that receive the benefit of care from both mum and dad, both very different styles, both very much essential to the child's successful development. But at the moment, as we'll see in the following chapter, our culture simply defaults to a primary custodian arrangement which leaves children with limited access to their other parent.

The problem of absent fathers has been noted earlier. It was considered a problem when I was young because fathers *chose* to leave the family home. Now our institutions *force* fathers out of the family home. Now we deal with fathers who are directed to be absent post-divorce by the institutions that purport to be looking after the best interests of the children.

The problem is complex. The current solutions for sharing custody post-divorce are simple but clumsy. The decision is openly made in the best interests of the custodial parent because it is presumed that this will also cater to the best interests of the children:

> The law of child relocation ... is a mess. It is not much better anywhere else. It has been dressed up in shibboleths and word formulations that make it look like we, as family court judges, know what we are doing – we don't. The law pretends that we can determine with some high degree of predictive accuracy whether a move by a child with one parent away from another parent will be in a child's best interest – we can't. The truth is this: there is no evidence that our decisions in these types of cases result in an outcome that is any better for the child than if the parents did rock-paper-scissors. In fact, in a relocation case, a judge is almost never deciding what is in a child's best interest.[34]

---

34   Duggan 2007.

This idea – that child custody decisions reflect the best interest of the mother not the child – was driven home to me with the force of a cricket bat to the skull in a conversation I had with a woman I know. Not an angry confrontation, as you might think. Quite the opposite.

She had asked me to meet up with her. I chose a café. She arrived, sat down and began to unburden herself.

A sad, disconsolate story. She was in the throes of breaking up with her second husband. She had had a child with him, and another child with another man previously.

She admitted that she had entered this latest relationship and this marriage with the full hope that this man could step up to replace the previous father.

This triggered me.

What exactly was wrong with the previous father? I didn't ask. This wasn't the time and place.

Tears were streaming out from under her large sunglasses. Her disappointment, her tragedy were manifest.

However, what was with the rejecting of the father of the first child? Sure, she didn't like him. But just because she didn't like him did not make him any less of a father. His rights to access to his child should in no way depend on the mother's like or dislike of the father.

Would she do this to the second father? Was she in the process of doing this now?

What 'right' is it that women operate under that makes them think that they can create a baby – which they don't do on their own regardless of their thoughts on the issue – and then can decide whether, when and how the father might have contact with the child?

What about the kids? Is she thinking about the kids? Or is she simply thinking about herself – and the kids are tagging along for the ride. Regardless of whether they want to or not.

I felt sympathy for her. The story was long and distracted. It covered ground that I really did not need to know. Nonetheless, I felt sympathy. I saw her pain, and I felt for the kids who can so often be the victims of parents' relationships – with one another and with others.

I reflected how I could feel sympathy for her, care about her, care about her children, and yet have no relationship with her. Or, at least, no longer. You see, I was (and am!) the father of the first child! I'm the one she admitted during our conversation that she had sought to replace!

Everyone loses in the divorce derby

Divorce sucks. Women, men and children lose. They lose in different ways. This is not about who loses the most – that's impossible to say. But it is clear that all these people lose. So why do people go through it at all?

Before looking at ways that men and women might better deal with divorce, it is probably important to consider whether divorce is the correct solution. Perhaps divorce has simply become too easy. Not easy to go through, but easy to *start*. What if the reasons for the divorce are not past wrongs but future gains? The no-fault policy dismisses the reasons for the divorce allowing either party equal access to initiate a divorce. But the train of consequences are not equal.

> No-fault divorce gave women the keys, feminism gave them permission to leave, and child support laws ensured they wouldn't starve. Under no-fault standards, anyone could abandon a marriage for any reason. Whereas it took two to say 'I do,' it took only one to say 'I don't' and 'I'm outta here.'[35]

It appears on reflection that many parents do perhaps ask whether divorce was the best thing to do. Regardless of whether they regret it, it is pretty clear that divorce is probably more selfishly motivated than with the interests of the children in mind.

Realistically and unfortunately, divorce is unlikely to decline dramatically in any near future. So how might dads better prepare for marriage? Well, women should step into an ugly stereotype and men should step away from one. Women fall victim to the poverty trap post-divorce. Therefore, their best strategy is to choose carefully the man they marry in order to later divorce. He should be rich.

---

35   Arndt 2012.

Fathers should spend a lot of time with their kids while married. This will have at least two major effects on his long-term status as a father. First, in the unfortunate event of a divorce, the 'status quo' arrangement will be to have roughly the same amount of time with his kids after the breakup as before.

But the second effect is likely to be far more pervasive and encouraging. It is my strong belief that if he makes a 50 percent contribution to raising his children, his wife will not want to divorce him in the first place! That's right! If you try helping out around the house with the kids (and other domestic responsibilities!), I believe that you have a far greater chance of staying married.[36]

But if it turns out that your contribution to child care is deemed inadequate by the powers that be, and she initiates a divorce, you need to stand up for yourself a bit. This is no time for stoicism, mate. Do not move out of the house when *she* says she wants a divorce. If she is the one who chooses to break up the family, let her choose to be the one to leave the family home. Let her scream, jump up and down, and shake her fists at you, but do not move out of the house because *she* chooses to break up the family.

Of course, refusing to leave the family home if she wants out for instance is not necessarily easy. But negotiating the challenge is possible, and of course, it can be done with respect and civility. As one single father explained it:

Sophie initially went out and said she wanted to separate: 'You need to move out.' ... She wanted me to go and move into my parents' old house which my sister was in the process of vacating and it was a long way and the kids would not be remotely interested in going there. And I said that. I said 'I'll never see the kids If I go out there,

---

36 A recent study in Norway apparently found exactly the opposite – that the more housework a husband does the more likely he is to be divorced later. At least this was the media take on the story. The researchers themselves offered a very different explanation. Couples with pragmatic, secular views about marriage are more likely to (a) divide housework evenly, and (b) seek divorce if the relationship goes sour. In short, *b* doesn't cause *a*. Rather, *c* (pragmatic, secular views) causes both *b* and *a*; Divorce Risk for Couples Sharing Housework, *Ninemsn*, 28 September 2012. Retrieved 2 October 2012 from http://news.ninemsn.com.au/world/2012/09/28/02/39/divorce-risk-for-couples-sharing-housework.

I'm not doing that – you know, if you find this relationship, for reasons that you haven't explained, suddenly is so horrible, it's up to you to move out' and so we kind of got into a Mexican stand-off for almost 12 months.

Then when the divorce is in progress, men might step back from being so silently resilient in the face of trauma. It *is* an emotionally traumatic time. Going it alone will leave him lonely. Being lonely at times like these leads to substance abuse, depression, etc. That does not help him, and it definitely does not help the children.

Men may be placed in an unenviable position when divorce strikes – but that does not mean he should give up. When the enemy is external, it is typically men that step up to protect their kith and kin. They go away to foreign lands to protect their family. But when the enemy is within, when it is the woman that is giving him a hard time, he gives up.

Nonetheless, it is one thing to give up on the relationship with his wife; it is another entirely for him to give up on the relationship with his children! Making the best of a bad lot, this is the strength of a dad. The divorce maybe the man's Waterloo, but there is no way he should be driven from the field.

In the interest of reconciliation for the purposes of raising happy, healthy children, here are a few things Australian society should reconsider in terms of how divorces are 'done'.[37]

Assume equal contact with both parents as the default option unless individual circumstances dictate otherwise. We had something like this in Australia (*Shared Parental Responsibility Act 2006*), but it is by no means universal. Regrettably, recent amendments by the Gillard government have undermined this provision.

Enforce violations of court ordered child custody arrangements immediately when they are reported. Mothers denying access are not martyrs or heroes, and fathers seeking access are not villains. It is essentially a criminal act to deny a parent access to his or her child.

The custodial parent after a divorce should not unilaterally be allowed to move more than 200 kilometres away without court approval.

---

37   McCann 2000, 201; Farrell 2001, 52.

Any decision to do so should require a reconsideration of custody arrangements, or at least, that the custodial parent compensate the non-custodial parent for the travelling costs incurred in seeing their children at the new residence.

In summary, if you are a dad, you should get involved with your kids now (long before any tensions emerge in your marriage), do not move out of the house without question (if a separation seems unavoidable), and seek support once the blues begin. And above all, remember this. You do not *deserve* this. It is not your *fault*. She is ending your role as her husband, but you can still be very much in charge of your role as the father of your children. *Your children.*

Epilogue: the compleat child

To lose one parent may be regarded as a misfortune; to lose both looks like carelessness.

Wilde [1895] 1986, 267

There's only about one thing worse than a single-parented child, and that's one with no parents.

Occasionally nature dishes up this unpalatable dish, and most adults would not hesitate to step up to trying to fulfil the role of one of the missing parents.

In the past, nature also occasionally dished up the loss of one parent. Sometimes it was the mother because of death in childbirth. Sometimes it was the father because of his death in war.

Today, the world is different. Today, roughly one-fifth of all children are living in single-parent households, and roughly one-third will live in a single-parent home at some point in their lives.[1] This is probably a higher rate than at virtually any other time in the history of humans.

Why are things this way? Is it because a single-parent household is considered better for the child? No. It does not seem that anyone is

---

1   McCann 2000, 6; Linacre 2007.

claiming that. No, it exists because one parent decides that they do not want to live with the other parent. It is *not* generally because one parent decides they do not want to live with their children. Single parenthood is the collateral damage arising from more flexible adult relationships.

Compleat is an archaic spelling of the word 'complete', meaning that a long time ago this was the spelling people generally accepted as being correct, even though it seems kind of weird by our modern standards. Even more archaic is the notion that it takes (at least) two parents to make a compleat child. I say 'at least' in full acknowledgement that, in the physical sense, one father and one mother is all you need to make a child.

By God or by Nature, whichever your preference, it takes two people, one female and one male, to create a child. No matter how much of the work is done by the woman versus the man, no matter if the fertilisation takes place on a petri dish underneath a microscope, there *has* to be a contribution from a man.

But for much of human evolution, children have been raised by more than two adults, in social groups where uncles, aunts, older siblings, friends, and the neighbour with the huge banana tree in her back yard filled in as surrogate mums and dads from time to time. Even today, in many cultures children are raised in extended families where there may be several adult figures in the home who look after the children. An African saying (with historical roots in multiple countries) has it that it takes a village to raise a child.

As we discussed earlier, raising newborns to adulthood is a tough gig given the human reproductive strategy of quality over quantity. Human babies don't pop out of an egg with a fully developed behavioural repertoire for survival in the rough and tumble world. They have to be taught how to behave, and this tuition requires a considerable amount of time and effort relative to damn near every other species.

If nuclear families are a relatively recent innovation on the evolutionary scale of human development, then the emergence of single parent families is a microscopically tiny dot at the most recent end of the time line. Think of it this way. If all of human existence could be reduced to a single year, nuclear families would have been around for only a few minutes, and single parent homes barely a second. Single parent homes are still very much an evolutionary experiment in progress.

Here's the kicker, compared to a proverbial village, the familiar Western notion of a nuclear family with only a mother and a father to look after the children may represent a shortage of childcare labour in the family home; and single parent homes almost certainly place constraints on the amount of parental guidance available to children.

Perhaps humans are forever improving, but it is not clear that this latest development is ideal. One parent, looking after all the children in the home, all the time? That doesn't even sound right. No-fault divorce, and the resulting phenomenon, the single parent home, can be thought of as an evolutionary gamble in the grand scheme of things. And the stakes are frighteningly high – the physical, emotional, and intellectual fates of future generations of children.

Early in the era of no-fault divorce and single parent – actually single *mother* – households, the potential limitations of this family arrangement were implicitly understood. Children growing up with only their mother at home were said to be from 'broken' homes. But somewhere along the line 'broken' became normal, and the perceived necessity of paternal influence on child development began a long, slow decline.[2] Now the term often used in the academic literature is simply a 'father-absent' home, as if dads were truant schoolboys playing hooky on their families.

And it's not just about dads being absent from the parenting process, it is about mums being absent too. Women have pointed out that to be involved in the world of paid labour on an equal footing with men is difficult because mothers bear the bulk of the responsibility for childrearing. And as we saw in the chapter 'Deadbeat dads', there is considerable evidence to support this contention. Mothers do more of the domestic and child care labour in the typical family home than fathers, regardless of whether they pursue careers full-time or not.

Women do, however, have a choice. They can choose to step away into the corporate world. Just as men have a choice to step away into the domestic world of childrearing. One of the great wins for women is to have achieved so much in a relatively short period of time; for women to have a place beside men and to have the options of careers that are available to men. But this great achievement has come at a great cost.

---

2   Radin 1981, 410; Shanley 2001; Hertz 2006.

Women must choose: children or career. Some choose not to choose – the supermum who can do it all – as portrayed by Sarah Jessica Parker in the popular movie *I don't know how she does it*. But these women are looking at two decades of stress, a lack of sleep, the loss of a social life, no time for leisure, physical decline, and possibly career burnout. A high price to pay.

By fighting for equal footing in the world of professional success, women have won – and lost. Peter Cook in his book *Mothering matters* highlights one of these losses – the tendency to view the role of mother as somehow being less important than pursuing professional success. Women who are 'just' mothers have somehow copped out or abandoned the great crusade.

Professional achievements are wonderful, but the notion that motherhood is less important than having a career is absurd on the face of it. In the grand, evolutionary scheme of things, there is no role more important than motherhood. Think about it. Imagine a world where all women chose careers over maternity. No mums – no more humans.[3] Women would be advised not to let their relatively sudden influx into the labour market lead them to adopt the wrong set of priorities.

But the revolution of the female workforce has created problems for men too. Not only have they been knocked off their perches as the sole breadwinners of the family, but they've had to learn a whole new range of roles and responsibilities. Men are just now learning to value and give priority to raising their own children after over a century of spending time in the labour market largely removed from family life. Men are partly to blame for their own exclusion, but society in general doesn't always reinforce fathers who adopt these kinds of priorities. It takes a deal of courage on their parts to 'step up' to the challenge of succeeding in their careers and being good dads.

And how has all this affected the kids? Children placed in day care as virtual foundlings as their parents return to the grind? Sure child care can be outsourced, but at what level and at what cost? Of all the players in this triangle, the one that we should have the most sympathy for is the children. Why? Because they don't get to choose. They have to adapt to the decisions mum and dad make.

---

3 Cook 2008.

I remember being in a counselling session with my ex. She announced to the counsellor that 'we' were pregnant. (I resisted the urge to say 'no, I'm not' in this particular instance). His reply remains in my head: 'That's good; for now you will both learn what unconditional love looks like.' Unconditional? That's a high parenting bar to clear, no matter how much you love your kids.

Most of our concerns as parents are about how our child will turn out.[4] But what does that mean, exactly? If I say I want my son to attend Oxford, is that for him or for me? If I say I want my daughter to be a neurologist, is that for her or for me? So often we do not give consideration to what is best for the children – we simply short-circuit to what is best . . . for ourselves! But we're great at deluding ourselves about our selflessness along the way.

Parents often discover only in hindsight that their actions were not in the best interests of their child. Many baby-boomer parents are beginning to have second thoughts about the motivations for their divorce.[5] It was not in the best interests of the child – it was in their personal best interests. S/he was bored, had found someone new, couldn't deal with the day-to-day schlock that comes with any long-term relationship – and s/he moved on. The children? Oh, they'll come with me (if she's the mum). Oh, their mother will look after them (if he's the dad).

So, the best social arrangement for raising children may be a village – with at least one male and one female who are particularly committed to the project. But over the millennia the village has dwindled to two, and sometimes only one. Parents aren't always around, for a variety of reasons. Perhaps they die in an accident, perhaps their work forces them to be more absent than they would wish.

But often a parent's absence stems from their failed relationship with the other parent. There is a divorce and one or the other partner wins custody and removes the children elsewhere, or in the worst case scenarios, perhaps one parent simply steals the child away.

---

4 See http://www.mamamia.com.au/parenting/
nothing-we-worry-about-really-matters/.
5 Arndt 2012.

So what are the ideal conditions if the parents cannot agree to be together – if one disagrees to stay with the other? Keep contact with the other parent – even if they're unwilling.

If the father (or mother) is completely absent, find a substitute parent. But a word of caution; new lovers are *not* the same as substitute parents. Bringing a new lover around your children is a selfish decision. It's all about you. It is an understandable choice for a divorcee – but it has nothing to do with meeting the needs of the child. It is sadly the case that one of the most common outside perpetrators of child abuse – sexual and physical – is mum's new partner. Clearly these men were not chosen for their nurturing potential.

Absent dads, exhausted mums, incompleat children

What happens if dad, or the symbolic equivalent of a father, is simply left out of the equation? The research accumulated over the last 50 years or so suggests some less than favourable outcomes as far as children are concerned. The studies vary in their approaches. Some compare children from 'father-absent' homes to children who grew up living with their fathers, while holding constant or statistically correcting for other factors known to influence children's development (i.e. socioeconomic status, marital conflict, etc.).

Some studies focus on the amount of time fathers spend with their children in a variety of activities and then look for correlations with various developmental outcomes. Other researchers measure psychological and behavioural characteristics of mothers, fathers, and their children and determine which parent–child correlation is stronger for numerous characteristics. There are variations on these approaches, but in general the findings are that having dad around matters – a lot!

Roughly one third of all boys in Australia live in a household that does not include their biological father.[6] Some of the consequences of father-absent homes are not pretty. Fatherless boys are:

---

6   Biller 1981; Hoffman 1981, 364; Lamb 1981; Abramovitch 1997; Biller & Kimpton 1997; Hosley and Montemayor 1997; Lamb 1997a, 1997b; Pleck 1997; Harris et al. 1998; McCann 2000, 6; Farrell 2001; Dalton et al. 2006; Ellis et al. 2008; Baxter & Smart 2010, 131; You & Davis 2011.

five times more likely to commit suicide
14 times more likely to commit rape
nine times more likely to drop out of high school
10 times more likely to use drugs or abuse alcohol
20 times more likely to be incarcerated
nine times more likely to end up homeless
six times more likely to exhibit behavioural disorders

The effects of not having a father around can be observed almost immediately. Infants who are not visited by their fathers in the hospital put on weight more slowly and take longer to leave the hospital than infants who are visited by dad. One study suggests, unbelievably, that infants actually prefer to be held by their fathers over their mothers![7]

Conventional wisdom has it mothers are essential in a child's life from the very point of conception, whereas a father's role emerges only after the child becomes much older. Conventional wisdom is wrong. Children who lose their fathers before the age of two are more negatively affected than children whose lose their fathers at later ages.

---

7   Lamb 1977.

Whatever it is that fathers do, it starts to matter almost immediately in terms of the child's emotional and intellectual development.[8]

And one additional benefit of getting fathers involved in infant care may be a lower probability of mothers suffering from postpartum depression.[9]

As they grow up, children from fatherless homes exhibit a variety of negative characteristics. They are more selfish, less altruistic, and more limited in their moral reasoning, exhibiting less guilt and acceptance of blame for their transgressions, and showing less willingness to obey or conform to explicit rules or guidelines for behaviour. They have a higher frequency of delinquent behaviour, are more likely to become teenage parents, and experience lower levels of psychological well-being.[10]

Perhaps one of the great ironies of boys who grow up without fathers is that they often wind up being hyper-masculine rather than feminine. They don't necessarily become more like their mothers; they become more like the thugs they see on TV and in the movies. Think about it. How would a son without a father figure around learn what it means to be a man? Schoolmates? The guy with 127 tattoos who hangs around the bowling alley? Watching *Jersey Shore*? Going to see the latest Bond movie?

Children's ambition in life is correlated with fathers' not mothers' ambition, suggesting that dads play a major role in shaping children's dreams and aspirations. The amount of time a child spends around their father is related to their openness to new experiences, self-esteem, and success in athletic competition. Indeed, a child's exercise and fitness regimen is determined by their father's behaviour not their mother's.

Children who spend a lot of time around their fathers have a better sense of self-discipline or self-control. In one study, the ability of primary school children to resist an immediate temptation (a cookie) in order to obtain a larger reward (several cookies) later was positively correlated with the involvement of their fathers in family life.[11] Given

---

8   McCann 2000, 39.
9   Fagan & Lee 2010.
10   Pleck 1997.
11   Atkinson & Ogston 1974; Mischel 1961.

this result, it is perhaps not surprising that children who spend little or no time around their father have a higher risk of obesity, and poorer eating habits in general.[12] The inability to resist all those cookies apparently adds up over time.

Kids who spend more time around their fathers are also more likely to develop what is called an internal locus of control, a belief that they are in charge of their own destinies based on the actions they take and the preparations they make for the future. When fathers are mostly absent, either due to death, divorce, or a preoccupation with work, children are more likely to adopt an external locus, accepting the idea that everything that happens to them is beyond their control. Their futures are in the hands of fate.[13]

The father's but not the mother's locus of control predicts their child's ability to distinguish between safe and unsafe activities. This too, is perhaps not all that surprising given that children tend to learn about the world of hard knocks from their dads. They learn that the world is a potentially harmful and dangerous place from their fathers, but also about what precautions they can take to reduce or eliminate many hazards. A father who believes that steps can be taken to reduce danger (an internal locus of control) is more likely to pass those beliefs onto his children and to explain what to do in potentially unsafe situations.[14]

Children who grow up without a father around have a tougher time in school.[15] For one thing, fathers seem to influence the intellectual development of children. The cognitive effects of not having a father around are numerous. Children in father-absent homes have lower IQs, perform worse academically, and score lower on various cognitive skills tests, including social skills, verbal reasoning, perception of visual details, quantitative skills, perceptual-motor skills, spatial tasks, vocabulary, general linguistic skills, even after controlling for socioeconomic status.

The influence of fathers on linguistic skills may seem somewhat surprising given that women have superior verbal skills in general. Researchers have picked up on this apparent anomaly. Sadly, one ex-

---

12   Johnson-Down et al. 1997; Stewart & Menning 2009.
13   Biller & Kimpton 1997; Coppens 1985; Lamb 1997a.
14   Coppens 1985.
15   Biller & Kimpton 1997; Harris et al. (1998).

planation for this effect invokes the 'incompetent father' stereotype. Dads are insensitive to the cognitive limitations of children and hence use language that strains the limits of their kids' understanding. So, 'as a result of their incompetence men may inadvertently stretch their children's linguistic skills'.[16] Right. Dads are insensitive louts, but they wind up teaching their kids something anyway.

But the effects of not having a father around during the school years go beyond intellectual development. Children from father-absent homes go to bed later and at different times each night compared to children growing up with their fathers, who go to bed earlier, and at the same time every night. Fatherless children miss school more frequently, receive more suspensions and expulsions, and are less popular with their peers than children who live with their fathers. In general, the number of years of school completed is positively correlated with the number of years living with a father present in the family home.[17]

Unfortunately, many of the negative characteristics that emerge during the school years create additional problems as children progress into adulthood. Although mums seem to hold the title when it comes to empathy, it is actually the amount of time a child spends around his *father* that better predicts their capacity to empathise with others later in life as an adult.[18]

Not only do children from fatherless homes score lower on university entrance exams, but this also affects them later in life when they experience higher rates of unemployment.[19] Indeed, the amount of time a father spends with his children is positively correlated with the career success of those children later on in life.[20]
This is, perhaps, not surprising given that fathers are still, by and large, the breadwinners of most family households. It's easy to see why kids would associate fathers with professional achievement.

Sons and daughters who grow up with their father in the family home have better, more satisfying relationships later in life, and are

---

16 Lewis 1997.
17 McLanahan et al. 2013.
18 Biller & Kimpton 1997; Lamb 1997a; Pleck 1997.
19 McLanahan et al. 2013.
20 Biller & Kimpton 1997; Harris et al. 1998.

more confident of their ability to form and maintain close social connections than sons and daughters who grow up in fatherless homes.[21]

Daughters growing up in fatherless homes may have difficulty developing satisfying romantic relationships with men. They also tend to seek the attention of adult males and are generally more promiscuous.[22] This may, in part, be due to a tendency for fathers to place restrictions on the sexual behaviour of their daughters. Consistent with the popular stereotype, fathers may be an intimidating influence on their daughters, and perhaps more importantly, their daughters' boyfriends!

But perhaps the saddest influence of all is that children from fatherless homes are less involved with their own children, especially their sons. The cycle is essentially perpetuated from one generation to the next.[23]

Freud on dads

Perhaps one of the most unusual views of the unique contributions of fathers to the well-being of their children comes from Sigmund Freud. Most of us are familiar with the notion of an Oedipus complex, wherein a son unconsciously wishes to kill his father and become his mother's lover. While this is commonly discussed in 'pop' psychology circles, it is more or less consistent with what Freud theorised.[24]

Specifically, according to Freud a son unconsciously perceives his father as a rival for his mother's, um, shall we say 'affection', and fears that his father will castrate him in order to eliminate the rivalry. The initial resolution to this conflict results in a desire to kill his father. However, over time the son begins to identify with his father. This allows the son to repress the sexual desire for his mother, resulting in the next step in psychological development. The son wishes to emulate his father rather than kill him. Isn't that nice?

---

21 Biller & Kimpton 1997; McCann 2000.
22 McCann 2000.
23 Lamb 1981, 21–23; Radin 1981; Mullen et al. 1998; Cabrera et al. 2000.
24 Biller 1981; Abramovitch 1997.

Whether Freud was right or not about the unconscious psychological urges of male children, and there is considerable debate about
the value of this 'hypothesis', he almost certainly forced the analogy
to the Greek myth. In the actual story, Laius, the father of Oedipus,
does not actually want to become a father. He has to be tricked by
his wife Jocasta into becoming intoxicated before they have sex and
she conceives the child. Moreover, it is Jocasta who actually hands
the infant Oedipus over to his would be assassins. Hardly the kind of
mum a son should fall for.

One interpretation is that Freud merely projected his own unconscious desires for his mother, who was considerably younger
than his father, to develop his theory, and then went looking for ancient myths and more contemporary literary works to support his
hypothesis of a universal theme in all sons. Either way, it's kind of
creepy.

So why *does* growing up without a father around have negative consequences for children? It affects them in at least five ways. First, children
need role models to learn how to behave in certain situations. As they
get older, more and more of this learning involves 'acting grown up',
and having a father around is an excellent way to obtain this tuition.
For boys, the lessons are straightforward and direct. For girls, it is more
about learning how to interact with adult males, especially with respect
to developing long-term, romantic relationships. A daughter who grew
up with a dad around knows 'how men tick', and this knowledge pays
big dividends when she starts dating.

Second, as I noted above, father-absent homes are associated with
lower household incomes than father-present homes, and socioeconomic status is directly related to several emotional, intellectual and
behavioural outcomes in children. Third, although society has started
to come around to the idea of single mother homes, the stereotype of
a 'normal' family home is still very much one of married couple with
children, despite demographic data to the contrary.

Fourth, although fathers do less of the parental disciplining overall,[25] they may be more rigid in terms of demanding adherence to
rules.[26] As one father explained it:

I would say I'm a little bit more strict or more of a discipline figure with the girls. I am a lot harder on them in certain respects in that I actually expect more from the girls.

... You know, the little tricks that kids do to get attention or get their way, I don't stand for any of it, so they know to not try it on me. But they will try it on their mother still. Because it does – it does work.

If I say 'no', I stick to it. And it doesn't matter how much they whinge, complain anything at all – I stick to my 'no'. I said 'no' that's it, end of story.

Many fathers take the notion of discipline and responsibility to perhaps its ultimate level – a duty roster for each child in the family. The refrigerator door seems to be the designated place for the roster, and a white board with coloured pens the preferred method for recording duties. Each child has a list of chores to be completed each day and puts a tick by his or her name to indicate completion of the task.

Some dads even have rewards – stickers seem to be a popular choice for kids of all ages – for completing all chores successfully for an entire week or fortnight. The similarity to an official time sheet or duty roster in the office seems like more than a coincidence to me.

Finally, there is perhaps the biggest influence of all – perceived abandonment. To a child, 'if daddy doesn't live with us, daddy doesn't love us', is an all too easily reached explanation for a divorce. In a more general sense, father absence deprives children of a potentially loving relationship with an adult, even if they believe their daddy still loves them to pieces. This was the single thought that motivated me throughout my divorce proceedings. My son was 6; my daughter 2. I would not lose them; I would not 'abandon' them. Take the family home; take the company assets; but you will not take my kids away from me. No, actually, you will not take *me* away from my kids.

Having summarised a lot of research showing how important it is for children to have their dads around, I'll now sprinkle in several grains of salt. We have to qualify some of the conclusions that can be drawn from all this research. First, if you remove a father's love from

---

25 Hosley & Montemayor 1997, 169.
26 Hoffman 1981, 360; Hetherington et al.1997; Farrell 2001, 47.

a child's life, these and other bad things are *more likely* to happen; but only *more likely*. None of the things discussed here are definite outcomes of not having fathers around.

A child from a father-absent home is perfectly capable of being psychologically well-adjusted, intelligent, law-abiding, happily married, of winning the Nobel Prize in medicine, and inventing a side rear-view mirror where the cars appear exactly as close as they actually are. He may even one day grow up to become President of the United States, as Barack Obama, the son of a single mother, did in 2008.

Indeed, there are many important contingency factors affecting the extent to which father absence results in psychological and behavioural deficits in children, but one of the most consistent determinants is the child's age when the father leaves the family home. Although there is no magic number, the effect on school-age children is not as great as when the father leaves prior to the onset of formal education.[27]

There is some evidence that boys may be affected more than girls by the absence of their fathers.[28] Much recent research suggests that fathers favour sons over daughters by spending more time with them, and being more involved with their general upbringing.[29] This bias even persists after divorce. A non-resident father is less likely to maintain contact if he has only daughters compared to only sons.

Does this indicate that fathers actually *prefer* to spend time with their sons more than their daughters? It seems at least as likely that fathers are restricted in what they can do with their daughters, by their spouses, and by society in general. Remember my experience trying to shop for my daugher's undies? Could this have something to do with the disparity in time fathers spend with sons versus daughters? Daughters need to learn about personal hygiene, using hair pins, wearing bras, periods, etc. How, exactly, is dad going to broach this territory if he can't even buy undies for his daughter?

Rather than favouring sons over daughters, fathers may simply feel freer to interact with their sons in a broader range of activities. Some research suggests that mothers interact with their daughters and sons

---

27 Biller 1981; Farrell 2001; Jeynes 2002; Lamb 2004b.
28 Biller & Kimpton 1997, 149.
29 Hosley & Montemayor 1997; Radin 1981, 384.

differently. It may be the gender match of the parent-child that influences how and how often parents interact with their children.[30]

For example, fathers may perform the simple act of buying clothes for their sons without any prompting. It's just a matter of selecting slightly smaller versions of what they wear themselves. But we already have an inkling of the difficulties fathers might encounter shopping for clothes for their daughters. Apparel purchases are just one small part of being a parent, but they provide a window of understanding into why fathers might wind up spending more time looking after their sons compared to their daughters.[31]

In addition to taking into account all of these contingency factors we have to be exceedingly careful in interpreting what all this research actually establishes. Are all these effects due to the absence of fathers, or could there be other factors involved? Single mother families and married couple families differ on many variables besides simply the absence of the father in the family home. For example, divorces are usually preceded by marital discord, and this conflict is often exacerbated by the official split.

Now it would hardly be a shocking scientific discovery if children from families with high marital discord were found to exhibit cognitive, emotional, and behavioural deficits relative to children from harmonious, loving family homes. Yet, this could well be the underlying difference of importance between single-mother and married couple homes, not the absence of the father per se.[32]

Likewise, financial difficulties are a major cause of divorces, and research shows a clear link between socio-economic status and child development, particularly with respect to academic performance. So, 'father absence' may be a surrogate for a more complex array of factors affecting the intellectual and emotional development of children.

Another related issue is that not all 'father-absent' homes are the same, particularly with respect to a child's exposure to father substitutes

---

30 Conrade & Ho 2001.
31 Some research suggests that fathers spend more time with sons than daughters at an early age, even when children are infants. So another part of the problem may involve the choices that fathers make about which children will receive the most attention (see Lamb 1981, p. 17).
32 Biller 1981, 490–92; Lamb 1997a; Jeynes 2002; Ghazarian & Buehler 2010.

who can facilitate the same kinds of psychological and behavioural outcomes. Research suggests that stepfathers, older brothers, uncles, male school teachers and community volunteers can provide meaningful substitutes for biological fathers in some areas of development, so it may really be the complete absence of any male role model that leads to many of the developmental deficits discussed here.[33]

Moreover, the research does not establish that fathers are more important than mothers or are somehow the primary source for all of these benefits to the intellectual, emotional, spiritual, and physical health of children. Indeed, research suggests the opposite – that mothers provide more of these benefits than fathers.[34]

For example, children derive feelings of emotional security more from their mums than their dads.[35] Nevertheless, a child raised by both parents will be more emotionally secure than a child raised by a single mother. Mothers facilitate the cognitive development of toddlers more than fathers, but a toddler who spends time with daddy as well as mummy will show higher levels of cognitive development on average.[36]

To a large extent these effects can be explained by taking into account the variance in the amount of involvement of fathers versus mothers. It is currently the case for many families that mums are the constants in their children's lives. The go-to parents. They are always there – reliable and dependable. Mums' involvement is the constant; dads' the variable. It's hardly surprising then that fathers' influence is more predictive of children's outcomes. You need variance in parental behaviour to predict variance in children's behaviour.[37]

Indeed this research may not be telling us about the effects of fathers at all, but rather about the effects of the lesser involved of the two parents. In short, sometimes mum is the second parent. Research on the involvement of non-resident mothers in their children's lives shows similar benefits to those provided by involved non-resident fathers.[38] Children with highly involved non-resident mothers do better on many

33 Biller 1981, 500–01; McCann 2000.
34 Lewis 1997, 140.
35 Markiewicz et al. 2006.
36 Averett et al. 2005.
37 Biller & Kimpton 1997, 157.
38 Hetherington & Stanley-Hagan 1997, 202–03.

of these same outcomes than children with relatively uninvolved non-resident mothers. In essence, It may be more about parental roles than gender per se.

Another related point is that, although I've focused on differences, much of what dads and mums do for their children is similar. Despite gender stereotypes to the contrary, dads provide warmth, nurturance, and a sense of closeness to their children, just as mums play games, enforce rules, and expose children to risks.[39]

And as one final point of qualification I might note that much of this research is based on self-reports of mums and dads about their parenting behaviour in the past. These memories are likely to be inaccurate and biased to convey socially desirable outcomes and contemporary stereotypes. Some studies even ask mums to answer questions about their spouses' parenting behaviours, exacerbating potential bias due to gender stereotypes. Nevertheless, on balance the research seems to show that having dad around in the family home is good for kids.

It's hard to let go

The message to mums then is to get your hubbies involved in the parenting gig as soon and as often as possible, for the good of your children ... and your hubbies ... and yourselves! But as the subtitle of this book implies, this involves giving fathers more responsibility and authority, and generally a freer rein to do things as they see fit; and as we noted earlier, this will be exceedingly difficult for mothers who love, care about, and more importantly, worry about their children. Can he be trusted? Will he do a good job? Can he cut the mustard in a crisis situation?

But mums simply can't have their cake and eat it too. Responsibility and authority go hand in hand here. If you want him to do half the work, he'll want more say about how things will be done. Otherwise he'll be nothing more than your personal assistant in the home. Sounds good you say? How do women feel about being nothing more than personal assistants in the office? Right. Thought so. Let's move on.

---

39   Lamb 1997a.

Here is a short list of the areas where mums are most likely to find it difficult to let go of their implicit positions of authority: children's fashion, risk taking, cleaning, play dates, and school activities.[40] Let's take a look at each of these domains in order to examine why mothers might want to retain control over these kinds of decisions.

We'll start with a relatively easy one – children's fashion. Let me just state at the outset that there are some pretty strong arguments for why mothers *should* retain ultimate veto power on all things related to children's clothes, hairstyles, shoes, school uniforms, and, near anything related to how the child looks when he or she ventures into the world. Let's face it men, when it comes to fashion, we are hopelessly outgunned.

My wife has 150 pairs of shoes; I have five. She has D'Orsays, wedges, loafers, Mary Janes, platforms, pumps, slingbacks, slip-ons and strappy dress shoes; leather, patent, satin, sequin, suede and synthetic dress shoes; espadrilles, gladiators, flip flops, platforms and slides; wedges, flat heels, low heels, high heels and ultra-high heels; casual, dress, outdoor and wedding sandals; hiking, lace-up, rain, slip-on, Western, zipper, career, ankle, midcalf and knee-high boots; slip-on, bootie, moccasin and slide slippers; athletic shoes and so on. And of course, many, many shoe accessories. I have dress shoes, casual shoes, sports shoes and thongs.

Research suggests that women buy 100 percent of their own clothes – and most of their husbands' clothes – and maybe this is a good thing.[41] Perhaps nothing is sadder than watching a wife in a department store sending her husband to the change room to try on clothes that she has picked out for him. He's bored and embarrassed; she's mildly annoyed.

And the very notion that a man could force his wife to try on clothes that he selected for her is positively absurd! Indeed, the very thought of buying a dress or a pair of shoes for his wife strikes fear and dread in the hearts of most husbands. Most men make a fairly direct transition from having their mums buy their clothes for them to having their wives take over this role. As a result, women have come to expect men to be crap at all things fashion.

---

40 Deutsch 1999, 227.
41 Miley & Mack 2009.

I used to work as a salesperson in an apparel shop. One of the turning points in my relationship with my wife was when I bought her a dress – and she actually liked it! Now I know what you women readers are thinking – she didn't really like the dress at all but she just didn't want to hurt my feelings. Shame on you! Here's how I know otherwise.

First of all, my wife doesn't give a damn about hurting my feelings. She does it all the time. Second, and perhaps more to the point, she wears that dress all the time, and the more important the occasion, the more likely she is to wear it. I actually got it right, and in this case, the exception sort of proved the rule. She just could not believe that I noted her clothing preferences over time then simply extrapolated to a green dress in a shop window display (and by this time I'd learned that green was her favourite colour for clothes). That I did this while away on a business trip got me extra brownie points.

(Note to male readers: If you want to be able to do this well, you must pay attention to what your wife wears and how she looks. Pay her compliments. Even better, ask her questions about her clothing preferences. You initiate conversations along these lines and I promise you that there will be benefits far and beyond the ability to buy her dresses.)

But when it comes to dressing children, most dads emphasise function to the point of complete disregard for form.[42] The very notion that clothes must 'match' seems completely lost on most dads, as Nigel Marsh, a stay-at-home dad trying to make inroads on the children's fashion front, conveys his book *Fat, forty and fired*:

> 'Oh no, not in that!' she exclaimed the first time I emerged from the girls' bedrooms with two dressed twins.
> 'Why not?'
> 'Because I never put those tops with those skirts,' she replied.
> 'Why not?' I asked.
> 'I prefer it if they wear their green tops with those skirts,' she explained.
> 'But you asked me to dress them,' I protested.
> 'Yes, but I like them in a different outfit.'

---

42 Bryant 2001, 121–22.

'Yes, but you asked me to dress them – I've dressed them. They look fine.'

'No need to get upset about it – I'll quickly change them.'

'No, you won't,' I replied.

'Why not?'

'Because I want them to wear what they've got on. What I, their father, chose for them to wear.'[43]

Good luck Nigel. Unfortunately, dads seem to lose this battle more often than not. I simply no longer challenge my wife when it comes to my daughter's clothes. In the grand scheme of things, most dads would probably concede fashion decisions, so this is not likely to be a make or break issue. Having acknowledged this, I'd warn mums about pushing this natural advantage to the point where dad eschews all clothing tasks and responsibilities. There will be mornings where you'll want him to dress the kids while you sleep late. Make sure you haven't shut him out of this space completely.

The next area, risk taking, is a little more delicate. It can ruin an otherwise idyllic marriage if not handled properly. Men take risks; women take precautions; and this basic difference transfers to parenting styles.[44] Not surprisingly, research indicates that mothers worry about their children more than fathers do.[45]

At least part of the risk fathers expose their children to involves cuts and bruises from physical play. Children are more likely to suffer minor injuries in rough and tumble with daddy compared to mummy.[46] More telling is the reaction to these little mishaps. Mums are often overprotective and mollycoddling,[47] and may even chastise dads for playing too rough right in front of the children.

This is precisely what happened when my three-year-old suffered a nose bleed after playing a little indoor footy with me. My reaction? Kids are going to get hurt. That's what happens in life. My son was better off suffering a minor injury and understanding this basic life lesson

---

43 Marsh 2007, 64–65.
44 Chira 1994, A22.
45 Walzer 1996.
46 McCann 2000, 40; Farrell 2001.
47 Baxter & Smart 2010, 29, 143.

with me there than to live an injury-free childhood before entering the world as a clueless adult.

Pre-school and primary school teachers, overwhelmingly women, also reinforce the stereotype that dads are 'too rough'. I was attending my son's pre-school and playing with several kids in the yard. We chased and tussled, kicked a ball, then a group of kids all started to wrestle me and play 'stacks on the mill'. They were having a blast all shrieking with pleasure. However, the women teachers (there were no men aside from me) rushed in and told us to stop. I was told this was 'inappropriate' behaviour. I think it was 'different' behaviour – different from what a mum would do.

But I think there's an important thing here about how men are a little looser with kids, and this isn't a bad thing! Despite the ouches from playing with daddy, fathers are generally the preferred playmates of children between the ages of two and six, the rough and tumble years for both genders. After the age of six, mummy often becomes the favourite playmate of girls.[48]

The tendency for dads to engage in physical play with their children emerges at a very early age. Even in the hospital in the nursery for preterm births, fathers are more likely to stimulate and play with their babies. By the ripe old age of six months, fathers promote physically stimulating and unpredictable play more than mothers.[49]

The world is tough, and children tend to learn this from fathers not mothers. If there is one, single area where it is most difficult for mothers to 'let go', this is probably it.

Indeed, fathers can (perhaps inadvertently) teach their children an awful lot about life through play. One study suggests that a father's contribution to his children's sense of attachment and security may have more to do with 'sensitive and challenging play' during primary and high school years than anything daddy did when his children were still in nappies.[50]

Dads just seem to have a knack for creating fun and exciting games out of seemingly mundane or even difficult situations. In his book *Dads, toddlers & the chicken dance*, Peter Downey describes a variety of

---

48 Lamb 1981, 18.
49 Lamb 1997b, 104–20.
50 Grossman et al. 2002.

games for toddlers that can turn eating into entertainment. Among the more promising are:

- Here comes the airplane! (An oldie but goody)
- Make a new funny face every time they swallow a mouthful
- Bury vegetables under mashed potatoes and tell them to dig for treasure
- Give foods interesting names (Squash, for example, becomes a Yellow Submarine, instantly improving its palatability)
- Present food in interesting ways (It's amazing what you can do by cutting an apple or a sandwich to resemble something far more interesting).[51]

Another area where daddy's playfulness can pay dividends is getting children to do chores regularly.[52] Some of the ideas are fairly obvious. For example, getting your kids to put their dirty clothes in the clothes bin is as easy as a simulated game of basketball. Designate the three-point line in their room; encourage slam dunk contests; off-the-wall trick shots; anything to inject a little enthusiasm into this simple act. One word of warning, however. Everybody knows that socks fly truer when they are balled up, so you may spend a bit more time than usual un-balling socks before tossing them in the washer (is 'un-balling' a legitimate verb?)

Now I'm not saying for a second that mums cannot or do not invent games like this for their kids. They can and do. But dads can be great at just this sort of silliness. One dad at the health and fitness centre where I exercise takes his two sons for swimming lessons every day. His sons look to be about 4 and 3 years of age, so the lessons probably require an enormous amount of patience. This is serious fathering folks!

Anyway, after the swimming lesson dad and his two boys must shower and change with the grown up men. Now any parent who's tried to guide their children through this kind of process knows that it is often hard for kids to focus long enough to actually dry off and get into their clothes. How does dad solve this little dilemma? By turning it into

---

51 Downey 1997, 29.
52 Levine 2000, 161.

a race of course. This may not seem all that imaginative. But dad calls the event as if it were an actual horse race.

'Billy is coming up fast with his undies and shorts on. But wait! Here comes Bobby with a quick pullover of his shirt. They're neck and neck with socks. First the left, then the right.' All the while dad's voice is rising in volume and intonation, the way an announcer calling an actual race would do it. 'Now it's all down to the tying of the last shoes lace. It's close! Ah, and it's Billy by a nose!' All the men in the shower are treated to this little routine at around 6:30 pm every weekday. But it works. Those kids get dressed fast!

Having hyped up daddy as the best of all playmates, let me now note a rather significant qualifier. Much of the time taken up by 'playing' with dad involves a rather mundane activity – watching television together;[53] and though I'm not aware of any research on the topic, I suspect another favourite playtime activity of fathers everywhere is videogaming. I especially like the games where you kill several species of aliens in a variety of planetscapes. I found this to be very educational for my six-year old daughter. In no time she was able to distinguish between numerous weapons and could articulate the relative advantages of each for killing one kind of alien versus another. Contingency learning. Hey, just trying to be a good dad.

Another likely area of contention is the level of filth deemed acceptable in the family home. Just an anecdotal observation here – women seem to have lower filth thresholds and lower filth tolerance levels than men. By the way, these two things are not the same. The filth *threshold* is the point at which something begins to look dirty – the point at which the filth first becomes noticeable. Women notice filth before men, but this is not as big a sticking point as you might think.

The filth *tolerance level*, on the other hand, is the maximum amount of filth that can be endured in the family domicile before it starts to drive you stark, raving mad! Women freak out sooner than men and this is potentially a big problem. As I mentioned in the opening chapter, one of the most obvious ploys dads use to avoid doing housework is simply ignoring the various domestic labour tasks that need to be performed to ensure a happy, healthy family home.

---

53   Hosley & Montemayor 1997, 166.

Nowhere is the ignorance tactic more effective than for household cleaning tasks. It is astounding to consider the extent of the difference in filth tolerance thresholds between men and women, and no doubt, it would be difficult to calibrate the exact figure; but to get an idea of the difference, women might consider taking a peek into any public male toilet.

No worries. We men won't care, even if we're in the act. Women, of course, abhor the idea of a man peeking into their toilet, but that's another gender difference I don't want to go into right now. Take it from me, the filth level in a typical male public toilet would astound women. In some pubs the men's toilets, literally, have a pool of urine on the floor which must be waded through to reach the urinals. Do men complain about these unsanitary conditions? Nope. It's just back to the bar for another beer.

What all this translates into is that giving dads cleaning tasks is likely to result in outcomes perceived as hopelessly inadequate and incompetent by mums. Mums will want to correct him right away. Fight the urge, or at least use very subtle, deferential language in doing so; something like 'I see how you're doing that and it really is an efficient way to clean [soften him up a bit – men like efficiency], but when I do it this way, it does take a lot longer but [proceed to obvious superiority in terms of actual cleanliness and hygienic state].'

Another potential minefield for mums wanting to get their husbands more involved is arranging play dates. Two parents, each responsible for one child, have a needy, attention-seeking, potentially irritable problem on their hands. But bring one kid over to other kid's house and you've got two entertained and happy children, one parent who's completely free to do as they like, and one parent who probably has more free time than they would have otherwise.

It should be fairly obvious that the quid pro quo, you-scratch-my-back-I'll-scratch-yours thing is built into this little arrangement.

But half the difficulty of actually arranging a play date is managing the logistics. You've got to know whether your son has a soccer match that day, what time your daughter's guitar lesson is, whether the birthday party for your son's schoolmate is today or tomorrow, whether your daughter's appointment for the optometrist is at two or three. All this must be taken into account, not only for the kids, but for the parents who are trying to obtain the maximum benefits from their newly created free time.

Many mums know these things. Many dads don't. Many mothers juggle the week-to-week, day-to-day, hour-by-hour, minute-by-minute routines of every member of the family. Many dads don't. If ever the subtitle 'Fathers stepping up' had meaning, this is the area. Taking your son to his soccer match because your wife told you to is *not* the same as knowing that your son's match is at Enfield Park, Oval 2, at 9:30 am for a 10 am match, and arranging for your son to get there on time, with his soccer uniform washed and dried, and all his equipment (shoes, shin pads, socks, etc.) cleaned up from the last match. Dads you have been advised. Learn this difference.

Then there is the big first step – when a dad makes the inaugural call – to another kid's mum – to invite her child over – with only him around – for a play date – and a sleepover! Go ahead dads! Buy the ticket! Take the ride!

The bigger issue with play dates is, perhaps, that mums want to select who their kids associate with. This is hardly a surprise. Husbands, be honest. Whose friends have you spent more time with since your marriage, hers or yours? Right. Women want to be in charge of the social relationships that connect the family with the outside world; and as with fashion, they are better at it.

So mums may arrange most of the play dates, but dads should at least be comfortable and capable of arranging them from time to time. Remember, mums will have to take the odd business trip or weekend getaway with her girlfriends, and dads will need to survive these little excursions. Play dates are perfect for these sorts of situations. Mums have known this for decades. Time for dads to climb aboard.

Finally, we have school activities. Primary schools are not generally places where you will find lots of dads. Not among the teaching staff, on the parent committee, at parent–teacher conferences, or even one-on-one parent teacher meetings. I remember meeting my daughter's Year 1 teacher at one of these. The first thing she said, innocently enough, was 'Oh, I don't get many dads.' Just an 'ice breaker' I'm sure, but one with the implicit message that dads just don't do this sort of thing. They should. And mums are in the best position to encourage (demand?) this kind of involvement.

One of my proudest moments was when I agreed to do some baking for my kids' school fete. I, of course, went with my go-to dessert – chocolate chip oatmeal cookies. Several of the mums also baked cookies – but mine were the hot ticket of the afternoon. Another proud moment involved impressing a group of mums with my 'invention' of freezing yoghurt tubes to create healthy fun-to-eat treats. The mums were impressed, surprised, and then surprised at how impressed they were. A dad came up with that? Suddenly, I felt like a part of the school parent fold.

More dads should experience the kind of pride that comes from being involved in their kids' lives rather than the kind that comes from a number on their fortnightly payslip.

What is a father?

A father is a person who is forced to endure childbirth without an anaesthetic.

He growls when he feels good and laughs very loud when he is scared half-to-death.

A father never feels entirely worthy of the worship in a child's eyes.

He is never quite the hero his daughter thinks. Never quite the man his son believes him to be. And this worries him sometimes. (So he works too hard to try to smooth the rough places in the road of those of his own who will follow him.)

A father is a person who goes to war sometimes . . . and would run the other way except that war is part of an important job in his life (which is making the world better for his child than it has been for him).

Fathers grow older faster than other people, because they, in other wars, have to stand at the train station and wave goodbye to the uniform that climbs on board.

And, while mothers cry where it shows, fathers stand and beam . . . outside . . . and die inside.

Fathers are men who give daughters away to other men who aren't nearly good enough, so that they can have children that are smarter than anybody's.

> Fathers fight dragons almost daily. They hurry away from the breakfast table off to the arena, which is sometimes called an office or a workshop. There they tackle the dragon with three heads: Weariness, Works, and Monotony. And they never quite win the fight, but they never give up.
>
> Knights in shining armour; fathers in shiny trousers. There's little difference as they march away each workday.[54]

Of all the findings regarding the influence of fathers on children, I'd like to close with perhaps the most important of all. The amount of time a father spends around his children is positively correlated with children's acceptance of egalitarian gender roles. When kids observe their father around the house doing things like cleaning, laundry, helping with homework, playing video games, arranging play dates, taking them to the beach, giving them medicine when they're sick, putting them to bed at night, and baking cookies for their school fete, they come to see mummy and daddy as being responsible for similar things. There are no breadwinners or homemakers in their family. Mummy and daddy both have jobs and both do things around the house. One of the basic causes of the glass ceiling is eliminated from society – one child at a time.

---

54 Fuller & Batura 2011. The author is unknown but it is often attributed to longtime US radio personality Paul Harvey.

Works cited

Abramovitch H (1997). Images of the 'father' in psychology and religion. In ME Lamb (Ed.). *The role of the father in child development* (3rd edn), (pp19–32). New York: John Wiley & Sons.

Agerbo E, Mortensen PB & Munk-Olsen T (2012). Childlessness, parental mortality and psychiatric illness: a natural experiment based on in vitro fertility treatment and adoption. *Journal of Epidemiology and Community Health*, 67: 374–76.

Alexander H (2013). False abuse claims are the new court weapon, retiring judge says. *Sydney Morning Herald*, 6 July [Online]. Available: http://www.smh.com.au/national/false-abuse-claims-are-the-new-court-weapon-retiring-judge-says-20130705-2phao.html [Accessed 4 August 2013].

Allen SM & Hawkins AJ (1999). Maternal gatekeeping: mothers' beliefs and behaviors that inhibit greater father involvement in family work. *Journal of Marriage and the Family*, 61: 199–212.

Arditti JA, Smock SA & Parkman TS (2005). 'It's been hard to be a father': a qualitative exploration of incarcerated fatherhood. *Fathering: A Journal of Theory, Research, and Practice about Men as Fathers*, 3(3): 267–88.

Areni CS (2014). Gender inequity in the family household: the more things change the more they stay the same. Working paper, Macquarie Graduate School of Management.

Areni CS (2008). Salvation of the second shift: are wives immune to Monday blues? In AL McGill & S Shavitt (Eds). *Advances in consumer research*, Vol. 36, (pp444–48). Duluth, MN: Association for Consumer Research.

Armour S (2007). Workplace tensions rise as dads seek family time. *USA Today*, 12 November [Online]. Available: http://usatoday30.usatoday.com/money/ workplace/2007-12-10-working-dads_N.htm [Accessed 28 August 2013].

Arndt B (2012). Divorced parents decry own selfishness. *The Australian*, 26 April [Online]. Available: http://www.theaustralian.com.au/national-affairs/ opinion/divorced-parents-decry-own-selfishness/ story-e6frgd0x-1226338293411 [Accessed 4 September 2013].

Atkinson BR & Ogston DG (1974). The effect of father absence on male children in the home and school. *Journal of Social Psychology*, 12(3): 213–21.

Averett SL, Gennetian LA & Peters HE (2005). Parental child care and children's development. *Journal of Population Economics*, 18: 391–414.

Baker R (1996). *Sperm wars: the science of sex*. New York: BasicBooks.

Barreto M, Ryan MK & Schmitt MT (2009). Introduction: is the glass ceiling still relevant in the 21st century. In M Barreto, MK Ryan & MT Schmitt (Eds). *The glass ceiling in the 21st century: understanding barriers to gender equality* (pp9–18). Washington DC: American Psychological Association.

Baxter J & Smart D (2010). *Fathering in Australia among couple families with young children*. Canberra, ACT: Department of Families, Housing, Community Services and Indigenous Affairs.

Bedard K & Deschenes O (2005). Sex preferences, marital dissolution, and the economic status of women. *Journal of Human Resources*, 40(2): 411–34.

Beitel AH & Parke RD (1998). Paternal involvement in infancy: the role of maternal and paternal attitudes. *Journal of Family Psychology*, 12: 268–88.

Bellis MA, Hughes K, Hughes S & Ashton JR (2005). Measuring paternal discrepancy and its public health consequences. *Journal of Epidemiology & Community Health*, 59(9): 749–54 [Online]. Available: http://www.ncbi.nlm.nih.gov/pubmed/16100312 [Accessed 4 September 2013].

Benatar D (2012). *The second sexism: discrimination against men and boys*. Oxford, UK: Wiley-Blackwell.

Berlatsky N (2013). What the rising number of single dads says about fatherhood. *The Atlantic Monthly*, 3 July [Online]. Available: http://www.theatlantic.com/ sexes/archive/2013/07/ what-the-rising-number-of-single-dads-says-about-fatherhood-in-general/ 277498/ [Accessed 28 August 2013].

Berry S (2012). Common regrets of the dying. *The Sydney Morning Herald*, 16 July [Online]. Available: http://www.smh.com.au/lifestyle/life/ common-regrets-of-the-dying-20120716-224y2.html [Accessed 11 September 2013].

Biller HB (1981). Father absence, divorce, and personality development. In ME Lamb (Ed.). *The role of the father in child development* (2nd edn), (pp489–552). New York: John Wiley & Sons.

Biller HB & Kimpton JL (1997). The father and the school-aged child. In ME Lamb (Ed.). *The role of the father in child development* (3rd edn), (pp143–61). New York: John Wiley & Sons.

Blair SL & Lichter DT (1991). Measuring the division of household labor: gender segregation of housework among American couples. *Journal of Family Issues*, 12(1): 91–113.

Boroughs DL, Hage D, Black RF & Newman RJ (1992). Love & money: the dark shadow of recession is contributing to the breakup of hearts and homes all across America. *US News and World Report*, 19 October, 54–60.

Bozett FW (1985). Male development and fathering throughout the life cycle. *The American Behavioral Scientist*, 29(1): 41–54.

Braaf R & Meyering IB (2011). *Seeking security: promoting women's economic well-being following domestic violence.* Sydney: Australian Domestic and Family Violence Clearinghouse.

Bratberg E & Tjotta S (2008). Income effects of divorce in families with dependent children. *Journal of Population Economics*, 21(2): 439–61.

Brinig M & Allen D (2000). 'These boots are made for walking': why most divorce filers are women. *American Law and Economics Review,* 2: 126–69.

Bryant T (2001). *Man with a pram: a year on the wild side with a stay-at-home dad.* Sydney: ABC Books.

Burnett SB, Gatrell CJ, Cooper CL & Sparrow P (2010). Well-balanced families? A gendered analysis of work–life balance policies and work family practices. *Gender in Management: An International Journal*, 25(7): 534–49.

Butsch R (1992). Class and gender in four decades of television situation comedy: plus ça change . . . *Critical Studies in Mass Communication*, 9: 387–99.

Cabrera NJ, Shannon JD & Tamis-LeMonda C (2007). Fathers' influence on their children's cognitive and emotional development: from toddlers to pre-K. *Applied Development Science,* 11(4): 208–13.

Cabrera N, Tamis-LeMonda CS, Bradley RH, Hofferth S & Lamb ME (2000). Fatherhood in the twenty-first century. *Child Development*, 71(1): 127–36.

Caldwell M, Henry P & Watson S (2007). A right to life: reducing maternal deaths in Pakistan [Online]. Available: http://vimeo.com/groups/136972/videos/ 11414359 [Accessed 3 February 2013].

Cancian M & Meyer DR (1998). Who gets custody? *Demography*, 35(2): 147–57.

Cannold L (2013). Should dads be in the birthing suite? *The Hoopla*, 13 July [Online]. Available: http://www.thehoopla.com.au/dads-birthing-suite/ [Accessed 4 September 2013].

Carson-DeWitt R (2009). How sex may relieve migraine pain? *About.com*, 27 January [Online]. Available: http://www.headaches.about.com/lw/ Health-Medicine/Alternative-treatments/ How-Sex-May-Relieve-Migraine-Pain.htm [Accessed 4 September 2013].

Casper LM & O'Connell M (1998). Work, income, the economy, and married fathers as child-care providers. *Demography*, 35(2): 243–50.

Chesters J, Baxter J & Western M (2009). Paid and unpaid work in Australian households: trends in the gender division of labour, 1986–2005. *Australian Journal of Labour Economics*, 12: 89–107.

Chira S (1994). War over the role of American fathers. *New York Times*, 19 June, A22.

Christiansen SL & Palkovitz R (2001). Why the 'good provider' role still matters: providing as a form of paternal involvement. *Journal of Family Issues*, 22(1): 84–106.

Clay MM (1989). *Quadruplets and higher multiple births*. London: MacKeith Press.

Cohen S (2012). Should buying donor eggs carry a criminal charge? *The Huffington Post*, 2 May [Online]. Available: http://www.huffingtonpost.ca/ sara-cohen/donor-eggs_b_1465807.html [Accessed 4 September 2013].

Collins L & Lapierre D (1997 [1975]). *Freedom at midnight*. London, UK: HarperCollins.

Conrade G & Ho R (2001). Differential parenting styles for fathers and mothers: differential treatment for sons and daughters. *Australian Journal of Psychology*, 53(1): 29–35

Cook P (2008). *Mothering matters: the sources of love, and how our culture harms infants, women, and society*. Balwyn, VIC: Freedom Publishing.

Cooper M (2000). Being the 'go-to guy': fatherhood, masculinity, and the organization of work in Silicon Valley. *Qualitative Sociology*, 23(4): 379–405.

Coppens NM (1985). Cognitive development and locus of control as predictors of pre-schoolers' understanding of safety and prevention. *Journal of Applied Developmental Psychology*, 6: 43–55.

Cox L (2008). Headaches and sex: 'yes, tonight dear'. *ABC News Medical Unit*, 5 February [Online]. Available: http://abcnews.go.com/Health/ PainManagement/story?id=4241193 [Accessed 4 September 2013].

Craig L (2005). The money or the care: a comparison of couple and sole parent households' time allocation to work and children. *Australian Journal of Social Issues*, 40: 521–40.

Craig L (2006a). Children and the revolution: a time-diary analysis of the impact of motherhood on daily workload. *Journal of Sociology*, 42: 125–43.

Craig L (2006b). Does father care mean fathers share? A comparison of how mothers and fathers in intact families spend time with children. *Gender & Society*, 20: 259–81.

Craig L (2007). How employed mothers in Australia find time for both market work and childcare. *Journal of Family and Economic Issues*, 28: 69–87.

Craig L & Sawriker P (2009). Work and family: how does the (gender) balance change as the children grow? *Gender, Work and Organization*, 16(6): 684–709.

Cunningham AS, Jelliffe DB & Jelliffe EF (1991). Breast-feeding and health in the 1980s: a global epidemiologic review. *Journal of Pediatrics*, 118(5): 659–66.

Dalton WT, Frick-Horbury D & Kitzman KM (2006). Young adults retrospective reports of parenting by mothers and fathers: associations with current relationship quality. *Journal of General Psychology*, 133(1): 5–18.

Davis SN, Greenstein TN & Marks JPG (2007). Effects of union type on division of household labor. *Journal of Family Issues*, 28(9): 1246–72.

Dawkins R (1976). *The selfish gene*. Oxford, UK: Oxford University Press.

De Beauvoir S (1972 [1949]). *The second sex*. Translated by HM Parshley. Penguin.

de Vaus D (2004). Lone parent families. In de Vaus D, *Diversity and change in Australian families* (pp39–56). Melbourne, VIC: Australian Institute of Family Studies.

de Vaus D, Gray M, Qu L & Stanton D (2009). The effect of relationship breakdown on income and social exclusion. Paper presented at the Australian Social Policy Conference: An inclusive society? Practicalities and possibilities. Social Policy Research Centre, University of New South Wales. Sydney, 32pp.

Deem R (1996). No time for a rest? An exploration of women's work, engendered leisure and holidays. *Time & Society*, 5(1): 5–25.

Deutsch F (1999). *Halving it all: how equally shared parenting works*. Cambridge, MA: Harvard University Press.

Deutsch F & Saxon S (1998). The double standard of praise and criticism for mothers and fathers. *Psychology of Women Quarterly*, 22(4): 665–83.

Devetter FX (2009). Gender differences in time availability: evidence from France. *Gender, Work and Organization*, 16(4): 429–50.

Dixon RB & Weitzman LJ (1982). When husbands file for divorce. *Journal of Marriage and the Family*, 2: 103–15.

Doiron D & Mendolia S (2012). The impact of job loss on family dissolution. *Journal of Population Economics*, 25(1): 367–98.

Downey P (1997). *Dads, toddlers & the chicken dance*. Sydney: Simon & Schuster.

Duggan WD (2007). Rock–paper–scissors: playing the odds with the law of child relocation. *Family Law Review*, 45(2): 193–213.

Durbin S & Fleetwood S (2010). Gender inequality in employment: editors' introduction. *Equality, Diversity and Inclusion: An International Journal*, 29(3): 221–38.

Dye P (2011 [1998]). *The father lode: a new look at becoming and being a dad*. St Leonards, NSW: Allen & Unwin.

Eliot G (1861). *Silas Marner: the weaver of Raveloe* [Online]. Available: http://www.gutenberg.org/ebooks/550 [Accessed 4 September 2013].

Ellis L, Hershberger S, Field E, Wersinger S, Pellis S, Geary D, Palmer C, Hoyenga K, Hetsroni A & Karadi K (2008). *Sex differences: summarizing more than a century of scientific research.* New York: Psychology Press.

Emery RE (1988). *Marriage, divorce and children's adjustment.* Newbury Park, CA: Sage Publications.

Equal Opportunity for Women in the Workplace Agency (2010). *Australian Census of Women in Leadership,* Australian Government.

Essock SM & McGuire MT (1989). Social reproductive histories of depressed and anxious women. In RW Bell & NJ Bell (Eds). *Interfaces in psychology: sociobiology and the social sciences* (pp63–72). Lubbock, TX: Texas Tech University Press.

Evenson RJ & Simon RW (2005). Clarifying the relationship between parenthood and depression. *Journal of Health and Social Behaviour,* 46(4): 341–58.

Eyer DE (1991). *Mother-infant bonding: a scientific fiction.* New Haven, CT: Yale University Press.

Fagan J & Lee Y (2010). Perceptions and satisfaction with father involvement and adolescent mothers' postpartum depressive symptoms. *Journal of Youth and Adolescence,* 39: 1109–21.

Farrell W (2001). *The father and child reunion: how to bring the dads we need to the children we love.* Sydney: Finch Publishing.

Fisher H (2005). *Why we love? The nature and chemistry of romantic love.* New York: Henry Holt and Company.

Fletcher R, Freeman E & Matthey S (2011). The impact of behavioural parent training on fathers' parenting: a meta-analysis of the triple p-positive parenting program. *Fathering: A Journal of Theory, Research, and Practice about Men as Fathers,* 9(3): 291–312.

Friedman B (2008). Unlikely warriors: how four US news sources explained female suicide bombers. *Journalism and Mass Communication Quarterly,* 85(4): 841–59.

Fuller J & Batura P (2011). *First time dad: the stuff you really need to know.* Chicago, IL: Moody Publishers.

Gadalla TM (2009). Impact of marital dissolution on men's and women's incomes: a longitudinal study. *Journal of Divorce and Remarriage,* 50(1): 55–65.

Ghazarian SR & Buehler C (2010). Interparental conflict and academic achievement: an examination of mediating and moderating factors. *Journal of Youth and Adolescence,* 39(1): 23–35.

Gill S & Davidson MJ (2001). Problems and pressures facing lone mothers in management and professional occupations – a pilot study. *Women in Management Review,* 16(8): 383–99.

Gimenez-Nadal JI & Sevilla-Sanz A (2011). The time-crunch paradox. *Social Indicators Research*, 102(2): 181–96.

Goldberg SB (1997). Make room for daddy. *ABA Journal*, 83(2): 48–52.

Goldscheider F & Kaufman G (2006). Single parenthood and the double standard. *Fathering: A Journal of Theory, Research, and Practice about Men as Fathers*, 4(2): 191–208.

Grossman K, Grossman KE, Fremmer-Bombik E, Kindler H, Scheuerer-Englisch H & Zimmermann P (2002). The uniqueness of the child-father attachment relationship: fathers' sensitive and challenging play as a pivotal variable in a 16-year longitudinal study. *Social Development*, 11(3): 307–31.

Hagy J (2008). No matter what the DNA test says. *Indexed*, 4 April [Online]. Available: http://www.thisisindexed.com/2008/04/ no-matter-what-the-dna-test-says/ [Accessed 28 August 2013].

Hall J (1978). Gender effects in decoding nonverbal cues. *Psychological Bulletin*, 85(4): 845–57.

Halrynjo S (2009). Men's work–life conflict: career, care and self-realization: patterns of privileges and dilemmas. *Gender, Work and Organization*, 16(10): 98–125.

Harris KM, Furstenberg FF & Marmer JK (1998). Paternal involvement with adolescents in intact families: the influence of fathers over the life course. *Demography*, 35(2): 201–216.

Hertz R (2006). *Single by chance, mothers by choice: how women are choosing parenthood without marriage and creating the new American family*. Oxford: Oxford University Press.

Hetherington EM & Stanley-Hagan MM (1997). The effects of divorce on fathers and their children. In ME Lamb (Ed.). *The role of the father in child development* (3rd edn) (pp191–211, 360–369). New York: John Wiley & Sons.

Hochschild A & Machung A (1989). *The second shift, working families and the revolution at home*. New York: Penguin Group.

Hoffman ML (1981). The role of the father in moral internalization. In ME Lamb (Ed.). *The role of the father in child development* (2nd edn), (pp359–78). New York: John Wiley & Sons.

Holden M (2013). 'Desperate father' spray paints British queen's portrait. *Reuters*, 13 June [Online]. Available: http://uk.reuters.com/article/2013/06/13/ uk-britain-portrait-queen-idUKBRE95C0KG20130613 [Accessed 28 August 2013].

Holden S & Areni C (2013). Gender stereotypes influence reactions to scenarios depicting work-life conflict for parents, working paper. Bond University.

Horwitz S & Lewin P (2008). Heterogeneous human capital, uncertainty, and the structure of plans: a market process approach to marriage and divorce. *Review of Austrian Economics*, 21: 1–21.

Hosley CA & Montemayor R (1997). Fathers and adolescents. In ME Lamb (Ed.). *The role of the father in child development* (3rd edn), (pp162–78). New York: John Wiley & Sons.

Howard S, McBride N & Hardy F (2003). Fathering roles, responsibilities and barriers – men speak out. In R Sullivan (Ed.). *Focus on fathering* (pp1–16). Melbourne, VIC: Acer Press.

Jamieson A (2010). British Airways changes 'discriminatory' seating policy for men. *The Telegraph*, 21 August [Online]. Available: http://www.telegraph.co.uk/travel/travelnews/7957982/ British-Airways-changes-discriminatory-seating-policy-for-men.html [Accessed 4 September 2013].

Jeynes WH (2002). Examining the effects of parental absence on the academic achievements of adolescents: the challenge of controlling for family income. *Journal of Family and Economic Issues*, 23(2): 189–210.

Johnson S (2008). Father's Day cards banned in Scottish schools. *The Telegraph*, 22 June, B2.

Johnson-Down L, O'Loughlin J, Koski KG & Gray-Donald K (1997). High prevalence of obesity in low income and multiethnic schoolchildren: a diet and physical activity assessment. *Journal of Nutrition*, 127: 2310–15.

Kendrick DT (1989). Bridging social psychology and sociobiology: the case of sexual attraction. In RW Bell & NJ Bell (Eds). *Sociobiology and the social sciences* (pp5–24). Lubbock, TX: Texas Tech University Press.

King E (2008). The effect of bias on the advancement of working mothers: disentangling legitimate concerns from inaccurate stereotypes as predictors of advancement in academe. *Human Relations*, 61(12): 1677–711.

Kitson GC (1992). *Portrait of divorce: adjustment to marital breakdown*. New York: The Guilford Press.

Klein KJK & Hodges SD (2001). Gender differences, motivation, and empathetic accuracy: when it pays to understand. *Personality and Social Psychology Bulletin*, 27(6): 720–30.

Kolb D, Williams J & Frohlinger C (2011). *Her place at the table: a woman's guide to negotiating five challenges to leadership success*. San Francisco, CA: Jossey-Bass.

Kvande E (2009). Work–life balance for fathers in globalized knowledge work: some insights from the Norwegian context. *Gender, Work and Organization*, 16(1): 58–72.

Kymlicka W (1991). Rethinking the family. *Philosophy and Public Affairs*, 20 (1): 77–97.

Laakso J (2004). Key determinants of mothers' decisions to allow visits with non-custodial fathers. *Fathering: A Journal of Theory, Research, and Practice about Men as Fathers*, 2(2): 131–45.

Ladd LD (2000). Fathers are important – for real! *Texas Cooperative Extension*, October [Online]. Available: http://eclkc.ohs.acf.hhs.gov/hslc/tta-system/ family/center/Fatherhood/FathersareImpor.htm [Accessed 4 September 2013].

Lamb ME (Ed.) (2004a). *The role of the father in child development*. Hoboken, NJ: John Wiley & Sons.

Lamb ME (2004b). The nature of father involvement. In ME Lamb (Ed.). *The role of the father in child development* (4th edn), (pp1–21). New York: John Wiley & Sons.

Lamb ME (2000). The history of research on father involvement: an overview. In HE Peters, GW Peterson, SK Steinmetz & RD Day (Eds). *Fatherhood: research, interventions and policies* (pp23–42). Philadelphia, PA: Haworth Press.

Lamb ME (1997a). Fathers and child development: an introductory overview and guide. In ME Lamb (Ed.). *The role of the father in child development* (3rd edn), (pp1–18). New York: John Wiley & Sons.

Lamb ME (1997b). The development of father–infant relationships. In ME Lamb (Ed.). *The role of the father in child development* (3rd edn), (pp104–20). New York: John Wiley & Sons.

Lamb ME (1981). Fathers and child development: an integrative overview. In ME Lamb (Ed.). *The role of the father in child development* (2nd edn), (pp1–70). New York: John Wiley & Sons.

Lamb ME (1977). The development of mother–infant and father–infant attachments in the second year of life. *Developmental Psychology*, 13(6): 637–48.

Lancaster JB (1989). Evolutionary and cross-cultural perspectives on single-parenthood. In RW Bell & NJ Bell (Eds). *Sociobiology and the social sciences* (pp63–72). Lubbock, TX: Texas Tech University Press.

Levine S (2000). *Father courage: what happens when men put family first*. New York: Harcourt.

Lewis C (1997). Fathers and pre-schoolers. In ME Lamb (Ed.). *The role of the father in child development* (3rd edn), (pp121–42). New York: John Wiley & Sons.

Linacre S (2007*). Australian social trends: one-parent families*. Canberra: Australian Bureau of Statistics.

Livingston G & Parker K (2011). A tale of two fathers. *Pew Social & Democratic Trend*, 15 June [Online]. Available: http://www.pewsocialtrends.org/2011/06/ 15/a-tale-of-two-fathers/ [Accessed 4 September 2013].

Lunn S (2008). Five minutes with dad is better than no time at all. *The Australian*, 28 October [Online]. Available: http://www.theaustralian.com.au/opinion/

five-minutes-is-better-than-no-time/story-e6frg71o-1111117870845 [Accessed 3 March 2014].

Lyons AC & Fisher J (2006). Gender differences in debt repayment problems after divorce. *Journal of Consumer Affairs*, 40(2): 324–46.

Lyubomirsky S & Boehm JK (2010). Human motives, happiness, and the puzzle of parenthood: commentary on Kenrick et al. (2010). *Psychological Science*, 5(3): 327–34.

MacKinnon C (1987). *Feminism unmodified*. Cambridge, MA: Harvard University Press.

Markiewicz D, Lawford H, Doyle AB & Haggart N (2006). Developmental difference in adolescents' and young adults' use of mothers, fathers, best friends, and romantic partners to fulfil attachment needs. *Journal of Youth and Adolescence*, 35: 127–40.

Marsh K & Musson G (2008). Men at work and at home: managing emotion in telework. *Gender, Work and Organization*, 15(1): 31–48.

Marsh N (2007). *Fat, fired and forty*. Kansas City, MO: Andrews McMeel Publishing.

Magill-Evans J, Harrison MJ, Benzies K, Gierl M & Kimak C (2007). Effects of parenting education on first-time fathers' skills in interactions with their infants. *Fathering: A Journal of Theory, Research, and Practice about Men as Fathers*, 5(1): 42–57.

Manson D (2012). *Daddy's OK: fathers' stories of separation, divorce and rebuilding*. Chatswood, NSW: New Holland Publishers.

Marriner C (2012). Father gives up custody battle. *The Sydney Morning Herald*, 19 August [Online]. Available: http://www.smh.com.au/national/father-gives-up-custody-battle-20120818-24f30.html [Accessed 11 September 2013].

Mauldin T & Meeks CB (1990). Time allocation of one- and two-parent mothers. *Lifestyles: Family and Economic Issues*, 11(1): 53–69.

Maume DJ (2011). Reconsidering the temporal increase in fathers' time with children. *Journal of Family and Economic Issues*, 32(3): 411–23.

McCann R (2000). *On their own: boys growing up underfathered*. Sydney: Finch Publishing.

McLanahan S, Tach L & Schneider D (2013). The causal effects of father absence. *Annual Review of Sociology*, 39: 399–427.

Miley M & Mack A (2009). The new female consumer: the rise of the real mom. *Advertising Age*, 16 November, A1–A22, A27.

Millar L (2008). Aussie dads 'spend 1 min a day with their kids'. *ABC Online* [Online]. Available: http://www.abc.net.au/am/content/2008/s2395427.htm [Accessed 3 March 2014].

Miller T (2010). 'It's a triangle that's difficult to square': men's intentions and practices around caring, work and first-time fatherhood. *Fathering: A Journal of Theory, Research, and Practice about Men as Fathers*, 8(3): 362–78.

Mischel W (1961). Father-absence and delay of gratification. *Journal of Abnormal and Social Psychology*, 63: 116–24.

Moir A & Jessel D (1991). *Brain sex: the real difference between men and women.* New York: Bantam, Doubleday Dell Publishing.

Mojo D (2013). My wife on NBC Nightly News about being the breadwinner. *Daddy Mojo*, 1 June [Online]. Available: http://www.daddymojo.net/2013/06/my-wife-on-nbc-nightly-news-about-being-the-breadwinner/ [Accessed 28 August 2013].

Monna B & Gauthier AH (2008). A review of the literature on the social and economic determinants of parental time. *Journal of Family and Economic Issues*, 29(4): 634–53.

Morell V (1998). New look at monogamy. *Science*, 281(5385): 1982–83.

Mulder CH & Wagner M (2010). Union dissolution and mobility: who moves from the family home after separation? *Journal of Marriage and Family*, 72(5): 1263–73.

Mullen K, Furstenberg FF & Marmer JK (1998). Paternal involvement with adolescents in intact families: the influence of fathers over the life course. *Demography*, 35: 201–16.

Murray D (2012). Australian Breastfeeding Association class baby formula 'was like AIDS'. *News.com.au*, 26 August [Online]. Available: http://www.news.com.au/breaking-news/hardline-counsellor-slams-bottlefeeding/story-e6frfkp9-1226458040994 [Accessed 4 September 2013].

Nelson, SK, Kushlev K, English T, Dunn EW & Lyubomirsky S (2012). In defense of parenthood: children are associated with more joy than misery. *Psychological Science*, 24(1):3–10.

Nielsen L (2011). Shared parenting after divorce: a review of shared residential parenting research. *Journal of Divorce & Remarriage*, 52(8): 586–609.

O'Neill BM (1992). Till debt do us part: financial consequences of divorce. *Journal of Financial Planning*, 5(4): 159–65.

Oddy WH (2001). Breastfeeding protects against illness and infection in infants and children: a review of the evidence. *Breastfeeding Review*, 9(2): 11–18.

Ortner SB & Whitehead H (1981). Introduction: accounting for sexual meanings. In SB Ortner & H Whitehead (Eds). *Sexual meanings: the cultural construction of gender and sexuality* (pp1–27). Cambridge: Cambridge University Press.

Owen K (2003). Mad, bad, or just plain sad dads: the relationship of post-separation parenting patterns and grief on the mental and physical health of fathers. In R Sullivan (Ed.). *Focus on fathering* (pp73–91). Melbourne, Vic.: Australian Council for Educational Research.

Pardo-Crespo R, Pérez-Iglesias R, Llorca J, Álvarez-Granda L, García-Fuentes M, Ángel Martínez-González M & Delgado-Rodríguez M (2004). Breast-feeding and risk of hospitalization for all causes and fever of unknown origin. *European Journal of Public Health*, 14(3): 230–34.

Parker K (2008). *Save the males*. New York: Random House.

Parker R (2013). Dolts, jerks, and schmucks: men in ads. *Parker & McSorley's*, 7 April [Online]. Available: http://www.parkerandmcsorleys.wordpress.com/2013/04/07/dolts-jerks-and-schmucks-men-in-ads [Accessed 4 September 2013]

Penttila IA (2005). Maternal milk cytokines and infant immune development. *Australian Journal of Dairy Technology*, 60(2): 104–05.

Petre D (1998). *Father time*. Sydney: Pan Macmillan Australia.

Phares V & Compas BE (1992). The role of fathers in child and adolescent psychopathology: make room for daddy. *Psychological Bulletin,* 111(3): 387–412.

Plato, *Crito* [Online]. Available: http://www.classics.mit.edu/Plato/crito.html [Accessed 28 August 2013].

Pleck J (1997). Paternal involvement: levels, sources, and consequences. In ME Lamb (Ed.). *The role of the father in child development* (3rd edn), (pp66–103). New York: John Wiley & Sons.

Pleck E & Pleck J (1997). Fatherhood ideals in the United States: historical dimensions. In ME Lamb (Ed.). *The role of the father in child development* (3rd edn), (pp33–48). New York: John Wiley & Sons.

Porter R (2011). We can't afford this obsession with the 'gender pay gap'. *The Daily Telegraph*, 1 September [Online]. Available: http://www.telegraph.co.uk/news/politics/8735044/We-cant-afford-this-obsession-with-the-gender-pay-gap.html [Accessed 28 August 2013].

Pous T (2011). 'Pregnant man' Thomas Beatie reveals plans to get hysterectomy. *Time*, 1 November [Online]. Available: http://www.newsfeed.time.com/2011/11/01/pregnant-man-thomas-beatie-reveals-plans-to-get-hysterectomy/ [Accessed 4 September 2013].

Pritchard D &Hughes KD (1997). Patterns of deviance in crime news. *Journal of Communication*, 47(3): 49–67.

Radin N (1981). The role of the father in cognitive, academic, and intellectual development. In ME Lamb (Ed.). *The role of the father in child development* (2nd edn), (pp379–428). New York: John Wiley & Sons.

Raisler J, O'Campo CA & O'Campo P (1999). Breast-feeding and infant illness: a dose-response relationship? *American Journal of Public Health*, 89(1): 25–29.

Rosenwasser S, Gonzales H & Adams V (1985). Perceptions of a house spouse: the effects of sex, economic productivity, and subject background variables. *Psychology of Women Quarterly*, 9: 258–64.

Rothman SM (1978). *Woman's proper place: a history of changing ideals and practices, 1870 to present*. New York: Basic Books.

Rotundo EA (1985). American fatherhood: a historical perspective. *The American Behavioural Scientist*, 29: 7–25.

Sanday PR (1981). *Female power and male dominance: on the origins of sexual inequality*. Cambridge, UK: Cambridge University Press.

Schroeder P (2000). *24 years of housework . . . and the place is still a mess*. Waterville, ME: Thorndyke Press.

Shah D (2010). BA seat policy made man 'feel like a child molester'. *BBC News*, 24 June [Online]. Available: http://www.bbc.co.uk/news/10182869 [Accessed 4 September 2013].

Shanley ML (2001). *Making babies, making families: what matters most in an age of reproductive technologies, surrogacy, adoption, and same-sex unwed parents*. Boston, MA: Beacon Press.

Shaw G (1903). *Man and Superman*. Westminster: Archibald Constable & Co., Ltd.

Smith DL (2007). *The most dangerous animal*. New York: St Martin's Press.

Smock PJ, Manning WD & Gupta S (1999). The effect of marriage and divorce on women's economic well-being. *American Sociological Review*, 64(6): 794–812.

Stewart SD & Menning CL (2009). Family structure, nonresident father involvement, and adolescent eating patterns. *Journal of Adolescent Health*, 45: 193–201.

Stevensen B & Wolfers J (2007). Marriage and divorce: changes and their driving forces. *Journal of Economic Perspectives*, 21(2): 27–52.

Swinton AT, Freeman PA, Zabriskie RB & Fields PJ (2008). Nonresident fathers' family leisure patterns during parenting time with their children. *Fathering: A Journal of Theory, Research, and Practice about Men as Fathers*, 6(3): 205–225.

Taffel R (2003 [1999]). *When parents disagree and what you can do about it*. New York: The Guilford Press.

The Royal Women's Hospital [Online]. Available: http://www.thewomens.org.au/ [Accessed 11 September 2013].

Thompson CJ (1995). Caring consumers: gendered consumption meanings and the juggling lifestyle. *Journal of Consumer Research*, 22(4): 388–407.

Todd JM (2003). Dairy products in infant nutrition – latest developments. *Australian Journal of Dairy Technology*, 58(2): 55–57.

Toussaint L & Web JR (2005). Gender differences in the relationship between empathy and forgiveness. *Journal of Social Psychology*, 145(6): 673–85.

Townsend NW (2002). *The package deal: marriage, work, and fatherhood in men's lives*. Philadelphia, PA: Temple University Press.

Tracy SJ & Rivera KD (2010). Endorsing equity and applauding stay-at-home moms: how male voices on work–life reveal aversive sexism and flickers of transformation. *Management Communication Quarterly*, 24(1): 3–43.

Triana M (2011). A woman's place and a man's duty: how gender role incongruence in one's family life can result in home-related spillover discrimination at work. *Journal of Business and Psychology*, 26: 71–86.

Trope Y & Liberman N (2003). Temporal construal. *Psychological Review*, 110(3): 403–21.

US Census Bureau (2009). Custodial mothers and fathers and their child support, 2007. Washington, DC: US Census Bureau [Online]. Available: http://www.census.gov/prod/2009pubs/p60-237.pdf [Accessed 29 January 2014].

US Divorce Statistics, *Divorce Magazine.com* [Online]. Available: http://www.divorcemag.com/statistics/statsUS.shtml [Accessed 11 September 2013].

Vijayasiri G (2011). The allocation of housework: extending the gender display approach. *Gender Issues*, 28(3): 155–74.

Volk AA & Atkinson JA (2013). Infant and child death in the human environment of evolutionary adaptation. *Evolution and Human Behavior*, 34: 182–92.

Walzer S (1996). Thinking about the baby: gender and divisions of infant care. *Social Problems*, 43(2): 219–34.

Ware B (2012). *The top five regrets of the dying: a life transformed by the dearly departing*. Hay House.

Ware B (nd). Regret of the dying. *Inspiration and Chai* [Online]. Available: http://www.inspirationandchai.com/Regrets-of-the-Dying.html [Accessed 11 September 2013].

Watson I (2010). Decomposing the gender pay gap in the australian managerial labour market. *Australian Journal of Labour Economics*, 13(1): 49–79.

Weiss Y & Willis RJ (1985). Children as collective goods and divorce settlements. *Journal of Labor Economics*, 3(3): 268–92.

Wentworth D & Chell R (2001). The role of househusband and housewife as perceived by a college population. *Journal of Psychology*, 135(6): 639–50.

Weston R (1992). Trapped in poverty. *Family Matters*, 31: 5–7 [Online]. Available: http://www.aifs.gov.au/institute/pubs/fm1/fm31/fm31rw.html [Accessed 25 February 2014].

Wilde O (1986 [1895]). *The importance of being earnest and other plays*. London: Penguin Books.

Yang S (2000). Men more likely to commit suicide after divorce, study finds. *CNN.com*, 15 March [Online]. Available: http://www.edition.cnn.com/2000/

Works cited

HEALTH/03/15/divorce.suicide.wmd/index.html [Accessed 4 September 2013].

You W & Davis G (2011). Childhood overweight: does quality of parental childcare time matter? *Journal of Family and Economic Issues*, 32: 219–32.

Index

Index

About the authors

Charles S Areni

I am professor in management at the Macquarie Graduate School of Management at Macquarie University and part-time consultant. I married in April of 2000 and had my first child, a son, born four months later. Sounds odd for a man to say he 'had' a child, doesn't it? Still not sure what other verb to use though. My daughter was born in November of 2004, and then came the separation in 2007 and the divorce in 2008. I was a 50 percent shared custody 'single' father for five years (2007–12), and this book is largely about my experiences during that period of my life. I remarried in 2012 and added a step-daughter in the process. My ex-wife also re-partnered and my kids happily refer to their 'two dads' and 'two mums' (which is incredibly confusing when all four of us are in the same place). In short, we're kind of like the Brady Bunch meets Modern Family!

Stephen S Holden

I am adjunct associate professor in marketing at the Bond and Southern Cross universities and business consultant who has never married. While I was always positive to the idea of children, I never managed to find 18 years clear in my diary to commit to being a parent. Fortunately, a relationship that was rocked by storms resulted in an accidental pregnancy (how is a pregnancy ever accidental?) that brought on a period of calm during 2002. Our baby boy was born late in 2002 – and the calm ended! After 11 months, my son's mother left the relationship and the family household. Despite the trials of the relationship and the separation, I was deeply committed to being an engaged parent. I am and remain to this day a single father caring for my son for one week out of every two: each Thursday my son travels from one home to the other. My son thinks he is genuinely blessed to have two homes. I think he is too.

We would like to hear from you!

Please visit our website to let us know what you think about this book at: www.theotherglassceiling.com

www.ingramcontent.com/pod-product-compliance
Lightning Source LLC
Chambersburg PA
CBHW072122270326
41931CB00010B/1639